Perfect Martyr

Perfect Martyr

The Stoning of Stephen and the
Construction of Christian Identity

SHELLY MATTHEWS

OXFORD
UNIVERSITY PRESS

2010

OXFORD
UNIVERSITY PRESS

Oxford University Press, Inc., publishes works that further
Oxford University's objective of excellence
in research, scholarship, and education.

Oxford   New York
Auckland   Cape Town   Dar es Salaam   Hong Kong   Karachi
Kuala Lumpur   Madrid   Melbourne   Mexico City   Nairobi
New Delhi   Shanghai   Taipei   Toronto

With offices in
Argentina   Austria   Brazil   Chile   Czech Republic   France   Greece
Guatemala   Hungary   Italy   Japan   Poland   Portugal   Singapore
South Korea   Switzerland   Thailand   Turkey   Ukraine   Vietnam

Published by Oxford University Press, Inc.
198 Madison Avenue, New York, New York 10016

www.oup.com

Oxford is a registered trademark of Oxford University Press

Library of Congress Cataloging-in-Publication Data
Matthews, Shelly.
Perfect martyr : the stoning of Stephen and the construction of Christian identity / Shelly
Matthews.
    p. cm.
ISBN 978-0-19-539332-3
1. Stephen, Saint, d. ca. 36. 2. Bible. N.T. Acts—Criticism, interpretation, etc. 3. Identification
(Religion) 4. Church history—Primitive and early church, ca. 30–600. I. Title.
BS2520.S8M38   2010
226.6'06–dc22   2009045766

1 3 5 7 9 8 6 4 2

Printed in the United States of America
on acid-free paper

For George

Acknowledgments

The completion of a manuscript so long in progress occasions many words of thanks. I am grateful to E. Leigh Gibson for inviting me to cochair a new program unit in the Society of Biblical Literature on Violence and Representations of Violence among Jews and Christians in 2001, which served as the opportunity for my first forays into Stephen scholarship. I acknowledge the American Association of University Women, for the award of a postdoctoral fellowship in 2004–05, which funded the sabbatical in which I laid the groundwork for this book. I also thank the Center for Ecumenical and Cultural Research at St. John's Abbey and University in Collegeville, Minnesota, for their gracious hospitality in providing the space and the library for that sabbatical year; along with Cal Roetzel and his New Testament Colleagues in Minneapolis/St. Paul for allowing me a forum to present my early research. Richard Pervo provided generous access to manuscripts in prepublished form. The following colleagues and friends were early and generous supporters of my project: Elisabeth Castelli, Lawrence Wills, Amy-Jill Levine, and Denise Buell.

At my home institution, Furman University, I am grateful to Provost Tom Kazee, and to David Rutledge, former chair of the religion department, for arranging course releases for me at critical junctures in my writing. I thank my colleagues in Furman's Ancient Greek and Latin reading group, Anne Leen and Matthew Gillis, for their collegiality and support. I thank my former student,

James Hoke, for his enthusiastic assistance with this project as a summer research fellow in 2007.

Melanie Johnson-DeBaufre and Laura Nasrallah have both read numerous, early drafts of this manuscript, which has been greatly improved by their insightful comments. I am deeply indebted to them for their assistance, collegiality, and friendship.

My beloved and good-humored family, George Frein, Nathan Louis and Alice Grace, have supported the completion of this manuscript in inestimable ways. Once more, I thank them most of all.

Contents

And thus Stephen fulfilled the perfect doctrine, imitating in all ways the Teacher of martyrdom and praying for those who were killing him, saying: "Lord, do not condemn them for this sin." Thus they were made perfect who knew that the one and the same God defends the human race through different dispensations from the beginning to the end. . . .

—Irenaeus, Against Heresies

The religion of mercy and forgiveness came into being through a sin that Christian culture considered unforgivable, the Jews' act of deicide. No repentance is possible, since the Jews cannot acknowledge the act of deicide without acknowledging Jesus as Christ, itself an act of conversion, not atonement.

—Susannah Heschel

Perfect Martyr

Introduction

Upon the martyrdom of Stephen came the first and greatest persecution of the Church in Jerusalem by the Jews [Γενομένου δῆτα ἐπὶ τῇ
τοῦ Στεφάνου μαρτυρίᾳ πρώτου καὶ μεγίστου πρὸς αὐτῶν
Ἰουδαίων κατὰ τῆς ἐν Ἱεροσολύμοις ἐκκλησίας διωγμοῦ]
—Eusebius, *Ecclesiastical History*

The Church of the Gentiles was baptized in the blood of Stephen.
—J. B. Lightfoot, "St. Paul and the Three"

The Jerusalem section of Acts is closed by the story of the stoning of
Stephen, the first Jesus believer to be killed by those who resist his
testimony. The story connects the death of Jesus in the Third Gospel
to the conversion of the Paul in Acts, for Stephen's death is closely
modeled on the death of Jesus and closely linked to the conversion of
Paul, the apostle to the Gentiles. As with many martyrdom tales, the
precise reason for Stephen's rejection and death is not clearly stated.
Stephen is charged with speaking against the law and the temple, the
central institutions of the Jewish people. But Stephen's defense
speech reveals his reverence for the law; the precise nature of
Stephen's temple criticism is difficult to discern; and, in any case, the
narrator marks those who make the temple/torah accusation as false
witnesses. The angry reaction of the crowd to Stephen's defense
speech is prompted not by proof that Stephen is against the law and
the temple but by Stephen's counteraccusation that his audience

is implicated in prophet persecution and law breaking. The stoning takes place after Stephen has shared his vision of the Son of Man.

While the grounds for the martyr's death are not obvious, the identity of the persecutors is. They are Jews living in Jerusalem, who come from the far reaches of the earth. Saul/Paul is also implicated as one who receives the coats of those stoning Stephen, his pre-conversion presence at the stoning standing as a sign of the violence of his former life, when he persecuted the church to the utmost. That the death comes by stoning makes clear that the *Ioudaioi* who murder Stephen are despicable rabble-rousers since, from a Roman imperial view, stoning is the crime of the barbarous. The vile persecutors serve as a perfect foil to the innocent and generous martyr who, filled with the Holy Spirit, prays an extravagant prayer of mercy upon them.

The death not only marks the close of the Jerusalem section of Acts but also paves the way for the mission into Judea, Samaria, and unto the ends of the earth. At the death, a severe persecution breaks out against the church in Jerusalem, causing all but the apostles to scatter, with some traveling as far as Antioch, the place where the disciples were first called Christians.

Martyrdom is not an event but a discourse. Throughout the course of Roman imperial rule of the ancient Mediterranean, hundreds and thousands of subjects were killed in state-sanctioned violence.[1] Nearly all of these subjects met their deaths without the consolation of being named and memorialized in any historical record. While all these deaths are events that "happened," language is required, specifically a narrative told by those empathetic to the victim and the victim's plight, to create a martyr. As Daniel Boyarin puts it, "For the 'Romans,' it didn't matter much whether the lions were eating a robber or a bishop, and it probably didn't make much of a difference to the lions, either, but the robber's friends and the bishop's friends told different stories about those leonine meals. It is in these stories that martyrdom, as opposed to execution, or dinner, can be found."[2]

As a discourse that attempts to wrest meaning out of violence through inverting categories of strength and weakness, victory and loss, and life and death, martyrdom narratives can subvert hegemonic powers, providing a language of, and hence a means for, resistance to those facing similar violent circumstances. Recent scholarship has also shown the discourse of martyrdom to do other kinds of complicated work as well in constructing the subjectivity of those who circulate the martyrs' stories. Reciting martyrdom tales can be a form of culture making,[3] a means of nation building,[4] and a process through which ethnoracial identity is constructed.[5] Paradoxically, the anti-judgment, anti-authority alignment of Christian martyrdom discourse can work in the service of generating new sites of authority.[6] In the first centuries of Judeo-Christian history, martyrdom tales work toward creating the very categories "Jew" and "Christian."[7] The primary focus of these studies has been on texts that might be considered full-blown martyrologies, such as those found in 2 and 4 Maccabees, in rabbinic literature, and in Christian martyrdom literature from the mid-second through the fourth centuries. This book contributes to the current conversation on martyrdom, memory, and identity by bringing the story of the stoning of Stephen in Acts into this conversation.

To be sure, Stephen is not a martyr according to recent typologies of martyrdom proposed by Jan Willem van Henten or Daniel Boyarin.[8] While later Christian tradition gives to Stephen a privileged place—in some versions, the first space—in the company of Christian martyrs, one might say that his death is first narrated before the elements that will constitute Jewish and Christian martyr acts of Late Antiquity have coalesced (or, following van Henten's typology, before Christian death narratives have more completely conformed to the framework established in the Jewish martyrdom narratives of Maccabees and Daniel). The trial proceedings are not formal enough, the ultimatum is not directly given so that the persecuted might directly resist or affirm, and erotic elements so common in later martyr texts are absent. A visionary element is present in Stephen's cry, "'Look' . . . I see . . . the Son of Man" (Acts 7.56) but is not developed. Stephen is not persecuted in a "pagan" court but rather by his own people. Therefore, in some renderings, his death might fall more precisely under the taxonomy of the persecuted prophet or the noble death rather than the Christian martyr. Yet, I want to suggest that the story of Stephen occupies an important place on the path toward Christian martyrologies proper and hence is too compelling to overlook for those who recognize the identity work that such texts do.

Dating Acts

As a supporting plank in my argument that the Stephen story should be considered for its relevance to the developing second-century discourse on martyrdom, I note recent reappraisals of the dating of the canonical Acts. While this text has long been dated by common consensus to the 80s or 90s of the common era, a surge of scholarship has now converged in arguing that it is better understood as a product of the early second century.[9] There is nothing in the reception history of Acts that precludes a dating to the second century rather than the first, as the first sustained and irrefutable witness to Acts is Irenaeus, ca. 180 CE. Recent and compelling reintroductions of the argument that Acts knows portions of Josephus's *Antiquities*, as well as several Pauline Epistles, set

a *terminus a quo* for the narrative at 100 CE.[10] Within this possible range of
dates, I assume a date in the second or third decade of the second century as
most probable.[11] As many have come to recognize, the political, social, and
ecclesial issues of concern in Acts, and the rhetoric employed to address them,
fit more squarely within debates of the third generation of the Jesus movement,
rather than the first or second. In terms of its depiction of persecutory Jews, its
defense of Christians in Romanized terms, and its understanding of proof
from prophecy, Acts is a document that lies close to the thought world of Justin
Martyr.[12] Its appropriation of Jewish symbols and Scriptures, its clear statement
that the ministry of Paul is authorized by the Jerusalem apostles, and its solution to questions of divine judgment and mercy, and violence and peace, place
the text within debates that might be considered "marcionite" in flavor.

Thus, Acts may be considered as a document near contemporary with 4
Maccabees (ca. 100 CE) and the Letters of Ignatius (ca. 110 CE); as a close relative of the Apocryphal Acts of Paul, both in terms of genre and dating; and not
so distant from the *Martyrdom of Polycarp* (ca. 150 CE), the text that is often recognized as the earliest Christian martyrdom narrative. Without making arguments for textual dependency among all these texts in which martyrdom
figures, I note the usefulness of considering them as products of the same
thought world, possibly the same geographic region, written under similar
social circumstances.[13] Viewing Acts as an early second-century text not only
prompts reassessment of its relationship to these texts but also raises questions
about what the canonical Acts does and does not say about the fate of revered
figures of the first generation of Jesus believers. If Acts is located in the second
century, its silence concerning the fate of its own hero Paul—to say nothing of
its silence concerning the deaths of James, the brother of Jesus, and of Peter—is
especially curious. Some sixty years after their deaths, it is difficult to explain
this silence as owing to paucity of source material. Because Acts contributes to
the shaping of second-century discourse of martyrdom, the silence concerning
the deaths of these early Christian leaders, Peter, Paul, and James, as well as the
prominence of Stephen's death require explanation.

Stephen in Acts' Construction of Categories

As is now commonly recognized, identities do not emerge whole and contained
at fixed points in time but rather are constructed over time through social and
linguistic processes.[14] This construction requires the imposition and continual
maintenance of boundaries among social groups whose identities would
otherwise remain in flux. The work of Daniel Boyarin especially has enabled

scholars to understand the development of identities from the time of the Jewish Jesus movement to the time in which Christianity came to be spoken of as a religion that was not-Judaism, not as the birth of a religion at a fixed point in time but rather as a massive unwieldy construction project. This construction involved constant negotiation across a number of sites where struggles played out over the precise architectural nature of the edifice and required the concurrent construction—over the same centuries, with related elements of contest and struggle—of Judaism as something Christianity was not.[15]

Adopting the model and terminology employed by Boyarin, one might say that the author of Acts is an early border agent working to fix barriers and hence to construct two unified and distinct social/religious entities called Judaism and Christianity (or better, working to fix barriers between his version of Christianity, with Judaism on the one side and heresy on the other). But he is an early player, laying bricks in his particular region of the ancient Mediterranean for the "borderline" between Judaism and Christianity that will not be firmly and broadly erected for some centuries.[16]

While Acts lays foundation stones for the edifice of a version of Christianity that is not-Judaism—a version so like that of many of our Protestant Christianities that is naturalized and nearly unquestionable—it should also be noted that its author is not in full possession of the categories that later constructors of Christianity as a religion distinct from Judaism will eventually possess. That is, Acts does not own the fully stocked semantic toolbox available to later constructors of Christianity as a religion distinct from Judaism, one that would enable him to confidently name fellow believers as "Christians/not Jews."[17] This leads to the conceptual awkwardness evident in passages such as Acts 18.24–28, where "the Jew Apollos" (Ἰουδαῖος τις Ἀπολλῶς) is noted for powerfully and publicly "refuting the Jews" (εὐτόνως τοῖς Ἰουδαίοις διακατηλέγχετο δημοσίᾳ). It could be said that the rupture enacted by "the Jew" upon "the Jews" in this particular passage—Ἰουδαῖος τις εὐτόνως τοῖς Ἰουδαίοις διακατηλέγχετο—captures precisely both the split Acts asserts and the confusion the narrative has in naming it. Acts is a book in which individual Jews— Stephen, Apollos, Peter, and, quintessentially, Paul—"vehemently refute the Jews" by proving Jesus is Christ (cf. Acts 9.22). While asserting two distinct groups, Acts has still not embraced unequivocally the name by which Jesus believers will come to be named.[18]

Boyarin, along with scholars including Jan Willem van Henten, and Judith Lieu have come to recognize that martyrdom narratives are key sites for identity construction among Jews and Christians. Readers of these narratives of men and women who choose to die rather than compromise their identities are instructed in what makes one Christian, what makes one Jewish. It is my contention that Acts' story of the martyrdom of Stephen participates in both a peculiar and a pernicious construction of Christian and Jewish identities. It is peculiar because it stands at odds with numerous martyrdom traditions concerning the earliest believers of Jesus. It is most obviously pernicious because of its anti-Judaism.[19] An analysis of both its peculiarity and its anti-Jewish edge occupies a large portion of subsequent chapters. To introduce the problem here, I identify a number of overlapping themes by which the Acts narrative, in general, and the Stephen story, in particular, tell a story of Christian origins that is problematically framed and ethically troubling.

The Swift, Linear, and Violent Break

In the past several decades, scholars of ancient Jewish–Christian relations have compiled a number of arguments demonstrating that, the angry rhetoric of the *Adversus Judaeos* literature notwithstanding, Jews and Christians in the ancient world did not always live in enmity. To name a few, Wayne Meeks and Robert Wilken have read John Chrysostom against the grain to find Christians in Antioch keeping kosher, meeting with Jews in the synagogue, and fixing their Easter celebrations according to Passover;[20] E. Leigh Gibson argues that Jews in Smyrna invited Christians into their synagogues at the time of Pionius (ca. 140 CE), noting that shelter there might have been extended as "an alternative to the grim choice between martyrdom and execution";[21] Daniel Boyarin argues that rabbinic literature hints at Rabbi Eliezer's pleasure concerning the teaching of Jesus;[22] and Annette Yoshiko Reed speaks of the irenic tone of the fourth- and fifth-century redactions of the Pseudo-Clementines, in which the Jewish Christians acknowledge both the Torah and Jesus as distinct but legitimate paths to salvation.[23]

These recent studies highlighting porous boundaries, common alliances, and occasional irenic relations cut deeply against the grain of the Acts narrative. Both the chain of succession established in Acts—from Jesus, to Stephen, to Paul, the apostle to the Gentiles—and the geographic progression of "the Way"—from Jerusalem to Judea and Samaria and unto the ends of the earth—have served to support linear models of Christian origins by which Christianity *emerges* and *diverges* from Judaism quickly and decisively. To be sure, Acts' view of Jews and Jewish symbols contains complications of its own, which will be subject to considerable analysis below. Here, I note in brief that, in spite of the narrative's repeated loops back to Jerusalem, where Paul's mission to the Gentiles receives the blessing of Jewish Jesus believers (15.1–29) and where myriads of such believers are said to reside (21.20), Paul's final speech to the Jews in Rome suggests a decisive break between Jews and Gentile followers of the "Way" within the lifetime of Paul himself (28.25–28).

The break is not only swift but also contingent on violence for, as I will demonstrate in greater detail in another chapter, the parting is ignited by Stephen's death at the hands of the riotous mob of Jews. Eusebius reinscribes Acts' narrative by which originary martyrdom is linked to the creation of two distinct social groups by noting that Stephen's death ignites the "first and great" persecution of one distinct social group, the Jerusalem *ekklēsia*, by another, "the Jews" (*Hist. eccl.* 2.1.8).[24] While recent scholars of early Jewish–Christian relations, adopting images used also by the rabbis and the church fathers before them, have invoked a story of gestation and birthing to speak of the origins of and contests between Judaism and Christianity—the rivalry of Jacob and Esau begun in the womb of their mother—Acts tells a more deadly story: the parting is ignited by bloodshed. Thus, in J. B. Lightfoot's nineteenth-century study of Acts, the significance of the parting is not captured by imagery of an actual birth but rather by sacramental language fusing the imagery of birth and death. "The Church of the Gentiles," he notes, "was baptized in the blood of Stephen."[25]

Polarized, Uncomplicated Identities

As exemplified in the violent murder of Stephen and its connection to the persecuting-Saul-turned-persecuted-Paul, Acts constructs Jewish and Christian identity along a simple binary: to be a nonbelieving Jew is to be an agent of violence; to be a Christian is to suffer.[26] The extreme polarity between these two subject positions is heightened by Stephen's dying forgiveness prayer for his persecutors. This extravagant prayer of mercy uttered by the dying victim on behalf of the villainous Jews marks the martyr as bound by a new and superior ethic. In Acts' construction, this distinctively merciful response is the inverse of the merciless deeds of the *Ioudaioi*; the peaceful Christian and the violent *Ioudaioi* are constructed in tandem.

Owing to the reinscription of the violent Jew–violated Christian binary in modern scholarship, the assertion that the first killers of "Christians" were "Jews" is one of the fundaments of the master narrative of Christian origins, standing largely uninterrogated into the twenty-first century. The influence of the lurking violent Jew, so distinctive to Acts' account of Christian beginnings, helps to explain the numerous modern histories of early Christianity in which scenarios of widespread Jewish violence against Christians seem otherwise gratuitous. One thinks of the understanding of the Jew as the *fons persecution is* articulated in the influential works of Adolf von Harnack and W. H. C. Frend.[27] This sentiment has been echoed recently by H. W. Tajra, who, in spite of not being able to cite any specific textual evidence in support, imagines that the execution of the Apostle Paul in the Roman capital owes chiefly to influential

Jews in the Roman synagogue who desire his death and who manipulate Roman officials to sate that desire.[28]

The reflexive reliance on this binary is problematic on a number of grounds. For one, it erroneously reduces the multiplicity of first-century Jewish experience under empire—a complex of alliances, negotiations, and antipathies—to a simple tale of conflict between two opposing sides. A related problem in depicting first-century "Jews" and "Christians" in this polarized way is that it forecloses the possibility of imagining that belief or disbelief in Christ was only one of many identity markers among first-century Jews. In the following pages, I will suggest that a better historical narrative than the one offered by Acts would evoke some of that multiplicity, imagining, for instance, situations in which Jesus believers and other Jews formed alliances, marshaled resistance, and/or faced common suffering from imperial overlords. Such an alternative narrative might also make space for imagining that a particular Jew's assent to messianic claims for Jesus need not have been a singular identity marker, adversely affecting every interaction with other, nonbelieving, Jews.[29]

The Masking of Imperial Violence

In contrast to legendary accounts of the martyrdoms of Peter and Paul, where Roman officials assume the central villainous roles, the death of Stephen takes place outside of any Roman interest or agency. In large measure, Romans are bracketed from the violence animating the entire book of Acts. Tellingly, in Acts' version of Paul's trials and imprisonments, the Romans serve to *rescue* Paul, not to inflict harm upon him. The message that "Romans do no harm" occludes the role of this ancient imperial power in the violence enacted upon colonized peoples of the Mediterranean, including Judeans. Another way to name this problem is to note that Acts makes claims of agency in Stephen's death that have long been made about Jesus' death—the Jews alone are the agents of death. While post-Holocaust scholarship on Gospel passion narratives has underscored Roman agency, whether through Pontius Pilate or the grinding wheels of the "Roman imperial system" as the first cause of Jesus' death, the Acts narrative has not been subject to the same scrutiny.

Further Authorizations and Reinscriptions

I have already made some reference to the manner by which anti-Jewish rhetoric in Acts is reiterated by subsequent interpreters. Because of the highly charged significance of the "Hellenists" in modern constructions of Christian origins, I conclude this section by considering at greater length how the anti-Judaism of the Stephen pericope is authorized and reinscribed in the racially inflected discourse of the nineteenth century concerning Hellenists and Hebrews.

The great conundrum at the heart of nineteenth-century supersessionist Christian self-understanding is the inescapable fact that the earliest Christians were Jews. Susannah Heschel has demonstrated with acuity the anti-Jewish racism and anxiety infusing many premodern and modern Christian attempts to grapple with that conundrum, especially as it pertains to Jesus' Jewish identity.[30] An explanation is needed for how the Savior of the West is born into an inferior racial group. As Heschel notes, attempted solutions to the problem of Jesus' Jewishness range from arguments that Jesus, born of "the virgin womb of the God of Judaism," comes into the world detached from and unscathed by the "Pharisaic Judaism" of his day, to arguments that Jesus was racially Aryan.[31]

Nineteenth-century scholarship on Acts attempts another way out of the conundrum, through a particular racial/religious coding of the Stephen narrative. A key interpretive move of this reading is the superimposing of nineteenth-century constructions of the (Western)Christian and the (Eastern)Jew onto the terms Hellenist (*Hellēnistēs*) and Hebrew (*Hebraios*) that appear in the Stephen narrative (Acts 6.1). To be sure, the author of Acts himself is also attempting to work his way out of a Jewish/Christian conundrum, and these early modern interpreters are responding to markers in Acts suggesting both that believing Gentiles have replaced nonbelieving Jews as the rightful heirs to the promises of Israel and that Stephen plays a pivotal role in that replacement. However, by racially inflecting the categories Hellenist and Hebrew, and by imposing them *even upon Jesus believers who are Jews*, modern interpreters have inscribed the distinctions and boundaries between Jews and Christians more starkly than the author of Acts himself. That is, in the Acts narrative, there is an interstitial category and an interim period in which one can be coded positively both as a Jew and as Jesus believer. In contrast, nineteenth-century interpreters of Acts, through coding Jewish Jesus believers as either Hebrews or Hellenists, the former trapped in Judaism and the latter liberated into Christianity, collapse the interstitial space.

I summarize the contours of this nineteenth-century reading here, with primary focus on the foundational work of F. C. Baur on Acts. This is not to deny that Baur had at least as many detractors as disciples in the nineteenth century, particularly among those who resisted his reading of Acts as a compromise document hammered out between Gentile and Jewish factions of Christianity. Yet, as a number of recent monographs have demonstrated, Baur's foundational work, heavily influenced by Hegel's racially inflected notions of the gradual self-revelation of Spirit in human history, sets the parameters for the debate on Stephen's significance and holds enduring influence.[32]

Stephen is first introduced in Acts among a group of seven appointed to serving tables as a means of solving the dissension that has broken out within the church between factions named Hellenists and Hebrews (6.1–6). The narrative does not specify what makes (Jewish)Hellenists distinct from (Jewish) Hebrews, nor does it explicitly identify Stephen himself as a Hellenist.[33] Yet, because Stephen bears a Greek name, because he argues in a synagogue with members of the Greek-speaking Diaspora, and—most crucially—because he speaks with wisdom and the Spirit against the temple and the law, he is coded as a Hellenist. Likewise, though the narrative does not explicitly indicate that the apostles are "Hebrews," majority nineteenth-century Acts scholarship assumes that the Twelve are representative of the "Hebrew" outlook, one that is Jerusalem located, temple focused, law abiding, and Aramaic speaking. Since the question of Gentile believers is not introduced in Acts until the Gospel spreads from Jerusalem into Samaria and beyond (Acts 8.1ff.), it is clear that both the "Hellenists" and the "Hebrews" in Acts 6.1–6 are Jesus-believing Jews. But nineteenth-century commentary generally elides this fact, reading Hellenist as Christian and Hebrew as Jew.

Stephen's position as Hellenist makes possible a bridge between (the Hebrew) Jesus and (the Hellene) Paul, thus enabling Christianity's escape from the shackles of fleshy Judaism into the Spirit of freedom. In Baur's schema, Stephen receives the higher consciousness first possessed by Jesus and then confronts Paul with it, making possible Paul's conversion from Jew to Christian, a conversion of a full 180 degrees:

> in Stephen, whom [Paul] had persecuted he had been confronted
> with the idea which to a Jew was most of all intolerable, which set
> aside the Jewish particularism, and substituted for it a universalism,
> in which Jew and Gentile stood with equal privileges side by side, *he*
> *could now in the revulsion of his consciousness adopt without any further*
> *mediation the exact opposite of all that he had hitherto clung to with a*
> *true Jew's feelings and instincts.*[34]

Though Baur wavers over the question of whether Stephen or a later hand is responsible for the speech as recorded in Acts 7.2–53, he nevertheless finds it a fitting reflection of Stephen's higher religious consciousness. Stephen's speech lays bare "the grossness of the people's perversity, ingratitude and disobedience, with that overwhelming bias towards materialism which the people had always manifested"[35] and levels a scathing critique against temple worship, which signifies the coarse materiality and inflexibility of Judaism. The temple stands as a place in which "the external, visible, and tangible machinery of worship assumed an overwhelming preponderance, and ceased to be a living and flexible expression of that invisible Ideal."[36]

Against the Hellenist Stephen and his championing of the Spirit of freedom stand not just the hostile and nonbelieving Jews but even the apostles themselves. The Twelve, as "Hebrews," prove as moribund as the rest of their race. Stephen stands alone, "[waging] this fresh and so momentous battle against the enemy; and while he considers the Temple worship, with all its outward forms, as a thing already antiquated and in ruins, *the Apostles always remain immovably true to their old adherence to the Temple.*"[37] Through attributing to the Jerusalem apostles themselves this state of lethargic imprisonment to the flesh, Baur moves significantly beyond the schema of Acts in his denigration of the Hebrew/Jew, for however much Acts privileges Paul above the Twelve, these Jerusalem apostles yet hold authorizing roles in the Acts narrative.[38] Baur elides this authorizing function, so that Christian Spirit transfers from Jesus directly to Stephen to Paul, avoiding the taint of the Hebrew apostles altogether.

Another way in which nineteenth-century readings inscribe the Jew–Christian divide even more starkly than the Acts narrative itself concerns the question of the "severe persecution" arising against the Jerusalem church at Stephen's death (8.1). As already noted, key to Acts' own construction of the two distinct social groups, Jews and Christians, is the sculpting of the former as persecutors and the latter as persecuted. To be a nonbelieving Jew is to inflict violence upon Christians; to be a Christian is to be subject to Jewish violence. This distinction already inscribed in Acts between the murdering Jew and the victimized Christian, coupled with the tendency to read "Hebrews" in Acts as Jews and "Hellenists" as Christians, results in a widespread exegetical consensus that the severe persecution following Stephen's death affected only the Hellenist wing of the church and not the Hebrew. The thin thread of text on which this very large scenario unfolds is one phrase in 8.1: "That day [of Stephen's death] a severe persecution began against the church in Jerusalem, and all *except the apostles* were scattered throughout the countryside" (emphasis added). That is, the clause in which it is reported that the apostles remain in Jerusalem, while the rest of the church scatters, is taken to mean that no part of the "Hebraistic" church was persecuted in the first place.[39] In Acts' construction of the persecutor–persecuted binary, a Jew may fall within the category of the persecuted so long as that Jew believes in Jesus as the apostles obviously do (cf. the persecution of Apostles in 5.17–40, 12.1–5). But the widespread acceptance of the "Hellenist-only" persecution scenario in modern biblical criticism suggests among scholars a strong inclination to withhold from the Hebrews the privilege of being counted among the persecuted—that is to say from the authentically Christian—subjects.

To summarize up to this point, the Acts narrative, in general, and the Stephen story, in particular, participate in an anti-Jewish construction of Christian origins. Owing to the wide-ranging influence of the Acts narrative, this anti-Judaism has been reauthorized and reinscribed in much modern biblical scholarship. One aim of this book, therefore, is to draw attention to the anti-Jewish rhetoric of the narrative and its continuing effects. A further aim is to decenter this narrative of Jewish violence, free from Roman involvement, by considering alternate models for writing the history of violent encounters among Jews and Christians under empire. But this is a difficult task—indeed, in the end it might be considered a quixotic undertaking—owing to the tenacious hold of the Acts narrative on collective Christian consciousness. It is to the question of this collective Christian consciousness that I now turn.

Stephen, Cultural Memory and the Limits of the Historical-Critical Project

As Boyarin, Lieu, and van Henten underscore how martyrdom narratives work in *constructing* Jewish and Christian identity, Elizabeth Castelli demonstrates the potential of cultural memory to *fix* these identities. Elaborating and refining the work of Maurice Halbwachs on cultural memory, Castelli argues that individuals, owing to their adherence to larger social groups, "lay claim to a much wider and deeper past than the one constituted by their own personal or historical experience *and* that they discern meanings of that past through the group's accounting of it."[40] In Christian cultural memory, martyrdom texts are especially relevant because of the relationship of suffering to Christian subjectivity. As Castelli notes, "Christian identity was indelibly marked by the collective memory of the religious suffering of others."[41] Owing to this indelible marking, the privileged place of the Stephen story in Christian collective imagination is understandable (especially in Protestant circles, where canonical texts hold considerably more sway than the extracanonical lives of the saints). But, here, I wish to raise the question of the relationship of Christian cultural memory to the historical-critical project undertaken by Biblical scholars in their analysis of the Stephen story.

Castelli distinguishes between Halbwachs' use of cultural memory as a means to analyze early Christianity, on the one hand, and traditional methods of historical analysis employed by biblical scholars, on the other. While the latter methods focus on questions of how best to adjudicate "what really happened," the former asks instead "what meanings are produced?" and "what ideological impulses are satisfied?" through a particular narration of a story. As she underscores both through examination of ancient martyr texts and through the study of how the tragic murder of a high school student in the Columbine massacre becomes a late twentieth-century martyrdom, cultural memory is deeply intertwined with the project of mythmaking. The workings of cultural memory, she suggests, are so disparate from the modern project of historical analysis employed in biblical scholarship that one might say in some respects that historical criticism is a form of "resistance to the predominance of memory as a governing value in these texts."[42]

But to what extent does the historical-critical approach to Acts really subvert the memory preserved by this narrative? Biblical scholars employing methods of historical criticism do recognize that the coherence of various aspects of Acts is ahistorical, imposed by Luke upon his sources because of his theological concerns, his apologetic tendencies, and/or his aim to delight his audience. For more than two hundred years, historians of Christian origins have approached the book of Acts presuming that its author's intrusive hand can be pulled away, freeing his sources to bear unencumbered witness to the historical events that occurred in the earliest decades of the church. Applying methods captured by metaphors of winnowing and digging, they have attempted to distinguish Acts' redactional/theological/fictional elements from the actual history presumed also to reside in the text. From these "kernels of history," from this "bedrock," scholars have then constructed their own versions of a coherent narrative of Christian origins understood to correspond with events that happened in history. In principle then, the historical-critical method when applied to Acts should produce different results than the project of cultural memory/mythmaking.

It is my contention, however, that scholarly conclusions concerning the Stephen pericope owe much more to the influence of the Acts' narrative on collective Christian consciousness than to the historical-critical method. While I will not ultimately situate my own work within the bounds of this method alone, I argue here that, were the historical-critical method applied rigorously in the case of the stoning of Stephen, at the very least, the result would be some question concerning the event's historicity. I suggest here in brief what I will demonstrate in greater detail in upcoming chapters: According to the ground rules of historical criticism, it is as reasonable to argue that Luke is constructing a symbolic character as to suggest that he preserves within his narrative a reliable record of the actual event of the violent death of a Jesus believer named Stephen. And yet, rather than acknowledge where the historical-critical method leads, biblical scholars have with near unanimity asserted that this death lies among the bedrock events of early Christian origins. I turn here to a consideration of the disciplining influence upon Biblical scholars of Acts, in general, and the Stephen story, in particular.

The Sure and Certain Martyr

In the preface to the two-volume work Luke-Acts, the author promises a *coherent* narrative—a narrative with a precise order—written to provide the most excellent Theophilus with certainty concerning the events that have been fulfilled in their midst.[43] On his promise to deliver a coherent narrative of divinely ordained events that could reassure his elite patron, the author of Luke-Acts succeeds mightily. Readers are met repeatedly with demonstrations that the events narrated unfold providentially—according to the plan of God, in fulfillment of prophecy.[44] Coherence is also underscored by the numerous thematic doublets and parallels within and across the two volumes, as well as between these volumes and Jewish Scripture. Consider the male–female pairings found in nearly every chapter of the Third Gospel and spread across the Acts narrative as well; or, the thickness of the list of thematic and verbal parallels between persecution narratives of Moses, Jesus, Stephen, Peter, and Paul. As with the explicit attribution of events to the providential plan of God, so also these multiple symmetries, these foreshadowings and echoes, and precedents and antecedents, serve to reassure that nothing in the narrative happens by accident.[45] Other signs of the stabilizing function of the book of Acts include the narrative's assertion of continuity over disruption, of unity over divisiveness, and of deference to political order over *stasis*.[46]

Theorists of history such as Keith Jenkins have noted that historical narratives, through their coherence, function to discipline the past.[47] It might be said that the Acts narrative functions not only to discipline the past by providing a coherent ordering of events for Theophilus but also that the narrative has disciplined the subsequent emplotments of early Christian origins by historical-critical scholars, in spite of scholarly efforts to resist Acts' framing.[48] Thus, though critics since the time of F. C. Baur have called into question various aspects of Lukan harmonizing, suggesting, for instance, that Peter and Paul did not speak with univocity or that Paul did not speak *first* in the synagogue and then to the Gentiles, the basic geographical sequencing of events—from Jerusalem origins and unto the ends of the earth—as well as the web of relationships—from the Hebrew apostles, to the Hellenist Stephen, to the apostle-to-the-Gentiles Paul—has remained largely in tact.

Lying at the bedrock layer of unquestioned Lukan narratives is the story of the stoning of Stephen at the hands of an unruly Jewish mob. Strong confidence in the historical truth of this event is expressed not only by biblical scholars who read large swaths of the Acts narrative as historically reliable but also by those whose skepticism concerning Luke as historian is widely recognized. This is as true for the principal early nineteenth-century critic of Acts, F. C. Baur, as it is for Gerd Lüdemann, a contemporary scholar famously known for questioning Christian orthodoxy.[49] After sifting through the chaff, Baur identifies the kernel in this way: "that Stephen was seized and stoned in a tumultuous insurrection is indisputably the fact which we have to regard as the nucleus of the story. What remains is then that Stephen fell a sacrifice to a popular tumult which suddenly arose on account of his trenchant public utterances."[50] Up unto the present day, it is near impossible to identify a biblical scholar who departs from this historical judgment.[51]

While Baur insists more than once in his work on Acts that the martyrdom of Stephen wears the "indubitable stamp of historical reality," he does not provide a rationale for this judgment. It is often assumed that his son-in-law Eduard Zeller does. Zeller argues in his nineteenth-century commentary on Acts:

> The death of Stephen is *beyond dispute the clearest point* in the history
> of Christianity before Paul. With this event we first find ourselves on
> *undeniably historical ground.* Evidence for that would already be the
> one decisive fact which was occasioned by the persecution of
> Stephen, namely the conversion of Paul, *if any further proof were
> needed* of the fact of an event which according to all sides had such a
> visible effect on the development of the Christian cause.[52]

I have added emphasis to the Zeller quotation to underscore phrases that strike me as suggesting a shrillness of tone belying the supposed objectivity of this Enlightenment critic. Zeller protests too much. Yet, while these two assertions—that Stephen's death must be historical because of the effect it had on the development of Christianity and that the historicity of Stephen's death is proven by Saul's subsequent conversion—may be considered nothing more than *prima facie* arguments, they continue to circulate. In his late twentieth-century commentary that systematically divides each Acts pericope into "redaction," "traditions," and the "historical," Gerd Lüdemann reaches for this precise quotation from Zeller as his only argument for placing Acts 7.54–8.3 within the category of the "historical."[53] As another means of illustrating the impasse at which historical critics find themselves when trying to probe the Stephen pericope for its historical kernel, consider a recent article by N. H. Taylor. In his introduction to the article, Taylor indicates that one aim of his argument is to demonstrate that the historicity of Stephen can be affirmed. Rather than developing such an argument, however, Taylor merely asserts this historicity as the consensus reading, by offering a long footnote to a line of scholars who have also affirmed that there is a historical kernel to the story.[54] To support my argument that in spite of this reflexive certainty, there is no indisputable core event concerning Stephen, I identify here a number of points at which biblical scholars wedded to the historical-critical method might find themselves questioning the narrative's historicity.

First, there is the matter of external evidence.[55] The external sources that might be mined for traces of a Stephen tradition are uniformly silent about him. The silence is most pronounced in the Pauline Epistles. Several of the persons known from these epistles do become woven into the Acts narrative—for example, Peter, James, Prisca, Aquila, and Apollos—but Paul never acknowledges that he owes his conversion to a martyr named Stephen.[56] It is also the case that early Christians who invoke the martyrs' witness are silent on Stephen. Both Clement of Rome and Polycarp write at the turn of the first century to exhort imitation of earlier Christian martyrs, but neither of them will push the chain of Christian martyrs from their own time back beyond the time of Paul. Clement cites the examples of the "pillars of the Church" Paul and Peter, who were "persecuted and contended unto death," due to "jealousy and envy" (1 Clem. 5.1–6.2). Polycarp's chain of martyrs goes no further than "Paul and the other apostles" (Pol. Phil. 9.1–2). Outside of the Acts account, there is no further mention of Stephen's martyrdom until the time of Irenaeus and it is clear that Irenaeus relies on Acts for his information.[57] Because it is quite close to the martyrdom of Stephen in structure and content, the martyrdom of James as preserved in Hegesippus also bears on the question of Stephen's historicity. But here the results are also negative, for this companion story suggests that while the *motifs* concerning the way the first martyr dies are crucial to the construction of group identity for early Christians, the precise identity of the first martyr is fungible.[58]

Since there are no outside sources that might be invoked to support the argument of the historicity of the Stephen story, the method of necessity for those aiming to reach a historical conclusion concerning it has been to separate redaction from source, with "source" understood to correspond in someway to historical event. It is fair to say that there are more than a few bumps along the road from Acts 6.1 to 8.2 and that therefore one might reasonably assert that Acts here is working over earlier materials. These earlier materials are recognized as somehow submerged in the dispute among Hellenists and Hebrews in 6.1–6 in which Stephen is introduced: the charges against Stephen in his trial (6.11–14), the actual murder itself (7.54–8.1), and possibly within Stephen's lengthy speech (7.2–53).

A broad-brush sketch of the scholarly consensus concerning the history preserved in these traditions would include the following elements:[59] (1) There seems an obvious breach between the prescribed role for the Seven in Acts 6.1–6 and the actual role of Stephen in 6.8–7.53. The earlier passage underscores a strict division of labor between the Twelve devoted to the word and the Seven, among whom Stephen is numbered, charged with serving tables. The assignment of Stephen to "table service" in 6.1–6, however, is followed immediately by a narrative in which Stephen's ministry is clearly linked not with table but rather with miracles, signs, wisdom, and a very long speech (6.8–7.53). Luke's hand, then, is seen in the imposition of this later ministerial division upon a source that knows the historical Stephen not as deacon but as Spirit-filled missionary.[60] (2) The conflict over the neglect of the widows abruptly introduced and then discarded by Luke seems to many a trace of some quarrel Luke himself has not invented. (3) The roster naming the Seven is regarded as having an aura of facticity about it. The identification of Nicolaus as an Antiochene in this list, along with subsequent connections between Stephen and the city of Antioch at 11.19 and 11.26, was famously part of Adolf Harnack's argument for an Antiochene source in Acts, a hypothesis that lives on, if in modified form, in many quarters.[61] (4) The anti-law and anti-temple charges (6.11, 6.13–14) are an exegetical thorn, in part, because the speech of Stephen apparently contradicts the former but not the latter and also because Luke explicitly brands the charges as false. Yet, consensus remains that hostility against Stephen owes to some combination of anti-law, anti-temple provocation on his part. (5) The impenetrable core of the bedrock remains the actual martyrdom account buried in 7.54–8.1. While traces of a formal legal trial in these verses are regarded as Lukan framing, the frame is built around a firm tradition: Stephen, the follower of the Way, was killed by a riotous mob of Jews who opposed his religious allegiance.

Part of the difficulty with this barebones sketch of what happened (martyrdom) to whom (Stephen), by whom (a mob of riotous Jews) for a certain reason (religious disagreement centering around temple and torah), as has been quite persuasively argued by Todd Penner, lies in the fact that upon careful scrutiny each decision about what is kernel and what is chaff seems in the end arbitrary. This is not to deny the existence of sources for Luke but to suggest the impossibility of pinpointing them.[62]

Given, for instance, the centrality of the temple/torah charge in the Synoptic Gospels, it is at least as reasonable to suggest that parallels in the Stephen episode owe to the motif of *imitatio Christi* than to a historical referent.[63] Or, consider the name itself, *Stephanos*, or "Crown." How remarkably coincidental for the first of the Christian martyrs to have borne the name that comes to be identified as the reward for those whose testimony to Christ results in the death. Eusebius recognized this coincidence as owing to the firm hand of

Divine Providence.[64] Given Luke's penchant for symbolic names—Lydia, the dealer in purple dye from Thyatira; Theophilus, the esteemed lover of God who functions as Luke's ideal reader—a historical critic might conceivably argue that the name Stephen signals Luke's hand at play.[65] Even if one assented for the sake of argument to the assertion that the list of names in which Stephen is mentioned provides a secure piece of historical data, it would be possible to emplot more than one relationship between that name and the martyrdom story. It would be as reasonable, for example, to imagine that the name "Crown" on the list inspired the invention of the subsequent story as to imagine that the name proves the historicity of the martyrdom.

As with the temple/torah charge, and the name itself, so could be said for every one of the elements that have been identified as "core historical events." Given Penner's convincing observation that verisimilitude is the coin of ancient historiography, it is difficult to insist that one aspect of the narrative or another is the deal breaker, the point that the author of Acts simply could not have invented.[66]

To summarize briefly my argument thus far, the book of Acts, in general, and the Stephen pericope, in particular, participate in an anti-Jewish trope by which Jews are constructed as vile killers and Christians as merciful victims. In spite of both the detrimental effects of the story and the fact that historical-critical methods could easily lead to questions concerning the historicity of the narrative, biblical scholars continue to evoke the martyrdom of Stephen as part of the *indubitable reality* of Christian origins. It appears that this reflexive insistence on the certainty of the martyrdom owes more to the vice-like grip of the Acts narrative on Christian collective consciousness than to the results of a traditional historiographical method rigorously applied. This confluence of circumstances leads to my argument for subjecting the book of Acts to an alternate method of historical analysis.

History, Narrative, and Ideology

This study resists the notion that there are authentic kernels of history to be winnowed from the chaff in the book of Acts or that there is a bedrock of historical truth that can be unearthed within its pages. Rather, it is situated within conversations taking place both among modern theorists and scholars of antiquity concerning the constitutive nature of language in creating the past and the formal similarities between historical and fictional narratives. That is, my work is framed by understandings of the relationship of language to events commonly categorized as "the linguistic turn." As metahistorians and ideological

critics have argued, the "raw events" of life are to be distinguished from historical narratives about such events. While events undoubtedly happened, events
in themselves do not speak. There is no singular and necessary correspondence between these events and any narrative about them; there is no singular
and necessary way to frame these events. Three historiographical principles
deriving from this view of the relationship of event to discourse are as follows:
(1) The shape of the historical narrative is contingent on the perspective of its
author. (2) Because historical narratives are perspectival, and furthermore
because they deal with issues of law, legality, and legitimacy, it is also the case
that they are inextricably bound up with issues of authority and the social
order.[67] Historical writing, then, can be understood as an ideological act, with
regnant historical narratives serving to "justify the exercise of power by those
who possess it and . . . to reconcile others to the fact that they do not."[68] (3) It
must also be noted that the language that creates the past—historical narrative—shares formal similarities with the language of myth and literature.
Events in themselves do not possess the qualities of coherence, integrity, fullness, and closure. These formal qualities are imposed upon events by historical
narratives (and mythic narratives and fictional narratives). In this sense, as
metahistorians and ideological critics (as well as some ancient historians) have
noted, all histories are in fact literary fictions.[69]

In the field of Acts scholarship, the broadest and most significant engagement with issues of history after "the turn" is Todd Penner's *In Praise of
Christian Origins*.[70] Situating Luke's second volume within a discussion of
the ancient generic classification, *historia*, Penner argues that for ancient his-
toriographers, the criteria of suitability, plausibility, and persuasiveness—
rather than "accuracy"—form the superstructure upon which their historical
narratives are built.[71]

Penner's study of ancient texts resonates with those of modern theorists
not only in his recognition that historical narratives are fictions but also in his
underscoring of the ideological work these narratives do. An explicit and conscious awareness that the project of *historia* was the construction of identity
and the inculcation of values for the benefit of the ruling classes—present
already in ancient Greek authors—was especially honed among later Roman
authors. Penner offers up a useful catalogue of instances to illustrate that, at
the time of Luke's writing, Roman historians are considerably more concerned
with narrating history as it should have been rather than history as it really was.
For example, Polybius faults Timaeus' disparaging of Demochares because "as
everyone knows" Demochares was of honorable lineage, and honorable men
simply cannot be depicted otherwise (*Hist.* 12.13.4–6); Plutarch dismisses large
sections of Herodotus because Herodotus is "pro-barbarian" and does not

flatter Greeks consistently (*Her. mal.* 857A–858F); and Lucian, while not knowing the actual cause of a certain Severianus' death, can construct the dying scene anyway since a man of his nobility "must" die in a "manly" or "virtuous" way (*Hist.* 25–26). What most distinguishes these accounts of ancient *historia* from the traditional model of the historical-critical method, which aims for objectivity, is the open acknowledgment among the ancients that their histories are not disinterested. These ancient authors know that they write in the service of regnant elite cultural values. As Penner notes:

> . . . while it is one thing to suggest, as Haydn White does, that all histories are in fact literary fictions, it is another to appreciate the cultural and social climate of antiquity that makes this not so much an unconscious truism but a conscious and compulsory literary exercise every time an ancient writer sat down to write *historia*. For in each record of the past, writers from Herodotus to Ammianus Marcellinus were aware that their present was being shaped and molded as a result, and that at stake was one's perceived status within either the empire more generally or the local community more specifically.[72]

This observation that historical narrative, for ancient authors, has an obvious ideological function bears crucially on my reading of the two-volume work of Luke-Acts. The author of Luke-Acts begins with a preface in which his stated desire is to write an orderly account so that his patron the most excellent Theophilus might find "surety" or "truth." Through this preface, the author signals that he too is constructing an account of Christian origins that conforms quite closely to what an elite male Romanized reader would wish such origins to entail.[73]

Working from the premise of the impossibility that the proper or "true" account of what happened could be ascertained, and from the acknowledgment that historical narratives, both ancient and modern, are often pressed into the service of dominant ideologies, shifts my study of Acts' story of the stoning of Stephen in the following ways.

First, the question of establishing the precise genre of Acts, frequently a central question in understanding Acts' relationship to Christian origins, recedes in priority. Once it is conceded that the rhetorical categories of suitability and verisimilitude govern ancient historical narrative, the assigning of Acts to a particular genre—whether a historical novel, an epic, an ancient scientific treatise, or historiography in the manner of Polybius and Thucydides proper—no longer serves as a standard by which one might judge the scope of Acts' historical reliability.[74] More crucially, the ontological and epistemological questions—did it happen and how can we know for certain—give way to questions of rhetoric and ethics.

Here, my work is to be distinguished from the conclusions of Penner's study, as he finds himself at the end of his monograph on Stephen and the Hellenists at something of a historiographical impasse. In his conclusion concerning the historicity of the entire pericope of Acts 6.1–8.3, he asks, "Could the narratives be historically accurate and true? Absolutely. Could they be completely fabricated? Absolutely. Could the truth rest somewhere in between? Absolutely. The problem of course is that it is impossible to prove any of these premises."[75] While conceding the impossibility of precise and certain answers to these questions, I do not view that impossibility as an obstacle to writing historical narrative but rather as a reason to frame historical questions differently. Compelling questions by which to frame a study of the Acts narrative of Christian origins include the following: What is it that historians claim to know about what happened? What frames of reference are utilized for situating these historical narratives? What are the proper names assigned to persons and social groups? And what causal links and explanatory relationships are emplotted? Because the choice to privilege one historical narrative necessarily involves the suppression of other possible tellings, the question arises whether and how one might do justice to submerged voices and alternate versions of past human experiences and events. Because historical narratives are written in the service of the present and have material effects, it seems important to ask who benefits from a particular telling of history and who might be harmed by it; does it inspire people to struggle or promote the status quo.[76]

This line of inquiry is inspired especially by the work of Elisabeth Schüssler Fiorenza, who has long advocated for the acknowledgment of the rhetorical, ideological (and kyriarchal) nature of all historical narrative, both ancient and modern, in arguments that are often comparable to those articulated in Penner's book on Acts.[77] Schüssler Fiorenza, however, moves from that argument to a consequent call for biblical scholars (and by extension, all modern historians) to be ethically accountable for their interpretive practices. "If texts are polysemous and have an oppressive history of effects," she notes, "their interpretation always requires judgment and evaluation."[78] Denise Buell has also argued compellingly for the historian of ancient sources to acknowledge the ethical consequences of their interpretive choices. While noting that it is now relatively common to accede the complex interplay between the interpreter and interpreted— the inevitable role the interpreter plays in shaping interpretation—she argues further, in line with feminist and postcolonial critics, "it is possible not only to acknowledge the specificity and limitations of one's interpretation, but also to advocate for it—even provisionally—on the basis of its particular, contingent implications for the present and future."[79]

From my own (provisional) awareness of the implications of reconstructing ancient Jewish–Christian relations for present and future relations among Jews and Christians, I analyze the Stephen story, advocating for a better model for understanding Jesus followers in their relations with other Jews under empire than this singular story allows. By situating the text within the context of empire, and setting the canonical version against related but noncanonical texts, my aim is to complicate our understanding of early Jewish–Christian relations, as well as to add more voices to the story. By underscoring the violent effect of the text's rhetoric—including the violent effects even of its most merciful rhetoric—my hope to is call those who regard this text as sacred Scripture to greater awareness of the power of this sacred text, and how that power might be employed for ill as well as for good. Such awareness might then become a step toward accountability and conciliation.[80]

Plan of the Book

In chapter 1, I analyze the general orientation of Luke-Acts[81] in terms of its anti-Jewish polemic, its appropriation of Roman imperial values and frameworks, and its usefulness in emerging second-century heresiological contests. I draw attention to the violence of the rhetoric by which Acts depicts nonbelieving Jews and note that the author appropriates Roman categories in shaping those depictions. Differently from the other Gospels, and in line with later Christian apologetic, the Third Gospel explicitly affirms that the Roman destruction of Jerusalem owes to Jewish rejection of Jesus. Subsequently, Acts constructs unbelieving Jews as villainous and savage, cut off from salvation, in part, through employing Romanized stereotypes of barbaric behavior. Through focus on this vilifying and vengeful rhetoric, and its conformity to Roman imperial values and frameworks, I call into question scholarly arguments that Acts holds an irenic view of unbelieving Jews, as well as arguments that the text is best understood as a form of "resistance literature" serving to challenge the *Pax Romana*. Finally, I address the recent argument of Joseph Tyson that Acts, along with the first two chapters of the Third Gospel, serves to counter emerging marcionite theology. Tyson's work focuses on how Luke's appropriation of Jewish symbols in these chapters responds to marcionite renderings of Christian distinctiveness. I add a supporting plank to Tyson's argument by noting how the martial imagery of these chapters provides swift rebuttal to any marcionite assertion that divine violence is the exclusive preserve of the Old Testament God.

While chapter 1 offers an argument for the general orientation of the two-volume work, chapter 2 focuses more specifically on the rhetorical function of the Stephen pericope within the book of Acts. Here, I note how the depiction of Stephen's stoning by a riotous and barbaric mob of Jews conforms perfectly to Acts' rhetorical attempt to bracket Romans from violence against Jesus believers, on the one hand, and to implicate Jews who do not accept messianic claims concerning Jesus as essentially murderous, on the other. I argue further that Stephen's typological function as the perfect martyr goes far to explain Acts' silence regarding the deaths of prominent early Christian figures at Roman hands, and especially its silence concerning the death of Paul.

As a means of challenging Acts' version of events as "natural" or "obvious," in chapter 3, I consider a set of related death narratives concerning James, the brother of Jesus. The chapter begins with the narrative of the death of James preserved in Hegesippus—a text with remarkable structural similarity to Acts' story of Stephen. It then takes up two texts that diverge considerably from the Stephen story: the death of James as recounted in Josephus' *Antiquities*, and the story of violent conflict between James and Paul in the Pseudo-Clementine *Recognitions*. The chapter ends with an assessment of the various merits of these texts in evoking and explaining first-century violence among Jews.

Having considered the "perfection" of Stephen in chapter 2, in terms of the rhetorical fittingness of the pericope, I turn in chapter 4 to the question of the traditional reason that Stephen is hailed as the "perfect" martyr: In early Christian thinking, the sign of the martyr's perfection is the dying forgiveness prayer he utters on behalf of his persecutors. Because the Stephen prayer is closely linked to the dying forgiveness prayer of the Lukan Jesus, both of these iterations are considered here. Against those who argue that the dying prayer conforms perfectly to Jewish scriptural precedent, and those who argue that it signals a clear break between Christianity and Judaism, I argue that the dying forgiveness prayers are part of a complicated rhetorical balancing act. Through these prayers, the author of Luke-Acts both attempts to assert Christian difference from Jews on the basis of their superior ethic of mercy while also challenging marcionite notions that this ethic overrides divine judgment against unrepentant sinners.

I draw on the discourse of Roman imperial clemency to account for how an early Christian text can both mark its heroes as extremely merciful, all the while engaging in the unmerciful act of depicting Jews villainously. Acknowledgment of the violence adhering to the "manly" virtue of Roman clemency helps to clarify the violence of merciful rhetoric in early Christianity. I also consider the Roman discourse of pardon to account for the ambiguity of the reception of the dying forgiveness prayers. In questions of appropriate pardon, the possibility exists that any purported assertion of the virtue of clemency might in actuality prove to be an instance of a more "womanish" vice, such as pity or softness that owes to weakness of mind. Pardon owing to such softness or irrationality is a breach of justice. I shall show that while some Christians hailed the forgiveness prayer as a sign of the martyrs' perfection, others were much more troubled by them since, standing alone, they might suggest just this breach of justice—an inappropriate use of the dying forgiveness prayer conjures an eschatological moment in which the evildoers do not receive the divine punishment which is their due. Here again are raised not only questions of Roman imperial framing—how do these prayers measure against Roman articulations of the manliness of clemency, the womanishness of pity; the justice of the former and the despicable nature of the latter—but also questions of a "marcionite" sort—what is the nature and extent of divine mercy? Is divine judgment with its hell of fire and brimstone to be dismissed as the preserve of the Old Testament God? And finally, might those who answered yes to this question have embraced a version of enemy love and non-retaliation that prevented them from participating in the ancient prejudicial practice of condemning Jews to just that place.

I

Situating Acts

It will be impossible to make our way through the thicket of scholarship on the martyrdom of the Hellenist Stephen, who dies petitioning God to forgive his Jewish murders and thus initiates Christian identity within the Roman Empire, without understanding the scholarly topography of Luke-Acts. In particular, we must understand the text's larger rhetorical aims regarding Jews, regarding the Roman Empire, and regarding other forms of Christian identity. My argument in this chapter is that these larger rhetorical aims include denigrating non-confessing Jews, asserting alignment between the visions and values of followers of "the Way" and those articulated by the Roman Empire, and recasting questions of Christian identity in response to percolating marcionite[1] ideas concerning judgment and mercy, and war and peace.

I stake out my own position on Acts (and, in as much as it is necessary to consider the two volumes together, on Luke-Acts), cognizant that many currently read the text otherwise—and in some cases dramatically otherwise—insisting that the text demonstrates compassion and openness toward Jews, or subverts the Roman Empire. (As we shall see, some even read Luke-Acts with a "marcionite" lens, as privileging a New Testament God of peace over an Old Testament God of war and vengeance, though those who do so generally do not reflect explicitly on the marcionite nature of their readings.) One reason for the multiple and wide-ranging interpretations of this text is the fact of the text's ambiguity and ambivalence both toward Roman authority and toward Jewish cult and ritual, an ambiguity and ambivalence that derive from the colonial circumstance of its composition.[2] Especially in view of these ambiguities and the variety of readings that have been produced to account for them, it seems necessary to begin this chapter with some consideration of the interpretive premises that inform my own reading.

First, I note that to identify the rhetorical thrust of Acts as anti-Jewish, pro-imperial, and particularly situated with respect to rival articulations of Christian identity is not to posit that the text *in itself*, apart from its readers, is an agent actively promulgating these agendas. Nor do I mean to suggest that modern readers are compelled to read the text in this way, or that all ancient readers did. That is, I acknowledge the rhetorical-critical principle that texts are "rhetorical . . . multi-voiced, and tensive-conflictive,"[3] and possess ideology or agency only within (or as an effect of) the specific histories in which they are read. To quote Regina Schwartz's felicitous articulation of this principle, "To know anything about the Bible is to know that it is heterogeneous and that, in the history of biblical exegesis, the same text has been understood to convey widely divergent meanings, used to justify widely divergent theologies and policies, and used to justify the oppression of peoples and the liberation of peoples, often the same peoples, usually the same verse."[4]

Since a text has no agency in and of itself, and since an actual reader may be a *resistant* one, it is always theoretically possible to read a text in the service of liberation, even when the rhetorical markers within it do not easily lend themselves to such a reading. But texts do contain rhetorical markers, and thus it is possible to distinguish between ideal readings that follow these markers and resistant readings that push against them.[5] To illustrate the distinction between readings that follow the rhetorical grain of a text and those that push against it, consider a stream of interpretation taken up by feminists and other theorists of domination who have engaged the book of Acts.

One strategy of reading resistantly has been to mine the text of Acts for traces of submerged voices and liberatory visions that might be lodged there. Acts contains a good number of such traces. It is common for liberation theologians, for example, to celebrate the depiction of the utopian community in Jerusalem, where material goods are held in common such that none among them experience poverty as an echo of utopian Christian beginnings (4.32–37). The conversion of the Ethiopian court official (8.26–40), along with affirmations of divine impartiality in dealing with the peoples of every nation (10.34–35, 17.26), has long been welcomed as part of an antiracist and universalistic impulse in Acts and has been employed within intra-Christian contexts to challenge notions of white supremacy.[6] The numerous passages in Acts depicting women are read as signs of women's historical agency within the early church.[7] Peter's reference to the end time's prophecy from Joel in his Pentecost speech conjures a relatively egalitarian vision of a Spirit poured out among all in the last days (2.17–18).[8]

Yet, while Acts preserves traces of a movement with utopian impulses, these traces are submerged beneath a surface narrative that is emphatically kyriarchal. This phenomenon may be illustrated through consideration of the Pentecost narrative. Peter's Pentecost speech includes a citation from the Prophet Joel explicitly marking sons and daughters, young and old, and male slaves and female slaves as prophetic agents (Acts 2.17–18). But, on further inspection, it is difficult to find any such persons in the text who might have prompted Peter to cite this particular prophecy. While the images Acts associates with Pentecost are vivid and dramatic—sudden and violent wind, flaming tongues, and the simultaneous outpouring of multiple languages—actual description of the speakers themselves is quite vague. Who stands behind the πάντες and the οὗτοι upon whom the Spirit's fire descends? Presumably, "these" in 2.15 who are not drunk but prophesying are distinct from Peter and the eleven who stand in their defense (2.14). Presumably, they are (of?) the one hundred twenty "brothers (and sisters?)" in 1.15, and possibly, they include the women in 1.14, of whom only Jesus' mother merits a name.[9] Yet, whatever the identity of the prophetic speakers, their language miracle is firmly embedded within a "manly" narrative. Preceded immediately by the story of the replacement of Judas, which explicitly restricts the apostolic role to men (1.21–26), the Pentecost pericope is staged as part of the public speech and deliberation taking place within circles of Judean men (ἄνδρες Ἰουδαῖοι; 2.5, 2.14), Israelite men (ἄνδρες Ἰσραηλῖται; 2.22), and men/brothers (ἄνδρες ἀδελφοί; 2.29, 2.37).[10] In the larger text of Acts, the only slave actually depicted as prophesying is also the only prophesying woman, but she is not a believer, her spirit is of an inferior sort, and her appearance in the text may be something of a joke (16.16–18).[11]

To fully appreciate Acts' rhetorical strategy here, it is instructive to compare the text's treatment of central controversies in Paul's Letter to the Galatians—Paul's apostolic authority, table fellowship, and circumcision—with its treatment of central controversies in the Corinthian correspondence—women's leadership and the ordering of charismata.[12] The issues from Galatians rise front and center in Acts: Paul's authority vis-à-vis the Jerusalem apostles is clearly demarcated; controversies regarding circumcision and table fellowship are explicitly raised, debated, and resolved. In contrast, the issues that are front and center in 1 Corinthians—gender roles and charismata—are not debated in Acts. No debate is necessary because no question is raised. Acts seems to have absorbed entirely Paul's expressed desires and concerns in 1 Corinthians 14.

The "tongues" of Acts 2 are intelligible (1 Cor. 14.9: διὰ τῆς γλώσσης ἐὰν μὴ εὔσημον λόγον δῶτε, πῶς γνωσθήσεται τὸ λαλούμενον;) and no woman is permitted to speak (1 Cor. 14.34).

The fact that Acts 2 evokes prophesying slaves and women even though the narrative obscures them from view may be considered a "rupture" in Acts—a gap in the text where the Acts narrative reveals what it otherwise works to conceal.[13] But here, as throughout the text of Acts, the author works to smooth over those gaps, reassuring his patron that, in spite of any indication to the contrary, those who follow "the Way" do nothing to turn the world upside down. As this rhetoric of reassurance functions with regard to prophecy, so it does with women's leadership roles in general,[14] as well as with any provocation of empire contained within the Pauline mission.[15] For this reason, the rapier of a liberationist exegete of Acts is double-edged. Hand in hand with the search for utopian impulses within a text comes the work of critically confronting its kyriocentric[16] markers, especially when those markers loom large in the text.

Through the arguments advanced here that Luke-Acts denigrates nonbelieving Jews and aligns with Roman imperial interests, this book positions itself within a long-standing line of scholarly interpretation.[17] But it also responds to a recent cluster of liberal scholarship that attempts to position Luke-Acts as possessing a radically different orientation, one that is "open" to Jews and subversive of empire. Many of these recent arguments may be predicated on laudatory theological and ethical concerns to address Christian anti-Judaism in a post-Shoah context, on the one hand, and to critique imperial domination in an era of heightened awareness concerning the evils of colonization, on the other. But as I will demonstrate, they owe in large part to an eliding of certain obvious and troublesome rhetorical markers in the text. That is, they position the text of Luke-Acts as above the fray of anti-Judaism and colonialism without direct confrontation with these ideologies as they are inscribed in it.

Acts on Jews and Judaism

The question of Jews and Judaism in Acts has been framed in scholarship for the past several decades as a matter of whether the author of Acts rejects all Jews or merely those who disagree with him. There has been surprisingly little acknowledgment of how thin the difference between these two positions is.[18] In spite of this thin difference, scholars who underscore how Acts embraces both Jewish symbols and Jewish converts frequently slide into the conclusion that the text holds a "positive" or "open" stance toward Judaism and hence that its rhetoric cannot be classified as anti-Jewish.[19] Four major argumentative strands are marshaled in support of this view of Acts' rhetoric: First, it is stressed that Acts' embrace of what may be termed "things Jewish"—for example, circumcision (16.3), Nazarite vows (21.23–26), and Pharisaic erudition (22.3)—along with its celebration of the Jewish credentials of its key leaders, preclude any argument that Acts is hostile toward Jews.[20] Second, it is argued that Acts' debate with Jews is merely an intramural quarrel and thus that its invective against Israel should be regarded as no harsher than that hurled by a Jeremiah or an Isaiah. Once the text is situated as an in-group prophetic critique, any suggestion that its author is inveighing against Judaism from the outside is precluded as anachronistic.[21] Third, it is argued that Acts' polemic is aimed only at Jewish leaders and not the entire Jewish people.[22] Fourth, it is stressed that Paul's final citation of Isaiah in front of his Jewish audience in Rome, which includes the ominous warning that his audience "will indeed listen, but never understand, and . . . look, but never perceive (28.26–27)," should not be viewed as indication that Acts has "written off" the Jews, as more traditional readings of Acts on Jews and Judaism would have it. Because Paul quotes Isaiah, a prophet of Israel, and because the quotation ends with the hint that God might "heal them" should they turn, it is argued that Acts' final signal to the Jews is one of openness.[23]

Acts is indeed careful to underscore the Jewish identity of key protagonists and to celebrate Jewish embrace of the Gospel. Consider Paul's twice-repeated emphatic ἐγώ εἰμι Ἰουδαῖος (21.39, 22.3),[24] along with the rejoicing at James' announcement that myriads of Jews have come to believe (21.20). In as much as Acts celebrates the Jewish credentials of the movement's first leaders, it is right to say that Acts' position on the distinction between nonbelieving Jews and followers of "the Way" does not presume that the former group possesses an inferior racial essence. In marked distinction to the racist anxiety provoked in the modern West by the question of whether a Jew, owing to his/her corporeal "Jewishness," might possibly become an authentically Christian subject,[25] Acts holds a relatively more positive view: Not only might Jews be saved by a repentance that leads to belief in Jesus but such Jews, through their leadership of the movement, are essential to its success. Owing to this rhetorical emphasis in Acts, it is not helpful to categorize the text as anti-Semitic, insofar as that category has been traditionally reserved for racial, rather than religious, animus (and insofar as race has been traditionally understood as essential and fixed, rather than mutable).[26] It is also clear that the text of Acts places a high value on Jewish ritual practice and—perhaps especially—Jewish Scriptures. Furthermore, while generic considerations weigh heavily against such a suggestion,[27] for the sake of argument, one might concede that the thrust of

Paul's final speech in Acts 28 lies in the direction of "openness" and "hope" concerning the Jews.

Yet, Acts' emphasis on the movement's Jewish leadership, practices, and institutions, or even its celebration of and hope for Jewish converts, is not out of synch with the developing supersessionist rhetoric of proto-orthodox, anti-marcionite Christianity. To be sure, Acts is a document that is part of a *developing* supersessionist rhetoric. That this development is in process explains the occasional slipperiness of the rhetoric of self/other in the text. But Acts is well on the way to dividing Christians from Jews, to marking Stephen as belonging somehow to a different social and religious group than that from which the unrepentant murderous mob springs. It is not participating in an intramural debate—a debate within a fixed set of walls—but rather working to construct a different set of boundaries and borderlines.[28]

Assertions of Acts' openness toward Jews are commonly predicated on two overlapping lines of argumentation that serve more to cloud than to enlighten: the elision of Acts' exclusivism under the rubric of Acts' universality and the elision of Acts' insistence on Jewish conversion under the rubric of Acts' call for repentance. The range of scholarly positions on the question of Acts and the Jews would narrow considerably were the fault lines in these modes of argumentation more widely conceded.

First, consider the idea that Acts' universalism takes precedence over any exclusivism that it may exhibit. Acts does make clear that the offer of salvation is open to all. Yet, there is an obvious condition laid upon the offer. Belief in Jesus is the *sine qua non* of salvation,[29] including salvation for Jews as, for example, prophesied in the first volume by Simeon (Luke 2.34), affirmed by Peter in his address to the Jews of Jerusalem (Acts 3.11–26), and reaffirmed by Paul in his inaugural sermon to a mixed audience in Pisidian Antioch (Acts 13.38–39). On occasion, judgment against nonbelieving Jews is articulated in graphically violent images. In his gloss on the prophecy of the rejected cornerstone, a prophecy of keen importance to early attempts to explain the forsakenness of Jesus, Luke puts into the mouth of Jesus the threat that "Everyone who falls on that stone will be broken to pieces [συνθλάω]; and it will crush [λικμάω] anyone on whom it falls" (Luke 20.18). In Acts, Peter's admonition to listen to the prophet like Moses is accompanied by the threat that those who do not listen will be "utterly destroyed/rooted out" (ἐξολεθρευθήσεται) from the people (Acts 3.23).[30] Though the literature on Acts, Jews, and Judaism is vast and scholarly positions vary widely, few have ventured to suggest that this text offers hope for salvation of the Jews outside of belief in Christ.[31] It is disingenuous, then, to celebrate this universalism without attending to its hegemonizing force.[32]

Second, consider how scholars have tended to emphasize Acts' call to repentance while masking its call to conversion. In its traditional formulation, repentance is the proper response of the sinner, one who has failed morally and ethically. It is a turning back toward what has been established as the good. An act of repentance leads to atonement, the restoration of the sinner. In Acts, however (as in much subsequent Christian literature concerning Jewish depravity), the language of repentance is meshed with the language of conversion, such that repentance is not understood as a turning back toward what has been established but a turning toward the new—toward Jesus as Christ and as fulfillment of the Jewish Scriptures.[33] Such a reading characterizes Acts' call to conversion as if it were merely a general call for sinners to atone for evil deeds, rather than a specific call for Jews to confess Jesus as Christ. But in the same way that a sanguine reading of Acts stresses its openness, rather than its exclusivity, in this reading, the condemnation of nonbelieving Jews in Acts can be explained as owing to moral and ethical failings—the dullness of their perception, and their ingratitude and rebelliousness—rather than their refusal to assent to Christological propositions about Jesus.

Scholars who wish to preserve Luke-Acts as a document above the fray of Christian anti-Judaism often employ this rhetorical sleight of hand concerning Acts' message of exclusive salvation contingent upon conversion. It is present, for instance, in Robert Brawley's analysis of Paul's closing speech in the final chapter of Acts. Paul ends his testimony to the Jews of Rome by quoting Isaiah 6.9–10. Isaiah, of course, does not make explicit reference to the people's rejection of Jesus but rather to their blindness and deafness, and to the healing that would come, if only they would turn (with the object of their turning left unspecified). This makes possible the framing of the question of Acts 28 and Jewish salvation in euphemistic terms such as "turning" or "healing" without direct reference to Christ as the exclusive object of the turning or the exclusive source of the healing. Thus, Brawley may speak of the message of repentance leading to salvation in Acts 28 without making mention of Jesus as the *sine qua non*:

> The use of Isaiah 6:9–10 . . . anticipates that *should the unpersuaded turn*, God promises to heal them. . . . Further the antepenultimate clue in the characterization of God is that *God will heal the Jews, who do not understand or perceive, but who turn* (28:27). The final clue is that Paul preaches *God's rule to all who come to him* (emphasis added).[34]

Brawley concludes that his is an "ethical reading," of Acts, because he has found the universal message in Acts 28, namely, that Paul preaches to all in his final speech, including the Jews. But should the high ground of ethical interpretation really be conceded to one who embraces Acts' message of exclusivistic salvation contingent upon conversion of the Jews?

While the rhetoric of Acts with regard to questions of Jews and Judaism celebrates the open and universal scope of Christianity, the simultaneous assertion of a supersessionist thrust cannot be overlooked. Those who understand Acts to serve an apologetic or legitimating function have long recognized that invoking the Scriptures and other symbols of a religion with roots in antiquity serves to prove that "the Way" is not a superstition but the flowering of ancient wisdom. The proofs cited from Jewish Scripture and other positive coding of Jewish symbols, along with the highlighting of the Jewish credentials of its key protagonists, demonstrate that this community has the rightful claim on Israel's heritage. Acts anchors itself to Israelite heritage as part of its rhetorical strategy of carving out a space for itself within the dominant culture. Yet, in as much as Acts embraces Jewish Scriptures and symbols, it appropriates them, forcefully asserting that true Israel has its true *telos* in the *ekklēsia* of Jesus Christ.

Acts' developing supersessionist rhetoric comes into clear focus in two recent articles treating central institutions of Judaism, that of Mogens Müller addressing the function of Scripture in Luke-Acts and that of Geir Otto Holmås on the temple in Acts.[35] Müller begins his argument by acknowledging that the establishment of proof from prophecy was an essential aspect of Christian supersessionist rhetoric. Such proofs confirmed the coherence of God's salvific acts while enabling the church to claim that it alone had true understanding of its contents. While Justin Martyr is the first to articulate explicitly this principle of proof from prophecy, Müller demonstrates how this principle also undergirds the use of scriptural quotations in Luke-Acts. In contrast, the Gospel of Matthew participates in a form of midrashic exegesis, whereby the Jesus event is understood to give specific passages from the Scriptures new and fuller meaning: Jesus reveals the true hidden content of these particular passages from the Law and Prophets.[36] In Luke-Acts, however, the Law and Prophets are regarded in a more totalizing way, as proof that Jesus fulfills the promise of Scripture in its entirety. "All the scriptures" or "Moses and the prophets" as a whole are invoked as proof that Jesus would suffer and that Paul would preach to the Gentiles (Acts 26.22–23; Luke 24.26–27, 24.45–47). Hand in hand with this understanding of proof from the Scriptures as a whole is the view that their meaning, far from being enigmatic, is clear for anyone who has eyes to see and ears to hear. The distinction between Luke's insistence on the clarity of Scripture in pointing toward Jesus and Matthew's assumption that the relationship between Jesus and Scriptures is more cryptic is illustrated by the way the authors of these texts position their citations of Isaiah 6.9–10.[37] While this prophecy concerning the people's blindness and deafness is applied to Jesus' preaching *in parables* in Matthew 13.14–15 (cf. Mark 4.12), the passage is reserved by the author of Luke-Acts for Paul's final speech at the end of Acts where it functions to condemn the Jews for refusing to see the obvious: Paul's preaching concerning Jesus and the kingdom of God is merely a literal explication of promises contained in the Scriptures.[38]

While the Scriptures function in Luke-Acts in this supersessionist way—as obvious and literal proof that Jesus is the Christ and fulfillment of the promises—assertions concerning the function of the temple in Luke-Acts are less univocal. There are scenes in which the temple is the arena for conflict—a site for arrests, imprisonments, and demonstrations of the conspiratorial machinations of the temple leadership. Yet, there are also instances in which the temple functions as the site for demonstrations of true piety. The infancy narrative privileges the temple as locus for the pious worship of Zechariah, Anna, and Simeon (Luke 1–2); the last verse of the Third Gospel depicts the disciples who have witnessed the resurrection as "continually in the temple blessing God" (Luke 24.53); the Jerusalem apostles continue to visit the temple after Pentecost (2.46, 3.1, 5.12); and Paul himself performs rites of purification in the temple to prove his steadfast observance of the Law (21.26) and also insists that his own religious observances align with the promise that the "twelve tribes hope to attain, as they earnestly worship [λατρεύω] day and night" (26.5–7). In spite of these ambiguous, and in some instances truly paradoxical, temple depictions,[39] Gier Holmås demonstrates an underlying coherence concerning the temple in Luke-Acts. To put it simply, temple worship retains a positive valence only for those recognizing that such worship leads to Jesus, the resurrected messiah who is the fulfillment of the Law and the Prophets. In as much as temple worship is practiced by those who do not recognize Jesus as Christ, it is a "den of robbers." Their blindness to Jesus' identity is the root cause of the temple's destruction. As Holmås concludes:

> The reader perceives the fall of the temple—that is now a *fait accompli*—to be a direct consequence of Jerusalem's blindness when confronted with the offer of salvation, and is connected to the fact that the temple did not manage to live up to its call as a "house of prayer." The expectation of salvation that was the temple's actual purpose . . . continues, however, in the Christian community that, in prayer, calls upon the name of Jesus.[40]

At the same time that Acts embraces Jews who confess Jesus as Christ, and asserts that Jewish Scriptures and worship, properly understood, lead to this confession, it also works to denigrate non-confessing Jews as prone to sedition and mob violence.[41] As Lawrence Wills has demonstrated, Acts' depictions of Jewish crowds that oppose the Way are aligned with perspectives on mob behavior expressed by elite late first- and early second-century Roman authors.[42] From the time of the stoning of Stephen onward, followers of the Way are subject to crowds of unbelieving Jews who throw stones, concoct vile plots, and incite riotous behavior. Thus, as Wills observes, the force of the anti-Jewish rhetoric in Acts lies in the plane of the sociopolitical world. Acts adopts the perspective of Roman imperial sociology to demonstrate that Jewish people who do not confess Jesus are unworthy subjects of empire.[43]

Through the distinct coding of Jewish *symbols* as good and non-confessing Jewish *people* as bad, the rhetorical strategy of Acts aligns precisely with the *Adversus Judaeos* tradition of anti-marcionite Christians in the second century and beyond. The marcionite solution to "the problem" of the Jews was to denigrate Jewish symbols and the Jewish God, presuming them to be inferior to Christian revelation, but at the same time to grant to the Jews that their (inferior) messiah would yet come and restore them to their own land, as their Scriptures predicted. Since Marcion did not need Jewish Scriptures, regarding them as irrelevant to the new revelation, he was able to concede to the Jews that their Scriptures did not predict Jesus as messiah. (And hence, without irony, Tertullian can disparage Marcion as one who reads the Scriptures like a Jew.)[44] The anti-marcionites instead embraced the Jewish Scriptures and the Jewish God, all the while disparaging the Jewish people as having been displaced, owing to their stiff-necked rebellion and rejection of Jesus. As Stephen G. Wilson framed the issue between marcionites and their opponents some time ago:

> Putting it simply, it is as if the Marcionite said to the Jew: "Keep your God, your Scriptures, your Messiah and your law; we consider them to be inferior, superseded in every way by the gospel." The Catholic [sic] said: "We'll take your God, your messiah, your Scriptures, and some of your law; as for you, you are disinherited, cast into a limbo, and your survival serves only as a warning of the consequences of obdurate wickedness."[45]

Acts is not completely mirrored in this description of "the Catholic" perspective as this text does have a preoccupation with persons who are both believers *and* Jews, which is not found in later *Adversus Judaeos* literature. But owing to its similar embrace of the symbols and rejection of the unbelieving Jews, the narrative method of Acts may be understood as part of this anti-marcionite and supersessionist trajectory.

Acts and the Roman Empire

Acts asserts the compatibility of the Christian faith with loyal subjection to the Roman Empire. Acknowledgment of this pro-Roman tendency in Luke-Acts is widespread in the scholarly literature. It was recognized as early as the eighteenth century and has been articulated by many leading scholars in the field, including those whose approaches to the text have been otherwise quite disparate.[46] In Conzelmann's well-known iteration of this phenomenon, Luke-Acts strives to dissolve tensions between the reign of God and the reign of Rome by deferring the parousia into the distant future so that its promised upheaval sounds no imminent alarm for present-day rulers. It does so by making clear that Pilate views Jesus as innocent, by presenting Paul on friendly terms with high-ranking Roman officials, by presenting as spurious any accusation that followers of the Way are prone to *stasis*, and by making clear that *stasis* comes from "the Jews," a social group distinct from followers of "the Way."[47] While many modifications have been suggested over the years for specific aspects of Conzelmann's argument, it yet remains in its broadest contours an incisive view of Acts' orientation toward Rome.

Among those holding to the view that Luke-Acts articulates a pro-Roman stance, major debates have centered on how to situate this text precisely with relation to the genre of apologetic literature, a task that has been complicated by the growing recognition that the two-volume work is not an apology in the traditional sense—that is, it is not a formal defense of the faith directed outward, toward an audience of skeptical Roman officials.[48] Philip Esler has contributed helpfully to the conversation by suggestion that Luke-Acts is better understood under the social science rubric of "legitimation," as a text directed inside rather than outside, and written to reassure this internal audience that adherence to the Way does not require one to sacrifice allegiance to Rome.[49]

Recent scholarship on identity and geography in the Roman Empire has also advanced our understanding of the nature of Acts' socially and politically conformist rhetoric. Laura Nasrallah has demonstrated that Acts is situated within wide-ranging cultural struggles over Greek–Roman–barbarian identity arising in the imperial period. Acts engages common cultural themes of the so-called Second Sophistic, including its appreciation of literary Greek, its interest in what constitutes true piety, and its embrace of an exotic archaic past. Furthermore, as a text that narrates Paul's travels across the spaces of empire, particularly the cities of the Aegean basin that were also of crucial importance to the Emperor Hadrian's program of cultural unification, it replicates an imperial geographical vision. According to Nasrallah, through this appeal to philosophical and geographical currents of its time, Acts constructs "a Christianity that hybridizes neatly with Rome."[50]

In opposition to this body of scholarship concerning Luke-Acts' embrace of imperial vision is a stream of argument that characterizes the work as a text that aims to subvert the empire. Richard Cassidy stands as an early champion of the view that Acts has an anti-Roman orientation. Cassidy articulates what might be classified as a traditional liberation theology reading, as he argues that the privileging of the poor and downtrodden in Acts signals a direct confrontation of the oppressive values of the ruling Roman elite.[51] This liberation reading often presumes that concern for the poor and marginalized articulated in passages of the Third Gospel—for example, the Magnificat, the Sermon on the Plain, and the inaugural Sermon at Nazareth—remains a governing theme in Luke's second volume. It celebrates the egalitarian practice of communal property sharing in Acts 4 and the concern for women and others presumed to be "outcasts" in subsequent chapters. The universalism driving the Gentile mission is evaluated as a positive and countercultural sign that the movement excludes no one, however marginal their status.

A recent cluster of arguments employing vocabulary of empire studies aligns rather closely with Cassidy's observations concerning Luke-Acts as a countercultural and subversive document. Equipped with a burgeoning literature on the significance of the emperor cult in the Greek East, Allen Brent and Gary Gilbert demonstrate that Acts employs many of the categories and concepts commonly associated with the Caesars and their assertion of rule over the entire inhabited world.[52] But they argue that this appropriation is in effect a rhetorical subversion since Acts co-opts and redirects this vocabulary toward Christ and the kingdom of God, and away from Caesar and the *Pax Romana*. Both scholars suggest that for the author of Acts, imperial language of virtue and magnanimity reaches its full and "true" expression through Jesus and the *ekklēsia*, in opposition to empire. Thus, Gilbert concludes from the geographic scope of nations invoked in Acts 2, "Luke-Acts dismisses the claim that Rome was ruler of the world and speaks of the true *oikoumenē* created through the Spirit, ruled over by Jesus, and mapped out by the list of nations in Acts 2."[53] Brent, likewise, in his (rather literal) reconstruction of the relationship between Theophilus and the author of Luke-Acts, notes that Theophilus and his community will find that "they had received the *true* means for obtaining the *pax dei* both for themselves and for the empire, and with the *pax* the *true saeculum aurem* initiated by the Divine Child who was the only *true filius dei*."[54]

In a subsequent treatment of Acts and the emperor cult, Kavin Rowe argues that readers/hearers of this text would have been alert to the subversive nature of the Jesus-following community owing especially to Peter's speech in the structurally and theologically pivotal pericope concerning Cornelius, the Gentile centurion in Acts 10. In this chapter, Peter receives the dream that "all foods are clean," a dream he is able to interpret as signaling the openness of his movement to the Gentiles when he is approached by this God-fearing Roman officer. Rowe asks his readers to consider the many aspects of this pericope that signal the presence of the Roman Empire—"the leading Gentile character, a ranking member of the Roman military; the city, founded in honor of Augustus; the audience, a group of Gentiles; the sermon, the inaugural for the mission." Noting that Peter's assertion in this setting that Jesus Christ—and not Caesar—is the "Lord of All" (κύριος πάντων; 10.36), Rowe concludes that this statement of allegiance "precludes ultimate allegiance to the emperor on the part of the Gentile neophytes" and subsequently paves the way for the resistance toward empire shown by the Christian martyrs.[55]

Finally, David Balch has recently proposed readings of Acts that are critical of the Roman Empire. Focusing not on language of emperor cult but on Roman discourses of peoplehood and ethnicity, Balch proposes that Romans, unlike Greeks (and Jews), embraced a policy of ethnic mixing. Pointing to Dionysius' *Roman Antiquities*, Balch notes that Roman growth was achieved through open practices such as the granting of citizenship to conquered foreigners and the embrace of intermarriage. This mixing of the foreign and the local in Rome's origins is celebrated by Dionysius as a combination of "the excellence of the two races" a welcome mixing of two sets of "customs, laws and religious ceremonies." Balch then proposes that Acts' insistence that Gentiles be received into Jewish–Christian assemblies is a comparable embrace of the foreign and hence should be understood as a "Romanization of the Gospel."[56] What makes this Romanization ultimately anti-Roman according to Balch is that Luke turns these values upside down by including in its "multiethnic" vision Asians, as well as Westerners, and by privileging slaves and the poor rather than the elite. While Alexander's crossing the Hellespont is a key symbol of Western supremacy, Luke reverses direction and "represents Paul crossing the Hellespont in the opposite direction of Alexander—from Asia to Europe."[57] Thus, Balch concludes, the geographical movement in Acts from East to West "is indicative of larger ideological agendas: the Jordan River muddies the imperial Tiber."[58]

Of the four scholars just discussed—Brent, Gilbert, Rowe, and Balch—only Gilbert makes explicit reference to the alignment of his arguments with those of Cassidy.[59] But the others also see the subversive message of Luke-Acts in its liberatory embrace of the poor and marginalized. Brent notes that the true embrace of the *pax dei* of Christianity involves a reversal of key Roman values, particularly in the realm of social class and status, as embodied in the story of the nativity of the peasant Jesus and the Magnificat sung by his peasant mother;[60] Rowe notes that unlike the overwhelming and intrusive power of the Caesar's lordship, the lordship of Christ in Luke-Acts entails humility and service;[61] and Balch presumes that a socially egalitarian reading of Galatians 3.28 somehow governs the theology of Acts.[62]

The value of these empire-critical readings of Acts is that they demonstrate possible ways that Acts might be read "against itself."[63] These arguments underscore the ambiguity of literature written in colonial situations, whereby an affirmation of allegiance to empire might be undercut with a subsequent insistence that "Christ"—and not Caesar—is Lord of all. Yet, the empire-critical analyses of Acts reviewed here are not offered as *resistant* readings of Acts' rhetoric but rather as mere explications of that rhetoric. As such, they ignore rhetorical markers in Acts that signal cooptation and reinforcement, rather than subversion, of Roman imperial logics.

Despite the fact that these readings affirm traces of liberationist/anti-imperial impulses that I too embrace, they are also problematic because they gloss over the major definitional shift that takes place between the Gospel of Luke and the book of Acts concerning the question of who qualifies as the "outcast."[64] As noted above, those who read Acts as critical of empire tend to invoke the Magnificat, the Sermon on the Plain, or another teaching of the Lukan Jesus associated with poverty and humility. They assume that these passages that privilege the destitute in the Third Gospel are representative of the outlook of both the Third Gospel and Acts. But there is little to indicate that the Third Gospel's privileging of *les misérables* remains a controlling theme in Acts. Once the narrative progresses beyond the idealized community in Acts 4, which shares communal property and distributes according to need, representative "outcasts" in the remaining chapters who come to be included in Acts' embrace include the exotic and elite Ethiopian eunuch, high-ranking officials in Asia, a Roman centurion, and a wealthy dealer in purple dye.[65]

The shift away from poor and downtrodden in the Third Gospel to the socially well placed in Acts may be illustrated by Acts 16. It would be difficult to argue for a better candidate to represent the socially downtrodden than the mantic prophet of Acts 16.16–18: a slave girl whose prophetic gift is exploited by her owners for financial gain. But the narrative shows no compassion for her, relegating her to the status of a prop (and perhaps a joke). The real story here centers on Paul, who exorcises the slave girl only because he finds her an annoyance. Likewise, the prisoners listening to Paul and Silas sing hymns in the jail at Philippi might also count among those in desperate need of liberation. Here, however, the narrative focus is not on these prisoners but on the jailor and his conversion. Consider, for example, the prison drama following the earthquake at 16.27–28: "When the jailer woke up and saw the prison doors wide open, he drew his sword and was about to kill himself, since he supposed that the prisoners had escaped. But Paul shouted in a loud voice, 'Do not harm yourself, for we are all here.'" A great distance has been traveled by the redactor of Luke-Acts from Jesus' Nazareth sermon in Luke 4.18–19 to this sympathetic portrait of the noble jailer who would commit suicide for his failure to keep captives from being set at liberty.

The empire-critical reading of Acts has also stressed that this text focuses some attention on women, with the presumption being that any focus on women must be an expression of countercultural values.[66] But this line of argumentation fails to convince, in view of numerous recent studies of how particular depictions of high-standing women in ancient texts serve to reinforce Roman ideologies of gender, including studies that focus specifically on gender ideology in Acts.[67] If the emancipatory value of a text is measured in terms of the extent to which it gives voice to the marginalized, Acts falls short. This is so, not only in terms of how it depicts the women it does mention in the narrative but also in terms of how it omits from this account of the history of the postresurrection *ekklēsia* many named women leaders of the Jesus movement known from other texts.[68]

Furthermore, the suggestions of Gilbert, Brent, and Balch that Acts' universal scope somehow subverts and confronts the hegemonic universalizing rhetoric of empire are problematic. I have noted above that "exclusivism" rather than "universalism" might best capture Acts' privileging of followers of the Way over non-confessing *Ioudaioi*. The question of how universalism figures in Acts' discourse concerning race/ethnicity/peoplehood can be considered more broadly here, especially in view of Denise Buell's groundbreaking work on the subject. Buell has demonstrated that while early Christian discourse, like imperial discourse, makes extensive use of universalizing rhetoric, this rhetoric should not be understood as an enlightened appeal to eradicate racism or ethnic prejudice. The sort of cultural mixity embraced in modern discourse of urban life in the age of globalization is not in view in the ancient Mediterranean.[69] Because membership in a *genos/ethnos/laos* was understood to be mutable in the ancient world, it was possible to speak of Christianity as being open to all, while also defining Christians as members of a superior ethno-racial group. Thus, Buell notes the resonance between the rhetoric of Acts and that of the second-century orator, Aelius Aristides. In the context of considering the common dichotomy between Greeks and barbarians, Aelius Aristides notes that the Romans constitute another option, a race that is "all encompassing"— one that "counterbalances the rest."[70] While Luke-Acts situates itself in terms of the Jew–Gentile rather than Greek–barbarian binary, it also poses a third option, with an equally all-encompassing universal vision.

Recognizing that Luke-Acts can both invoke the universal, while also considering Christians as a particular and superior people, helps to account for its particular take on ethnic/cultural difference. As Acts charts Paul's travels across the Mediterranean, it does not bespeak a universalism that embraces Edamite or Phrygian or Cyrenian culture and values. Rather, Acts' perspective on the foreign mirrors Roman perspectives and includes typical imperial views of the subjugated: Athens provides the proper stage for philosophical exchange, and Paul's ticket onto that stage is his possession of *paideia* (17.16–34); Lystra is inhabited by yokels (14.8–18); the natives (*barbaroi*) of Malta are exotic, but friendly (28.1–10); and the *Ioudaioi* are prone to stasis.[71]

Finally, the argument that the author of Acts distinguishes himself from imperial agents by employing the beneficent ideology of empire in an innocent and true way, while remaining free from the taint of violence inherent in that ideology, does not do justice to the text of Luke-Acts in its redacted form.[72] In subsequent chapters, I will expose the problems in this line of argumentation as they pertain to the sayings on forgiveness and enemy love. Here, I shall merely mention how it skims over the violence of the Roman slave system. Both Rowe and Balch cite the dominical saying concerning the master who serves his watchful slaves (Luke 12.35–38) as a sign of the countercultural power relations asserted in Luke-Acts. But such an argument is possible only if one isolates this particular saying from the larger collection of logia in which it is situated. The master might serve the dutiful slaves as Luke 12.35–38 suggests, but the larger sayings collection makes clear that the master retains his power over the bodies of slaves with whom he is not pleased. Degrees of penalty from the master for these slaves range from light beating to dismemberment (Luke 12.45–48). Such disciplinary measures indicate no countercultural practice but are part and parcel of the logics of the slave society in which Luke-Acts is finally redacted.[73]

In conclusion, the empire-critical readings reviewed here may serve as a valuable window onto the ambiguity inherent in this text written in colonial circumstance and demonstrate possibilities for reading "Acts *against* Acts." Yet, the problem that remains unacknowledged in this scholarship is that Theophilus himself is not directed to read in this oppositional way. There may indeed be a subversive "hidden transcript" located in this text, but the surface transcript is one of accommodation. While Peter speaks to Cornelius of Jesus—and not Caesar—as the one who is Lord over all (10.36), nothing in the narrative suggests that this claim has subversive consequences. This Roman centurion suffers no charge of treason consequent to his baptism; there is no hint in the narrative that his conversion requires him to separate from his Italian cohort. While the charges of social disturbance leveled against Paul in both Philippi and Thessalonica (16.20–21, 17.6–7), along with the famous riot instigated by the artisans in Ephesus (19.23–41), may signal traces of a Pauline movement that challenged the status quo, these traces are trapped in a rhetorical frame insisting otherwise. Against any accusation to the contrary, Acts' final word on these men representing "the Way" is that they do not advocate lawbreaking, do not disrespect pagan gods, and do nothing that would turn the world upside down.

Acts and the Marcionite Heresy

While scholars in large numbers jostle to position Luke-Acts precisely in relation to questions of Jews and Romans, fewer pen arguments situating Acts' composition within emerging heresiological quarrels.[74] The relative paucity of interest in Acts as a text written in response to intra-Christian dissension may be accounted for by the traditional dating of Acts as a first-century text, a date considered too early to be linked to such a *Sitz im Leben*. Reading Acts as a second-century text, however, allows one to position it as fully engaged with emerging internal ecclesial debates concerning matters of practice and doctrine, debates that retrospectively come to be known as controversies between orthodox and heretical parties. Acts' awareness of such conflicts is explicitly signaled by Paul in his farewell speech at Miletus: "I know that after I have gone, savage wolves will come in among you, not sparing the flock. Some even from your own group will come distorting the truth in order to entice the disciples to follow them" (20.29–30). This prediction of dangerous divisiveness, along with the subsequent exhortation to follow Paul's teaching and example as a means of combating these divisive forces (20.31–35), aligns Acts with the Pastoral Epistles, also early second-century documents with provenance in Asia Minor that assert Paul as their authorizing voice against dissenters.[75]

The heretic of greatest interest to scholars who situate Acts as a second-century composition is Marcion of Sinope, the shipping magnate who sets up a shop in the city of Rome in the middle of the second century of the Common Era to promulgate his Christian message. None of Marcion's writings are extant, and we can only reconstruct his teachings from the heresiologists who outline his arguments to refute them.[76] In Marcion's schema, the creator god of the Jews is distinct from the Father God of Jesus Christ. The appearance of Jesus as envoy of this Father God is something entirely novel, and radical discontinuity exists between this new revelation of Gospel and anything revealed previously in the creator's Law or anticipated by the Hebrew prophets. The antithetical nature of Law and Gospel is especially evident in matters of judgment and mercy, and war and peace: While the Old Testament emphasizes vengeance in its formulation of the *lex talionis*, Jesus counsels his followers to turn the other cheek (*Marc.* 4.16). While the Old Testament Prophet Elijah sends bears to kill unruly children, Jesus opens his arms to embrace all children (*Marc.* 4.23.4–5). While the God of the Old Testament is capricious and warlike, Jesus embodies the Father God's higher principles of peace and compassion (*Marc.* 1.6.1). Though Marcion allows that Jesus did suffer on the cross, he espouses the view that Jesus did not suffer a human nativity. Rather than being born and enduring a human infancy, Jesus appears as an adult during the fifteenth year of the reign of Tiberius.[77]

Rejecting the Scriptures of the "Old Testament" God, Marcion draws upon two early Christian writings that he regards as the new Scriptures for the new revelation, one Gospel and one "Apostle." His Gospel is a version of what comes to be known as the canonical Gospel of Luke, though Marcion's version is shorter. While the precise content of Marcion's Gospel is difficult to ascertain, it is clear that it lacks the first two chapters of canonical Luke in which Jesus' human nativity is detailed.[78] The "Apostle" is an abridged version of a collection of the Epistles of Paul, who in Marcion's mind is the only apostle of the new revelation, standing in opposition to the Judaizing message propagated by the false apostles of the creator god. Fronting Marcion's "Apostle" is the Letter to the Galatians, the Pauline Epistle most easily read as constructing Law and Gospel in binary opposition (Gal. 3.16, 10–11) and as distancing the divine apostleship of Paul from the human/false authority of the Jerusalem apostles (Gal. 1.1).

Both Irenaeus and Tertullian accuse Marcion of mutilating the Third Gospel and the Pauline Epistles to create his heretical version of Scriptures. Though scholars reading Marcion through these accusations have assumed that Marcion abridged a canonical form of Luke in his possession, Andrew Gregory now presents a convincing hypothesis that Marcion only knew a form of a proto-Luke that was shorter than the canonical Luke.[79] Recent scholarship on Marcion's Apostle has also concluded that Marcion's tendency was more toward conservation than expurgation.[80]

In terms of structuring the early Christian story, Marcion's new Scriptures share something in common with the two-volume work of Luke-Acts. Both situate Jesus and his followers within a "Gospel–Apostle" frame, with one volume devoted to the life and teachings of Jesus and another devoted to the ministry of Paul.[81] But while these texts may frame the story similarly, they each fill the frame with radically oppositional content. Marcion's Gospel depicts Jesus "appearing" as an adult and revealing a new message that is distinct from the Torah and not anticipated by the Hebrew prophets. In contrast, the first two chapters of canonical Luke—the chapters absent from Marcion's Gospel—narrate Jesus' nativity, situate this advent squarely within Jewish cultic practices, and underscore his status as the fulfillment of Jewish prophecy. The canonical Acts embrace and idealize Paul as the most significant messenger of Jesus; but unlike Marcion who imagines Paul in opposition to the Jerusalem apostles, Acts asserts continuity between Paul and the Twelve. In Acts, Paul acknowledges the authority of the Twelve, works obediently under their direction, and is accredited by them to preach to the Gentiles. While Paul receives this accreditation gladly, Acts makes clear that the Twelve pave the way for Paul's Gentile mission, through conversions of the Ethiopian eunuch and the Roman Centurion Cornelius along with the pre-Pauline revelation concerning the dissolution of dietary laws. Moreover, in both canonical Luke and Acts, the refrain is repeated that everything that comes to flower in the life of Jesus and the ministry of Paul has been anticipated in the Hebrew Scriptures.

Because of the way that canonical Luke and Acts, taken together, serve to refute marcionite teaching, citations from both of these volumes are essential to the anti-marcionite arguments of both Irenaeus (ca. 185 CE) and Tertullian (ca. 207 CE).[82] A traditional understanding of how Acts comes to be utilized for this purpose is that the text, written in the first century, but underappreciated at that time, is dusted off and redeployed by the heresiologists who discover its usefulness for their arguments.[83] A more controversial assertion, articulated by John Knox some sixty years ago, and recently reintroduced by Knox's student Joseph Tyson, is that Acts, along with the final redaction of the Third Gospel, is published for the purpose of combating Marcion's proclamation.[84]

A key difficulty in positing Acts as a direct response to Marcion's proclamation lies in questions of dating and provenance, even among those who champion Acts as a second-century text.[85] Acts is a text composed in the East, quite possibly in the city of Ephesus, sometime between 110 and 135 CE. Marcion's ministry in Rome was established ca. 140–50 CE. Though he comes to Rome from an Eastern province, traces of that pre-Roman life are faint, and therefore, few scholars would venture to say anything about it.[86] Knox and Tyson are compelled to make this venture, arguing that Marcion would have been active in the East some decades before he traveled to Rome and therefore that marcionite teaching was one significant impetus for the publication of Acts in this region, some decades before 140 CE.[87]

The arguments of Knox and Tyson are intriguing, insofar as they bring to the foreground themes of Acts that serve as stark counterpoint to marcionite views, particularly in terms of the status of Hebrew Scripture in relation to the new revelation and of Paul in relation to the Jerusalem apostles. It is more persuasive to posit Acts as written in a milieu in which marcionite ideas are circulating, than to imagine its author writing in isolation from these ideas while still, almost preter-naturally, composing a text that comes to serve as a near-perfect rebuttal of them.

While the textual base for positing the nature and extent of Marcion's pre-Roman ministry is admittedly thin, it is not unreasonable to imagine that Marcion taught in the East for some decades before he arrived in Rome. Yet, the Knox/Tyson's arguments for "anti-marcionite" impulses in Luke-Acts may be strengthened, if they need not rise or fall on the question of the precise pre-Roman itinerary of Marcion of Pontus. Therefore, I tweak the thesis offered by these two scholars to accommodate an alternate model for the development of the categories orthodoxy and heresy.

In Tyson's recent restatement of Knox's thesis on the relationship of Luke-Acts to Marcion, he proceeds first by identifying texts that suggest traces of Marcion's presence in the East, so that he might establish the point at which Marcion's opponents encounter him. He then proceeds, in a second step, to outline Marcion's theology and practice and the challenge Marcion posed to his opponents.[88] But this two-step procedure by which one first finds the heretic and then identifies the teaching, which is assumed to originate with him, rep-licates the ideology of the ancient heresiologists, who also constructed each heresy as a teaching promulgated by an identifiable outsider—generally an "Easterner"—seeking to contaminate and hence to destabilize a preexisting orthodoxy.[89] As Karen King notes in her work on defining Gnosticism, how-ever, this model of a polluting heresy corrupting a pure orthodox essence oc-cludes the fact that "there was no predetermined orthodoxy that was simply there."[90]

A better model of how orthodox positions come to be constructed against Marcion of Pontus recognizes that the question of the proper relationship of "Judaism" to "Christianity," and of Law to Gospel, was a question animating texts identified with the Jesus movement from early on. In these internal debates, positions that eventually come to be projected onto the man Marcion arise before Marcion comes onto the scene. Obvious examples come from the Pauline Epistles: The question of Paul's authority vis-à-vis the authority of the Jerusalem apostles and questions of the relationship of Jewish Law to Jesus revelation are questions arising already at the writing of Galatians; the question of whether Paul's preaching on the relationship of law verses grace leads to the abolishment of punishment for sin is one he needs to address already in the Epistle to the Romans (Rom. 3.8). Consider also the Matthean tradition. Owing to the structure of the contrast between the law of Moses and the teaching of Jesus in the Sermon on the Mount ("you have heard it said . . . but I say . . . "), it is not difficult to imagine a reader of Matthew before the time of Marcion concluding that Gospel was somehow antithetical to Law.

That is, recognizing that the debates that animate the author of Luke-Acts are "marcionite" in character need not be contingent upon pinpointing Marcion's whereabouts before his departure for Rome. One might speak instead of marcionite ideas—with a lower case "m"—circulating in a particularly high concentration in Ephesus when Acts is written and the Third Gospel is redacted, including ideas about the antithesis of Law and Gospel and the sole authority of Paul as bearer of the new revelation. While these ideas are eventually projected onto Marcion as a means of distinguishing between internal orthodox purity and external heretical contamination, they need not be identified as originating with him.[91] In this model, the urgency of the question, did the author of Luke-Acts *really* know Marcion, recedes.

To illustrate the shift in models suggested here, consider the following text from Polycarp's *Letter to the Philippians* 7.1: "Whoever distorts the words of the Lord for his own passions, saying that there is neither resurrection nor judgment—this one is the firstborn of Satan" (Ehrman, LCL). Much ink has been spilled over the question of whether Polycarp has Marcion in view when he pens this admonishment.[92] Those who see Marcion here argue that such views concerning resurrection and judgment reflect his influence. As further support for the argument that Polycarp is thinking of Marcion here, they note that the moniker, "firstborn of Satan," is also employed by Irenaeus in the dialogue he stages between Marcion and Polycarp.[93] But for purposes of the arguments developed in this book, the crucial import of this passage is not that it enables us to identify the person Marcion as "the firstborn of Satan" denounced by Polycarp—this is possible but not certain. What is more firmly ascertainable from this passage is that Polycarp knows of Christians who are circulating ideas, eventually projected onto the outsider Marcion, that call into question traditional concepts of resurrection and final judgment.[94]

In short, I imagine that Acts is composed, and the Third Gospel receives its final canonical redaction in a milieu in which these questions are percolating and in which answers that come eventually to be associated with Marcion are being tested. There is merit, therefore, in considering "marcionite" theology and practices in relation to Luke-Acts, regardless of whether one accepts the premise that Acts' knowledge of this theology and practice comes directly from Marcion of Pontus.

YHWH God, Strong in Battle

In this final section, I demonstrate how the textual base for the thesis of Knox and Tyson may be expanded through consideration of an anti-marcionite thematic that appears to animate the author of Luke-Acts. In its redacted form, this two-volume work is well suited to address marcionite thinking concerning the balance of divine mercy to divine judgment, the question of divine propensity for war, and the nature of divine peace.[95] Because of the relevance of these questions specifically to the function of the Stephen pericope in Acts, I take up these questions in considerable detail in subsequent chapters centered on this pericope. Here, I introduce a discussion of the relevance of Luke-Acts for refuting marcionite assertions concerning mercy and judgment, and war and peace, by focusing on martial imagery in chapters 1 and 2 of canonical Luke.

As noted above, Marcion's Gospel does not include the first two chapters of canonical Luke. Knox had suggested that these two chapters were appended to a proto-Luke for the specific purpose of refuting marcionite theology, a position Tyson elaborates at length.[96] These scholars are most concerned with aspects of the infancy narrative that affirm Jesus as born into a community of pious Jews, according to Hebrew Scriptures. Tyson notes, for example, how the births of Jesus and John are described with emphasis on the fleshiness of conception and gestation.[97] The parents of John and Jesus, along with the prophets Simeon and Anna, are depicted as models of Jewish piety, affirming the Jewish priesthood and the importance of the temple, the connection between the Hebrew prophets and Jesus' arrival, and the importance of Jewish festivals and ritual observance. Luke 2 contains the only canonical reference to Jesus' circumcision, thereby marking Jesus as a savior who enters the world with an infant, fleshy, Jewish body. These first two chapters contain an unusually high concentration of Septuagintal language and echo prominent Septuagintal narratives. In addition to clear allusions to the story of Hannah and Samuel, there are explicit references to eight characters from the Jewish Bible—Aaron and Abijah (1.5), Abraham (1.55, 1.73), Asher (2.36), David (1.27, 1.32, 1.69, 2.3, 2.11), Elijah (1.17), Jacob (1.33), and Moses (2.22).

Once again, whether or not the author penned these words *directly* in response to Marcion's arrival on the scene, Tyson well demonstrates the serviceability of these first two chapters to an anti-marcionite polemic. The strong insistence in these two chapters that Jesus is the Jewish messiah, born of the flesh, in accordance with Hebrew Scriptures seems likely penned in awareness that others affirm Jesus as Christ in alternate ways. In connection with the anti-marcionite emphasis on Jewish piety and scriptural fulfillment in Luke 1 and 2 elaborated by Tyson, it is striking to note also the high concentration of vocabulary related to violence and military conquest in these chapters. These martial images blur any marcionite distinction between the war god of the Old Testament and the Father God of peace. For here, at the opening of canonical Luke, appears not the marcionite God of pure love and compassion but the militant God, swift to execute vengeance upon enemies.

The two canticles in Luke's infancy narrative, commonly known as the Magnificat (1.46–55) and the Benedictus (1.68–79), set the births of Jesus and John within a larger narrative of God's relationship with Israel. While the canticles include language celebrating divine mercy and peace for the elect, this beneficent language is interlaced with images of God as mighty warrior fighting enemies on Israel's behalf. Through their structure and vocabulary, these songs show affinity with martial psalms and hymns from the biblical and intertestamental periods, as well as with the *War Scroll* at Qumran. Phrases from Mary's song, including "the Mighty One has done great things" (v. 49) and "He has shown strength with his arm; he has scattered the proud in the thoughts of their hearts" (v. 51)," evoke YHWH God girded for battle (cf. Pss 24.7–10; Zeph. 3.17; 1QM I, 14). As Paul Winter has noted, Zechariah's prophecy in 1.68–74 echoes the prayer of Judas Maccabeus before he leads his army off to fight the Syrians:[98]

1 Macc. 4.30–33:	Luke 1.67–71:
When Judas saw that [the Syrian] army was strong, he prayed, saying,	Then . . . Zechariah was filled with the Holy Spirit and spoke this prophecy:
"Blessed are you, O Savior of Israel, who crushed the attack of the mighty warrior by the hand of your servant David, and gave the camp of the Philistines into the hands of Jonathan . . . Strike them down with the sword of those who love you, and let all who know your name praise you with hymns."	"Blessed be the Lord God of Israel,for he has looked favorably on his people and redeemed them. He has raised up a mighty savior for us in the house of his servant David . . . that we would be saved from our enemies and from the hand of all who hate us."

Among those who take the violent allusions of the canticles seriously, including Paul Winter, Richard Horsley, and Lloyd Gaston, a common endeavor has been to pinpoint their *Sitz im Leben*. Each of these three scholars identifies the canticles as pre-Lukan and also pre-70, positioning the songs at considerable remove from the cataclysmic violence of the Jewish War and the temple's destruction. Winter sees Maccabean resonance in the canticles and thus proposes that the Benedictus and Magnificat originate as Maccabean battle hymns sung, respectively, at the beginning and close of the fighting.[99] Horsley dates them near to the time of Jesus' birth. He affirms—one might even say he celebrates—their violent thrust by situating them as the songs of oppressed peasants of that era who longed for the overthrow of Roman and Judean overlords.[100] Lloyd Gaston employs a negative argument to situate the composition of these canticles to the era pre-70, reasoning that these chapters could not have been composed after the Jewish War since they are addressed specifically to Israel and they speak of peace, redemption, and rescue from enemies. Noting that after 70 CE, such optimism about peace as a real possibility for Israel would have sounded like "bitter mockery," he concludes that such statements must have been written before the tragedy.[101]

Yet, it must be noted, no matter what the original setting of the canticles, that these texts are known to readers in only one form, the redacted narrative of the Third Gospel.

No less important than the issue of their original life setting is the question of why they are privileged in the opening chapters of Luke's two-volume work. Even scholars who do not accept the hypothesis concerning a second-century, anti-marcionite setting for the redaction of Luke 1 and 2, as proposed here, will agree that these chapters are redacted post-70. Given this post-destruction redaction, the observation of Gaston concerning the sound of "bitter mockery" emanating from such triumphal assertions concerning Israel's fate should yet give pause.

Consider the way that the Lukan canticles inversely mirror sentiments in the lament from 2 Esdras concerning the destruction of the temple:

2 Esd. 10.21–22a:
our sanctuary has been laid waste, our altar is thrown down, our temple destroyed, our harp has been laid low, our rejoicing has ended . . .

Luke 1.46–47:
My soul magnifies the Lord, and my spirit rejoices in God my savior

2 Esd. 10.22b–23:
our righteous men have been carried off, our little ones have been cast out, our young men have been enslaved and our strong men made powerless. And worst of all, the seal of Zion has been deprived of its glory, and given over into the hands of those that hate us.

Luke 1.68–71:
Blessed be the Lord God of Israel, for he has looked favorably on his people and redeemed them. He has raised up a mighty savior for us in the house of his servant David . . . that we would be saved from our enemies and from the hand of all who hate us.

After the city of Jerusalem stands in ruins, what possible audience might assent to Mary's song that God has scattered and overthrown the proud and the powerful or Zechariah's prophecy that "By the tender mercy of our God, the dawn from on high will break upon us . . . to guide our feet into the way of peace" (1.78–79)? What resonance may be found in Simeon's praises addressed to God in the Jerusalem temple, "now you are dismissing your servant in peace" (2.29a) after the time in which the golden vessels of that temple reside in a distant "Temple of Peace," the one erected by Vespasian in Rome to celebrate the destruction of Judea (Josephus, J. W. 7.161)? These songs of victory in battle, affirmations that the enemy has been vanquished and proclamations of peace among those favored by God, have a distinctive ring after the Judean War. As Gaston notes, they would indeed sting in the ears of those mourning the destruction of Jerusalem.

Yet, they do adumbrate the perspective on vengeance, peace, and the constitution of Israel that is advanced in the two-volume work, Luke-Acts. Differently from the other Gospels, and in line with later Christian apologetic, the Third Gospel explicitly affirms that the Roman destruction of Jerusalem owes to Jewish rejection of Jesus.[102] In a passage distinct to the Third Gospel, Jesus weeps over the city of Jerusalem and its impending destruction, lamenting that it did not recognize "the things that make for peace" (εἰρήνη; 19.42). He proclaims that the destruction of the temple, along with the crushing of Judean bodies to the ground, owes to the inability of nonbelieving Jews to recognize the time of their visitation (ἐπισκοπή; 19.43–44). This is the consequence of not recognizing that visitation and that peace heralded by Zechariah in Luke 1 (1.68: "he has looked favorably [ἐπισκέψατο] on his people and redeemed them"; 1.79b: "to guide our feet in the way of peace [εἰρήνη]"). Acts subsequently makes clear that the promise of blessing for Israel is reserved for "the people" who accept Jesus as the Messiah, a group that promises to be increasingly Gentile in makeup by the narrative's close.[103] In a post-70 context, these assertions demonstrate the affinity of Luke-Acts with the imperial perspective that Jewish suffering in the war was deserved, and the emerging Christian appropriation of the term Israel for its own group.[104]

Whether these canticles are indeed appended to a proto-Luke in response to marcionite concerns, as proposed by Knox and Tyson, or whether they are part of an earlier form of the Third Gospel, as others insist, their usefulness for rebutting a particular strand of marcionite thought when they are read in the second century should be recognized. In praising one divine agent, who both engages in war and establishes peace, and who administers both mercy and judgment, the canticles serve well to refute any marcionite schema that assigns these disparate functions to two different gods revealed in two different testaments.

Finally, it should be noted that martial imagery in canonical Luke 1 and 2, so useful for refuting marcionite dualism, is not reserved for the canticles alone. As has been stressed in the work of J. Massyngbaerde Ford, these introductory chapters are replete with militaristic allusions.[105] These include the presence of the Angel Gabriel, one of the angels associated with eschatological holy war in the intertestamental period, along with the heavenly army (στρατιά) attendant on the annunciation to the shepherds. While the phrase πλῆθος στρατιᾶς οὐρανίου is commonly translated into English as "a multitude of the heavenly host," it might be more literally translated as "a large number of soldiers from heaven." As noted by Ford and, also more recently, by Brittany Wilson, even Mary the mother of Jesus receives the taint of a violent association in Luke 1. In the house of Zechariah and Elizabeth, Mary is hailed as "blessed among women" (1.42).[106] This affirmation is used twice in the Septuagintal narrative, which the author of Luke 1 and 2 strives to emulate, in both instances celebrating women who single-handedly execute enemies of Israel. Jael is poetically memorialized in Judges as "most blessed among women" for the fact that she has driven a hammer through the skull of the enemy Sisera (Judg. 5.24–27). Uzziah proclaims Judith, the decapitator of Holofernes, to be "blessed above all other women on earth" in the context of praising the God who guided Judith "to cut off the head of the leader of our enemies" (Jdt. 13.18–20).

In short, the first two chapters of canonical Luke well serve an antimarcionite program not only because they affirm Jesus as savior for the Jews, as predicted in the Scriptures of Israel, but also because they insist that the warlike God, who in marcionite distillation is a deity associated exclusively with the old revelation, oversees Jesus' advent. This advent is heralded through canticles praising the warrior God of Israel, through Gabriel's annunciation and the appearance of the heavenly army, through the hailing of Mary as "blessed among women," a Septuagintal acclamation that places Jesus' mother in the company of her "pugnacious precursors," Jael and Judith.

To conclude this chapter, I return to the question of resistant and conformist readings. While it is possible to read Luke-Acts as affirming Jews and Judaism, and as subverting Roman imperial logics, these readings require their own act of subversion, for they must push against the grain of the pervasive anti-Jewish, pro-Roman rhetorical markers lodged within the text. Recognizing the rhetorical thrust of Luke-Acts with respect to marcionite questions requires a somewhat different set of reading skills, capable of resisting the widespread, if unarticulated, modern propensity to read this text itself with a marcionite lens. This lens will be examined with respect to the forgiveness prayer of Stephen in the analysis of subsequent chapters. Here, I note the marcionite influence that extends over the readings of Ford and Wilson reviewed above. While these scholars both make compelling arguments concerning the rhetorical violence that imbues Luke 1 and 2, they move from this analysis to the somewhat baffling conclusion that the Third Gospel introduces this violence only as a prefatory foil for the author's subsequent program of peace. Thus, Wilson argues that the relationship of Mary to Judith and Jael is one of radical juxtaposition, signaling that "Mary ushers in a new age, in which women are called most blessed for their acts of peace rather than for their acts of violence."[107] Massyngbaerde Ford argues that while chapters 1–2 of Luke set up expectations of Jesus as a revolutionary messiah, the remainder of the Gospel is devoted to refuting this revolutionary messiah in favor of Jesus' nonviolent resistance.[108] Such conclusions, if unwittingly, read the Third Gospel as Marcion did: as a Gospel that truly begins with the third chapter of canonical Luke, in which the peaceful Jesus stands in opposition to the warring God of the Old Testament.

2

Perfect Martyr

Situating Stephen within Acts

And Stephen was the first after the Lord with respect to his ordination, and in addition—*as if he had been brought forth for this very
purpose*—because he was stoned to death by those who murdered the
Lord. And so, he was the first to carry off the prize gained by the
worthy martyrs of Christ, the crown, well suited to his name.
—Eusebius, *Ecclesiastical History* (emphasis added)

The previous chapter has addressed Luke-Acts in broad overview,
identifying rhetorical aims of the two-volume work with respect to
the questions of Romans, Jews, and other forms of Christian identity.
This chapter focuses more narrowly on the Stephen pericope within
the context of Acts' treatment of persecution and martyrdom. Under
analysis here are questions of how Acts plots relationships of
violence leading to death; the proper names assigned to executioners
and would-be executioners; the tropes related to martyrdom
employed; the gaps and silences in this narrative concerning violence
against followers of Jesus; and finally, the significance of the Stephen
pericope to these questions.

The perfect suitability of Stephen to the Christian story is noted
by Eusebius, who remarks on the uncanny nature of his name (τὸν
αὐτῷ φερώνυμον[1]) and the providential nature of his appearance in
Acts: *Stephanos*, or "Crown," is stoned to death, "as if he had been
brought forth for this very purpose" (ὥσπερ εἰς αὐτὸ τοῦτο
προαχθείς; *Hist. eccl.* 2.1.1). My concern here is to underscore

Stephen's perfect suitability to the text of Luke-Acts, not in the providential terms employed by Eusebius but in terms of rhetorical fittingness. To begin this analysis, I first raise questions concerning the place of Acts within emerging Christian discourse of martyrdom.

Acts Alongside Early Christian Martyr Tales

Among stories of early Christian martyrs beginning to circulate in the second century, the book of Acts may be categorized as holding an eccentric, if not a contrarian, view for several reasons. For one, Stephen, the persecuted prophet/ martyr raised up most prominently by the author of Acts, is unknown outside of this work until the church fathers begin to quote Acts at length, beginning with Irenaeus, ca. 180.[2] Furthermore, the only death of an apostle mentioned by Luke is that of James the brother of John, who receives relatively little attention in the martyrologies of the second and third centuries.[3] In contrast, narratives of the deaths of prominent early Christian "pillars"—James the brother of Jesus, Peter, and Paul—while preserved in a variety of genres in the second century, are (in)famously absent from Luke's account.[4] Finally, while no martyrdom of Paul is recounted, his repeated number of "near martyrdoms" at the hands of the Jews, along with his proclaimed willingness "even to die *in Jerusalem*" (Acts 21.13), suggest a desire to assign a Jewish agency and also a Judean locale to Paul's martyrdom that is dramatically out of synch with other Pauline traditions.

The case may not be made that the author of Acts is singularly responsible for the Christ-killing charge laid upon Jews since this charge surfaces in a number of first- and second-century sources. Nor does Acts distinguish itself among early Christian texts merely because it repeatedly portrays Jesus followers as persecuted to the point of death. The pervasiveness and necessity of Christ-like suffering is presumed across a large swath of early Christian literature and becomes an essential component of early Christian identity.[5] The peculiarity of Acts among second-century death narratives owes instead to its mapping of interactions of Jews and Romans with Jesus followers. The almost total absence of pagan authorities wishing to inflict harm on early Christian leaders in Acts sets this work apart from a set of near-contemporary martyrdom texts where the machinery of the state comes into play as executioner—for example, in the Letters of Ignatius or the *Martyrdom of Polycarp*. The Roman officials depicted in Acts, with few exceptions, not only refrain from persecuting the Way but also take great pains to "rescue" Paul from his persecutors.[6] Concerning the relationship of Jesus

followers to "the Jews"—*hoi Ioudaioi*—the force of its assertion is unre-
lenting: The dividing line between these two groups lies at the point of the
persecution of the former by the latter. In the schema of Acts, unbelieving
Ioudaioi kill and desire to kill; Jesus followers are persecuted and killed by
unbelieving *Ioudaioi*.[7]

A brief comparison of extrabiblical sources on the death of Paul with the
story of Paul in Acts well illustrates this peculiarity. While accounts of Paul's
death in early Christian tradition are notoriously opaque and have elicited a
variety of scholarly proposals concerning its nature and timing, it yet
remains that none of these extrabiblical sources, in distinction from the
Acts narrative, feature Jewish involvement. Both Clement of Rome and Polycarp refer to Paul's death within the context of exhortations concerning the
martyr's endurance (1 *Clem.* 5–6; Polycarp 9.1–2) but make no mention of
Jewish executioners. Indeed, the focus on jealousy and envy (ζῆλος καὶ ἔρις)
as the cause of the martyrdom in 1 *Clement* has led scholars to argue that
Paul was a victim of intra-Christian intrigues.[8] Eusebius preserves quotations that locate Paul's martyrdom in Rome under Nero, coterminous with
that of Peter (*Hist. eccl.* 2.25.5–8). In this broad outline—a Roman death
under Nero—Eusebius' sources conform to the details of Paul's death offered up in the mid- to late second-century *Acts of Paul*, a text that might be
understood as the canonical Acts' closest generic relative. In spite of generic
similarities between the *Acts of Paul* and Acts, their ideologies are poles
apart; the former rages against Nero as arch-persecutor, the latter presents
Paul preaching in Rome "unhindered" (ἀκωλύτως).[9] None of these extrabiblical sources single out Jews, Judeans, Jerusalemites, or the Jewish religious leaders as either having caused or having taken pleasure in Paul's
execution.

To be sure, the explanation for this peculiar avoidance of Roman violence,
in general, and Roman execution of Christians, in particular, is related to Acts'
legitimating function, as many scholars have suggested.[10] In a narrative
designed to reassure its readers of their place in the empire, the loss of
prominent leaders of the movement through state-sanctioned execution is a
subject best avoided, or if not avoided, at least deflected. In what follows, I
argue that the stoning of Stephen, the only execution of a Jesus believer with
significant import in Acts,[11] provides the author of this text with a means to
engage in such deflection by underscoring the centrality of persecution to the
Jesus movement, while avoiding any mention of Roman involvement in this
pivotal execution. The flip side of veiling Roman agency in violent actions
toward Jesus believers is to assign this agency to Jews, a phenomenon I now
turn to explicate.

Jews, Jerusalem, and the Killer Impulse in Acts

Jews as Christ Killers

If the importance of an idea in a text is ascertained merely by counting the number of times it is repeated, it becomes clear that assigning responsibility for the crucifixion of Jesus to Jews ranks among the chief concerns of the first half of the book of Acts. The accusation that Jews living in Jerusalem killed Jesus runs rhythmically through its opening pages like a pulse. The charge occurs most often in speeches of Peter and often employs a form of address suggesting an "Israelite agency" above and beyond that of Judeans/Jerusalemites alone:

[PETER]   Men, Israelites, listen to what I have to say: Jesus of Nazareth . . . this man . . . you crucified and killed by the hands of those outside the law. (2.22–23)

[PETER]   Therefore let the entire house of Israel know with certainty that God has made him both Lord and Messiah, this Jesus whom you crucified. (2.36)

[PETER]   Men, Israelites . . . The God of Abraham, the God of Isaac, and the God of Jacob, the God of our ancestors has glorified his servant Jesus, whom you handed over and rejected in the presence of Pilate, though he had decided to release him. But you rejected the Holy and Righteous One and asked to have a murderer given to you, and you killed the Author of life, whom God raised from the dead. (3.12–15a)

[PETER]   Rulers of the people and elders . . . let it be known to all of you, and to all the people in Israel, that this man is standing before you in good health by the name of Jesus Christ of Nazareth, whom you crucified. . . . (4.8b–10a)

[PETER]   The God of our ancestors raised up Jesus whom you had killed by hanging him on a tree. (5.30)

[STEPHEN]   You stiff-necked people, uncircumcised in heart and ears, you are forever opposing the Holy Spirit, just as your ancestors used to do. Which of the prophets did your ancestors not persecute? They killed those who foretold the coming of the Righteous One, and now you have become his betrayers and murderers. (7.51–52)

[PETER]   We are witnesses to all that he did both in Judea and in Jerusalem. They put him to death by hanging him on a tree. (10.39)

[PAUL]   Because the residents of Jerusalem and their leaders did not recognize him or understand the words of the prophets that are read every Sabbath, they fulfilled these words by condemning him. Even though they found no cause for a sentence of death, they asked Pilate to have him killed. (13.27–28)

Differently from these speeches, which lay responsibility for the death of Jesus squarely on Jews, the narrative of the community at prayer (Acts 4.25–30) assigns blame to a larger number of people, including Gentiles, kings, and rulers. Consider, especially 4.28–29: "For in this city, in fact, both Herod and Pontius Pilate, with the Gentiles and the peoples of Israel, gathered together against your holy servant Jesus whom you anointed to do whatever your hand and your plan had predestined to take place." Those who argue that Acts minimizes, rather than underscores, Jewish involvement in Jesus' death privilege this passage in making their case,[12] an argument that does not convince for the following reasons: (1) Unlike the speeches, this passage does not owe to Lukan redaction but rather to a preexisting traditional exegesis of Psalm 2.1–2, which assigns the roles of king and ruler to Herod and Pilate, respectively (cf. the similar exegetical association in Justin, *Apol.* 1.40). While the author of Luke-Acts concedes elsewhere that Romans are implicated in Jesus' death, the manner in which Roman culpability is assigned here is atypical. Note how Pilate's role as coconspirator in Jesus' death in this traditional exegesis stands slightly out of synch with the distinction the author of Acts builds into Peter's speech at 3.13: "You handed over and rejected Jesus in the presence of Pilate, *though he had decided to release him*" (emphasis added); (2) while the tradition preserved in 4.28–29 casts blame against all the people—Gentile and Israelite—who stood against Jesus, in Luke's redaction of the passage, ultimately *Israelite* hostility is privileged, for the prayer concludes with a petition for the Lord to now "look at *their* threats" (v. 29). In Acts, the only antecedent who has issued threats against the community of believers in Jerusalem is the Jewish leadership (4.17, 4.21); (3) even if this one passage is pointed to as ameliorating Jewish responsibility for Jesus' death, its ameliorating force wanes when it is placed alongside the several passages highlighted above implicating only Jews.

Sometimes the accusation that Jews are responsible for Jesus' death, because it is addressed directly to rulers, appears to single out the leadership for special blame (cf. 4.8–10, 5.27–30). Particularly in two instances from the Diaspora—Peter's speech before Cornelius in Caesarea (10.39) and Paul's before a gathering of Diaspora Jews (13.27–29)—care is made to mark the culprits in third-person form as Judeans/Jerusalemites and their rulers. Because the specifics of agency vary, with Jewish/Judean rulers and Jerusalemites bearing the brunt of the charge, it has been argued that Luke is minimizing blame through limiting Jewish culpability for Jesus' death to a subgroup, either within the walls of Jerusalem or the larger borders of Judea.[13] From this argument flows the conclusion that Acts is not anti-Jewish.[14]

Yet, while it is the case that Acts privileges Jerusalem as the city that kills its prophets, and hence does assign a primacy of agency for the death of Jesus to those living in Jerusalem, the text does not foreclose the possibility of reading "Jewish responsibility" for Jesus' death more broadly. The accusations in the Jerusalem section are not always exclusively addressed to Judeans/Jerusalemites. Frequently, markers are present that allow for a larger reading of the addressees. The Pentecost speech is prefaced by note that devout Jews "from every nation under heaven" were living in Jerusalem and gathered to hear Peter's speech (2.5, 2.14). In verse 22 of that speech, Peter does not single out Judeans but rather addresses Israelites as "you" who have crucified and killed. In the speech near the temple, Peter addresses "the people," "you Israelites" (3.12), as those who have handed over and rejected Jesus. Stephen's speech addressed to the "stiff-necked people" who have become Jesus' betrayers and murders is not limited to Judeans but is addressed broadly to all the rebellious descendents of Abraham (7.51–53). Even more to the point, and certainly calling into question the argument that Acts is limiting Jewish murderous impulses to a subgroup, are the many ways in which Acts demonstrates that Jews from the Diaspora are as eager to kill Jesus' emissaries as Jerusalem Jews were to kill Jesus himself.

Jews as Disciple Killers

Incidents of Jews wishing to kill leaders of the Way include the following: After a speech of Peter before the council and high priest, they are said to wish to kill Peter and all the apostles (5.27–33). By setting up the Stephen episode with accusations from Jews of "Cyrene, Alexandria, Cilicia and Asia" (6.9), Acts lays his death at the feet of Jews representing a vast expanse of territory—from the far reaches of North Africa to the provinces of Asia. In his unconverted state, Saul, a Jew from Tarsus, approves the killing of Stephen and breathes threats and murder on other followers of the Way. Herod's killing of James the brother of John brings "pleasure" to the Jews (ἀρεστόν ἐστιν τοῖς Ἰουδαίος; 12.3) and then further "expectation from the Jewish people" (προσδοκία τοῦ λαοῦ Ἰουδαίων; 12.11) that he will also kill Peter.[15] Once Paul is introduced onto the stage, the chief obsession of Jews is to take his life. From chapter 9 through chapter 26, there are more than a dozen references to Jewish plots to kill Paul. Jews in Damascus plot to kill Paul (9.23–24), as do Hellenists in Jerusalem (9.29). In Iconium, Jews stir up Gentiles resulting in a plot by both groups to stone Paul and Barnabas (14.2–4). Jews from Antioch and Iconium both work to win over the crowds in Lystra, to the end that Paul is stoned and left for dead (14.19). Unbelieving Jews of Thessalonica are responsible for inciting riots against Paul and Silas in that city as well as in Beroea (17.5, 17.13). While Paul is in Greece, with plans to travel to Syria, Jews concoct a plot against him (20.2–3). When Paul returns to Jerusalem and worships in the temple, it is not Judean Jews, but rather Jews from Asia, who incite the riot that leads to the attempt to kill Paul (21.27–31). The entire crowd in Jerusalem shouts for Paul's death after his speech from the temple steps (22.22). A conspiracy of more than forty Jews plot to kill him, and the chief priests and elders have full knowledge of this plot (23.12, 23.14, 23.21). According to Festus, Jews in Caesarea as well as Jerusalem petition for Paul's death (25.24). In sum, threads depicting perse-cutory Jews are woven throughout the narrative. While Jerusalem might be the source of the murderous impulse, the impulse is not contained within the city walls but rather flows from there outward. With few exceptions, unbelieving Jews are depicted as murderous, regardless of city of origin or current resi-dence. The aim of their murderous desire depends on the accident of time and geography. Those living in Jerusalem at the time of Jesus shout to crucify him; those in the post-crucifixion era, no matter their current residence or natal city, set their sights on the apostles (5.33); Stephen (7.58–60); James, the apostle (12.2–3); Peter (12.11); and, finally, Paul and his traveling companions, Barnabas and Silas.[16] Before turning to an analysis of the significance of the role of these Jews specifically in the martyrdom of Stephen, I consider here both the manner by which Acts depicts Paul himself as martyr, and the limits of that depiction, owing to the constraints of the Acts' narrative.

Paul as Both Martyr and Anti-Martyr

Numerous markers in the text of Acts suggest that Paul dies a martyr's death, following in the footsteps of Jesus. Paul's farewell address in Miletus at 20.17–38, with its foreboding references to his imminent absence (vv. 25, 38) has long been recognized as one of these markers.[17] The subsequent sign prophecy of Agabus at 21.10–14 addresses the issue of Paul's martyrdom more explicitly. Through symbolic enactment, Agabus demonstrates that Paul will be "bound" and "handed over to the Gentiles," like Jesus before him (cf. Mark 10.33, 15.1; Luke 18.32). Paul's response, "For I am ready not only to be bound but even to die in Jerusalem . . ." (21.13b), aligns his resolve with that of Jesus, who also reconciled himself to the fate of dying in Jerusalem (Luke 13.33). That Acts is sculpting Paul as a martyr in this scene is further indicated through the juxtaposition of Paul's expressed resolve to die and the weeping supporters who attempt to persuade him to avoid this fate (21.13–14). This feature of the pericope resonates with depictions of the martyr in near-contemporary early Christian literature, where similar conflicts obtain between the martyr, who is determined to die, and the martyr's friends, who would prefer that he flee.[18] Furthermore, Acts aligns the death of Paul with that of Jesus by strongly underscoring that both are the victims of Jewish machinations.

In considering the multiple ways by which Acts suggests that "the Jews" are the primary force behind Paul's death, it might be noted that one rhetorical effect of the silence concerning Paul's fate at the end of Acts 28 is to reinforce such a conclusion. Daniel Marguerat has argued that the silence concerning Paul's death in the final chapter of Acts, far from being an accidental and "empty" silence, conforms to the "rhetoric of silence" in Greco-Roman historiography.[19] With reference to the poetics of Homer and Virgil, whose epic narratives conclude without recounting developments that have been announced in the preceding body of the work, Marguerat speaks of "open closure" as a common rhetorical device in ancient literature. When reaching the end of a text in which a predicted outcome is left unspoken, readers are invited to fill in the gaps, by extrapolating from the previous narrative. One version of John Chrysostom's homily on the final chapter of Acts acknowledges this process of extrapolation, by explaining how the author "tells not what things came afterwards, deeming it would be superfluous for those who would take in hand the things he had written and who would learn from these how to add on to the narration: *for what the things were which went before, such doubtless he found these things which came after*" (*Hom. Act.* 55 [trans. *NPNF*[1] 11.326, n. 1181], emphasis added). Given that scenes in which Jews attempt to kill Paul are staged repeatedly in Acts, a reader versed in the practice of completing the ending of a work through extrapolating from "the things which went before" could reasonably assume that Jews were primary agents in causing Paul's death.[20]

Yet, even if the gap at the end of Acts begs to be filled with the image of Jews bearing primary responsibility for Paul's death, the text does not provide a fully developed and consistent depiction of Paul as martyr, killed by Jews in the footsteps of Jesus, as the hearing before Festus in Caesarea at Acts 25.6–12 makes especially clear. Paul had expressed before Agabus a martyr's resolve to die *even in Jerusalem*, and it might be said that here Festus gives Paul the opportunity to risk just that possibility, by asking whether he desires "to go up to Jerusalem" to be tried there (25.9). Paul's response contains a significant qualification: "*If I am in the wrong and have committed something for which I deserve to die, I am not trying to escape death*; but if there is nothing to their charges against me, no one can turn me over to them" (25.11ab, emphasis added).

The terms on which Paul here expresses willingness to face death in Jerusalem—only if the sentence is deserved—stand outside of the developing conception of Christian martyrdom.[21] To be sure, some early Christian discussions of martyrdom allow that there are legitimate reasons for fleeing the executioner, most specifically if escape is a temporary respite for the sake of continued teaching and ecclesial leadership on the part of the one threatened with death.[22] But since, by definition, the martyr is always innocent and the executioner always unjust, it is oxymoronic for a martyr to propose that his or her willingness to face death is dependent upon the justice of the sentence. Acts may have pressed "the crown of martyrdom upon his head" in the Miletus speech, as Dibelius noted long ago,[23] but it slips off in Paul's appeal to Caesar.

Paul's stipulation that he is prepared to die only a deserved death and his subsequent appeal to Caesar (25.11c) are, of course, the well-known plot device by which Acts propels Paul into the city of Rome. These are dueling and irreconcilable portraits of Paul: on the one hand, a Jewish prophet/martyr following the footsteps of Jesus to his death in Jerusalem; on the other, a Roman citizen confident that the Roman legal system will exonerate him from this unjust death penalty. They spring from the tensions between Acts' rhetorical strategy of denigrating Jews as killers and the importance of ending with Paul in Rome speaking "unhindered." The irreconcilability of these two Pauline portraits goes far to explain the importance of the pivotal role assigned to Stephen within the Acts narrative, a role to which I now turn.

Stephanos: The Perfect Martyr

Gamaliel Sets the Stage

A speech by Peter and the apostles prompts the first explicit statement of desire to kill the apostles in Acts by a Jewish party, here comprising members of the Jewish council (5.33). The Pharisee Gamaliel is introduced as a member of the council who urges the body to refrain from violence. In an effort to quell their murderous desire, Gamaliel exhorts his audience to consider the fates of a certain Theudas and of Judas, the Galilean. Both men are acknowledged as those who "rose up" and attracted a following, but whose movements were scattered subsequent to their deaths. The sage conclusion drawn from these examples: ". . . turn away from these men and leave them alone for if this plan or work be of humans, it shall be dissolved, but if it is of God you will not be able to destroy it, you would rather be found to be 'God-fighters'" (θεομάχοι; 5.39).

The notion that "plans and works" fail or succeed depending upon divine approval is a typical Hellenistic Jewish affirmation of *pronoia*.[24] The use of the word θεομάχος gives the speech something of a Dionysian flavor, for the plight of King Pentheus, who resists the will of Dionysos in Thebes, was famously sketched in Euripides' *Bacchae*. Yet, in terms of formal considerations, Gamaliel echoes Josephus even more than Euripides. Compare Gamaliel's "lest you be found to be God-fighting" (μήποτε καὶ θεομάχοι εὑρεθῆτε) with Josephus' admonition in his direct speech to rebels desiring to war with Rome: "you are fighting not only against the Romans, but also against God" (μὴ μόνον Ῥωμαίοις πολεμοῦντες ἀλλὰ καὶ τῷ θεῷ; *J.W.* 5.378).[25] Gamaliel's words set the stage for how an ideal reader will perceive the subsequent aggression of unbelieving Jews aimed at followers of the Way. This Pharisee may have succeeded in temporarily restraining his colleagues from their impulse to engage in one of the most egregious of follies—opposing God and his works.[26] But their restraint evaporates almost immediately after the closed-door session ends. From the stoning of Stephen onward, the incidences of Jewish God-fighting only increase.

It is also instructive to compare the mention of Theudas and Judas the Galilean in Acts with Josephus' earlier treatment of these two charismatics. Theudas appears once in a short Josephan summary of the Roman procurator Fadus' rule. Here, the brief flowering and brutal suppression of this sign prophet's movement are the sole events recounted as befalling the Jews under Fadus:

> During the period when Fadus was procurator of Judaea, a certain imposter named Theudas persuaded the majority of the masses to take up their possessions and to follow him to the Jordan River. He stated that he was a prophet and that at his command the river would be parted and would provide them an easy passage. With this talk he deceived many. Fadus, however, did not permit them to reap the fruit of their folly, but sent against them a squadron of cavalry. These fell upon them unexpectedly, slew many of them and took many prisoners. Theudas himself was captured, whereupon they cut off his head and brought it to Jerusalem. These, then, are the events that befell the Jews during the time that Cuspius Fadus was procurator. (*Ant.* 20. 97–99 [Feldman, LCL])

The story of Judas the Galilean is more complex. While the six references to Judas in the Josephan corpus do not entirely cohere, he is consistently identified as a rebel against Rome, whose misguided refusal to submit to the yoke of the first Roman procurator of Judea sows the seeds of unmitigated disaster. As the founder of the Fourth Philosophy, he is linked to the destruction of Jerusalem in the Jewish War (*Ant.* 18.23–24). His progeny include the rebel commander Menachem who is dealt a violent death of the sort he has inflicted upon others (*J. W.* 2.433) and two sons crucified under Tiberius Alexander (*Ant.* 20.102). He is also said to be a distant relative of Eleazar, the leader of the *Sicarii* who hole up in Masada (*J. W.* 7.253).[27]

The most plausible explanation for the overlapping tradition in Acts and Josephus is Acts' dependence upon the *Antiquities*.[28] Luke's departure from Josephan chronology so that Theudas, who died under Fadus (ca. 44–45 CE), is placed before Judas the Galilean, who resisted the census under Quirinius (ca. 6 CE), can be accounted for by (1) (first and foremost) the author's creativity in reworking his sources, (2) the constraints of his narrative that require Theudas' death to be something Gamaliel can speak about in the past tense, and (3) the link between these two rebels via a reference to Judas' sons in *Antiquities* 20.97–102, in which the mention of Theudas precedes that of Judas.

While Acts depends upon Josephus for information on Theudas and Judas, his account diverges significantly with respect to the manner and agency of death. In the case of Josephus' treatment of the Theudas incident, Fadus initiates the brutal suppression of the movement, sending out the cavalry who slaughter hundreds including Theudas himself (*Ant.* 20.97–99). Though Josephus does not recount the death of Judas the Galilean, he holds him responsible for carnage on all sides and relates him to rebels who die at the hands of Rome as well as by fellow countrymen. In contrast, Luke gives no hint of a swooping cavalry, a massive slaughter, or a chopped head raised up as a trophy. The leaders of the two movements suffer nondescript agent-less deaths: Theudas was killed; Judas also perished (θευδᾶς . . . ὃς ἀνῃρέθη . . . Ἰούδας Ὁ Γαλιλαῖος κἀκεῖνος; 5.36–37); their followers are passively "dissolved" (διελύθησαν) and "scattered" (διεσκορπίσθησαν). It is clear that Josephus grants to Rome an instrumentality in the execution of God's *pronoia* as it pertains to the violent dissolution of various Jewish religious–political movements that Acts does not. However much Josephus defers to Roman authority, he does not have qualms about demonstrating that this authority exerts itself through brutal police action.[29] In contrast, the Acts' narrative refrains here from depicting Romans with blood on their hands.[30]

Stephen Is Introduced

The pericope introducing Stephen places him first within a controversy among the Hellenists and Hebrews concerning widows and the distribution of food (6.1–6).[31] It then depicts him suffering false accusations from Diaspora Jews with synagogue affiliation in Jerusalem. They charge him with speaking against the pillars of institutional religious practice—temple and torah. Key indications that Acts is working with sources here include the introduction of a controversy concerning widows and food that is immediately dropped, along with the dissonance between Stephen's assigned role—table service—and his subsequent role as prophetic witness and performer of wondrous signs.[32] The enigmatic designations Hellenists and Hebrews appear not to be invented by Luke.[33] The list of the seven Greek names is also regarded as a sign that Luke draws from a source. While *Stephanos/Crown* has a name perfectly suited for the one destined to be the first Christian martyr, the rest of the names are not similarly pregnant with symbolism. Philip is known from other sources; Nicolaus the proselyte has been tantalizingly, if speculatively, associated with the Nicolaitans of Revelation 2.6;[34] and Prochorus, Nicanor, Timon, and Parmenas are obscure.

Without denying that the author of Acts is working over sources here, I note that, in their redacted form, many of them serve well to communicate Stephen's symbolic role as pivot between Jesus and Paul and as prototypical Christian martyr. While Stephen is in the midst of controversy between two groups of "Jews," the Hebrews and the Hellenists, this intragroup division adumbrates the subsequent division between Jewish and Gentile believers that will come to the fore in the Pauline mission. That Stephen faces controversy in the synagogues, but is tried before a council (*synedrion*) and the high priest, makes him a transitional character: like the Jerusalem apostles, he faces a hostile temple leadership; like Paul in the Diaspora, his enemies also spring from the synagogues. Even the seemingly arbitrary list of the seven names may be viewed as conforming to the plotline of Acts. Beginning with the prominent names of Stephen and Philip, and ending with the Antiochene proselyte, the order bespeaks the movement from "Stephen's mission to Greek-speaking Jews to the evangelization of Gentiles at Antioch."[35] Finally, regardless of precisely how many synagogues his accusers are imagined to inhabit,[36] that they include natives of Cyrene, Alexandria, Cilicia, and Asia means that Stephen's enemies come from the far reaches of the earth. If they include "Libyans," the geographic reach is further extended; if the textual witnesses that read "libertines" or freedmen are preferred over those reading "Libyans,"[37] then Stephen's opponents are variegated with respect to class as well as geographic origin. In either case, Acts 6.9 makes clear that the scope of Stephen's opposition is wide.

The Import of Stephen's Death for the Mission's Progress

Within the book of Acts itself the Stephen episode functions as a geographic marker of the mission's progress, closing the Jerusalem section of Acts and propelling the mission into Judea and Samaria (and eventually through the agency of Paul, to the ends of the earth). The closing verse of the martyrdom story, "That day [of Stephen's death] a severe persecution began against the church in Jerusalem, and all except the apostles were scattered throughout the countryside of Judea and Samaria (8.1)," confirms the prophecy of Jesus in 1.8 concerning the geographic progress of the apostolic witness. The fourfold sequence by which the death propels the mission forward—death-persecution-scattering proclamation (8.1, 8.4)—anticipates in narrative form what Tertullian will famously proclaim some years later: the blood of the martyr is the seed of the church. The seed planted by Stephen's martyrdom bears fruit in four missionary endeavors that follow immediately upon it:[38] (1) the mission of Philip in Samaria (8.4–40), who, like Stephen, is one of the seven (6.5); (2) the conversion of Saul (9.1–31), whose association with the death of Stephen is underscored (9.1, 22.20), who turns immediately upon his conversion to the work of "confounding" (συγχέω) the Jews, and who will take center stage from Acts 13 to the close of the book; (3) the mission of Peter (9.32–11.18), who goes about as result of the scattering (8.4, 9.32) finding himself in Lydda, Joppa, and, finally, Caesarea; and (4) the nameless missionaries, who, scattered because of the persecution at Stephen's death (11.19), proceed as far as Antioch, the place where disciples of the Lord Jesus are first named "Christians" (11.26).

The Import of Stephen's Death for the Making of Christians and Jews

This last branch of mission activity foregrounds another means by which the death of Stephen is pivotal: the death ignites the process of naming the two distinct religious groups in Acts. While the assertion that Stephen himself is the "first Christian" overreaches, verses 11.19 and 26 do connect Stephen's death with the first naming of Christians. Because Acts does not embrace wholeheartedly the name Christian for his group—it is used only twice in the entire narrative—the suggestion that Stephen's death is connected to the "making of Christians" in Antioch is only a suggestion rather than a sustained narrative theme. In contrast, a shift that is sustained after the death of Stephen concerns the way that Jews are named in Acts. Preceding the martyrdom of Stephen, hoi Ioudaioi is used only three times, marking a portion of the audience for Peter's Pentecost speech (2.5, 2.10, 2.14). After the death of Stephen, the use of hoi Ioudaioi increases dramatically, becoming Acts' preferred term of vilification for those who persecute and/or desire the persecution of Jesus followers (e.g., 9.23, 12.3, 12.11, 13.50, 14.5, 14.19, 18.12, 20.3, 20.19, 23.12, 25.24, 26.21).[39] Concurrent with the increase in negative employment of the phrase hoi Ioudaioi in Acts after the Stephen episode is the abrupt cessation of sympathetic depictions of Jews as ho laos—the people of God. In the Jerusalem chapters, ho laos is portrayed positively, as open to the messengers of the Way.

The people are convinced by the apostles and serve to protect them from a malicious leadership (e.g., 4.17, 4.21, 5.13, 5.26). However, once they are stirred up against Stephen in 6.12, "the people" lose their receptivity and act only with hostility toward the apostles. Thus, as Augustin George notes, after the death of Stephen, "the Jews," are no longer "the people" of God.[40] Their agency in the death of Stephen is integral to the making of *hoi Ioudaioi*.[41]

The Import of the Speech

Stephen's speech rehearses a history of Israelite heroes faithful to the promises of God met by an increasingly rebellious, idolatrous, and persecutory people. Abraham is identified as "our ancestor," the common link between Stephen and his audience of "men, brothers, and fathers." This common ancestor receives the promise of future deliverance from slavery and proper worship "in this place" (7.7). In this citation of Exodus 3.12,[42] the substitution of "place" (τόπος) for "mountain" (ὄρος) as the locus of worship prepares for the critique of the temple as the locus of true worship in Acts 7.47–50. As Todd Penner notes, "'This mountain' is the place of the temple. But Luke intentionally reconfigures the promise so that the mountain/temple associations are subordinated to 'the land.' By telescoping the narrative, Luke has heightened the connection between deliverance and land to the exclusion of Mount Sinai."[43]

Joseph is next in the sequence of heroes, a man who extends generosity and mercy (7.13–14) toward his brothers who have persecuted him (7.9).[44] Moses receives lengthy treatment as gracious liberator, lawgiver, and prophet, who intercedes on behalf of a people that scorns him and prefer to worship the golden calf, "reveling in the works of their hands" (7.41). The merciful comportment of Joseph and Moses in the face of their vile treatment from the people makes them both obvious types for Jesus (and Stephen). This is especially the case with Moses, as the speech invokes a Christology that understands Jesus as fulfillment of the promised "prophet like Moses" in Deuteronomy 18.15 (7.37).[45] The historical recitation ends with a critique of the temple, followed by a castigation of the audience as Christ killers in line with their prophet-persecuting ancestors. Both of these issues require close analysis.

THE NATURE OF STEPHEN'S TEMPLE CRITICISM. The story of deliverance from Egypt through Moses' hand ends with the forging of the golden calf to venerate. This blatant act of idolatry then explains the exile (7.41–43). From there, the speech moves to a complicated distinction between the "tent of testimony in the wilderness" (ἡ σκηνὴ τοῦ μαρτυρίου ἐν τῇ ἐρήμῳ; 7.44) and the temple or "house" built by Solomon for God (Σολομὼν δὲ οἰκοδόμησεν αὐτῷ οἶκον; 7.47–50). The idea that God would dwell in such a house, one made "with human hands" (ἐν χειροποιήτοις), is then refuted, through citation of Isaiah 66.1–2:

> Heaven is my throne, and the earth is my footstool.
> What kind of house will you build for me, says the Lord,
> or what is the place of my rest?
> Did not my hand make all these things? (Acts 7.49–50)

Part of the puzzle in understanding these verses is that the accusers who levy the formal charge that Stephen is speaking against the temple and the law (6.13–14) are explicitly marked by the narrator as false witnesses. It can be argued that Stephen demonstrates the baselessness of the anti-law charge by speaking favorably about the lawgiver and the law itself (7.38). But, on a straightforward reading of 7.47–50, it is difficult to deny that Stephen's speech has an anti-temple slant and thus seems to confirm the accusation of "false" witnesses that "this man never stops saying things against this holy place" (6.13). Indeed, the stark contrast drawn between the wilderness tent that was modeled on an ideal heavenly pattern (7.44) and the house built under Solomon with human hands indicates that Stephen's temple critique is drawn in extremely radical terms, as a suggestion that it would have been better had the temple never been built.[46]

To be sure, in the minds of F. C. Baur and those following his lead in the nineteenth and twentieth centuries, there was complete clarity concerning the nature of Stephen's temple criticism. The problem with the temple was that it enabled "the godless and carnal temper of the people [to manifest] itself more openly." Possession of the temple enabled the people's religion to become "a formalism composed of outward rites and ceremonies." The temple stood as a place in which "the external, visible, and tangible machinery of worship assumed an overwhelming preponderance, and ceased to be a living and flexible expression of that invisible Ideal."[47] In Baur's final analysis, Stephen's temple criticism proved a sure sign of his supersessionist insight:

> That the essence of true religion did not consist in outward
> ceremonials, connected with a temple service confined to one
> appointed spot—this was the great idea, through which, even at that
> time, Judaism saw itself in danger of being superseded by
> Christianity. This inevitable rending asunder of Christianity from
> Judaism, whereby Judaism would cease to be considered an absolute
> religion, and by which its final extinction was threatened, had been
> clearly perceived and even expressed by Stephen.[48]

From a twenty-first-century perch, it is painfully obvious that Baur pegged Stephen's problem with the temple to the fact that it was too pre-Enlightenment, too Jewish/too Catholic.[49]

In arguments that might owe to this painful awareness, a cluster of recent scholarship has attempted to swing the pendulum in the opposite direction. Building from a much greater appreciation for the place of cult and ritual in Hellenistic Judaism than Baur and his school could muster, many now argue that the speech of 7.44–50 is not temple-critical.[50] Yet, however valiant these efforts to the contrary, it remains difficult to sustain the argument that a speech that has excoriated a people for "rejoicing in the work of their hands" ($\kappa\alpha\grave{\iota}$ $\epsilon\grave{\nu}\phi\rho\alpha\acute{\iota}\nu o\nu\tau o$ $\grave{\epsilon}\nu$ $\tau o\hat{\iota}s$ $\grave{\epsilon}\rho\gamma o\iota s$ $\tau\hat{\omega}\nu$ $\chi\epsilon\iota\rho\hat{\omega}\nu$; 7.41) in the idolatry leading to exile might abruptly shift to a neutral or positive reference to the "handmade" ($\grave{\epsilon}\nu$ $\chi\epsilon\iota\rho o\pi o\iota\acute{\eta}\tau o\iota s$) house for God that Solomon built (7.48).[51] In the same way that the prophetic condemnation of idolatry from Amos in 7.42–43 follows from the making of idols in 7.41–42, so the critique of idolatry from Isaiah in 7.49–50 follows from 7.48. As Richard Pervo notes, "By inference, innuendo, and insinuation, the temple of Solomon (and its successors) is drawn into the belly of the golden calf."[52] To be sure, it is more fitting to situate Stephen's rebuke of temple cult within second-century concerns rather than to account for it anachronistically within the problematic frame of Protestant spirit and Jewish/Catholic carnality.[53] But even in this second-century context, the speech is slanted against the temple.

The confusion of the pericope, which both asserts the falseness of the anti-temple charge levied against Stephen and attributes to him a speech that culminates in an attack against that temple, is best explained as owing to the same impulse that leads to Acts' confusion in depicting Jews and Judaism as a whole. As noted in the previous chapter, the temple is a staging point for key scenes in the two-volume work, although the import of this staging seems ambiguous at first glance. Passages in which Acts seems to hold a marked reverence for the temple stand alongside passages in which the temple seems nothing more than a "den of robbers." Yet, there remains a clear condition attaching to positive temple references: belief in Jesus. Only those making the connection between the promises to Israel of restoration and their fulfillment in the incarnate and resurrected Christ understand the true purpose of temple worship.[54] Those who do not recognize Jesus as Christ engage in futile temple worship leading (ultimately) to its destruction. To make this distinction, the narrative employs categories somewhat awkwardly, as already seen in the case of "the Jew" Apollos vehemently refuting "the Jews."[55] Those who worship in the temple—Zechariah, Simeon, Anna, the Twelve, and Paul—vehemently refute those who worship in the temple—nonbelieving Jews—by demonstrating that

Christ is the *telos* of such worship. In as much as Stephen would not critique the former, charges against him are "false"; since he cannot but condemn the latter, he is temple-critical in the end.

THE CHARGE OF PROPHET PERSECUTION. From the critique of temple worship as idolatry through third-person historical recitation, Stephen shifts to an accusation of prophet persecution in direct address:

> You stiff-necked people, uncircumcised in heart and ears, you are
> forever opposing the Holy Spirit, just as your ancestors used to do.
> Which of the prophets did your ancestors not persecute? They killed
> those who foretold the coming of the Righteous One, and now you
> have become his betrayers and murderers. (7.51–52)

Here, Acts employs a topos already present in Deuteronomistic understandings of Israelite disobedience leading to judgment—Israel kills prophets and then suffers for that crime.[56] But Stephen has changed the referent, from "our" ancestors to "yours," a one-word shift with significant import.

In its earliest settings, assumption of blame for prophet persecution functions as an intra-communal means of explaining present tumultuous circumstance.[57] Nehemiah 9.7–31, a recitation of Israelite history highlighting incidents that Acts 7 will also cover (the promise to Abraham, deliverance from Egypt through Moses, and the forging of the golden calf), serves as an answer to the question of how Israel has arrived at its status as vassal slaves to Persia. The answer is one that keeps covenantal theology in tact: "We suffer not because our God has been defeated, nor because our God has been unfaithful; but because we killed the prophets and turned aside from their oracles. We ourselves are to blame for our current plight" (Neh. 9.16–17, 9.26–27, 9.29).[58] Communal blame for prophet persecution persists as a means to account for the temple's destruction in rabbinic literature as indicated, for example, in haggadic tradition concerning the death of Zechariah, son of Jehoiada (2 Chron. 24.20–22; cf. *b. Git.* 57b; *Lam. Rab.* proem 23; *Eccl. Rab.* 3.19).[59] In these traditions from the era post-70 CE, the razing of the second temple, as well as the first, is in view.

While it is often assumed that any instance of the prophet persecution topos employed by Jesus believers must mark this group's difference from and persecution by nonbelieving Jews, Melanie Johnson-DeBaufre proposes that the Q oracles on prophet persecution are participating in the *intra-communal* self-blame of the earlier scriptural tradition. Noting that the final form of Q may be dated to the time of the Jewish War, she considers the import of Q's message of prophet persecution, shaped within the context of war:

Perhaps it was the experience of communal suffering at the hands of
Roman imperial occupation that burned at the heart of Q's theologizing
about communal blame. Perhaps the community of Q was moved *not
only* by the brutal crucifixion of one righteous and prophetic Jew, but
also by the deaths of *thousands* of Jews at the hands of the Romans in
the first century C.E. Perhaps it was the smoking ruins of rebellious
Jerusalem that brought the Q people to ask, "How did it come to this?"[60]

The Q prophet persecution oracles in their original setting may indeed
be assuming a form of intra-communal blame, within the larger context of
accounting for national calamity within the bounds of covenantal theology:
God is not unfaithful; Rome is not the cause of our suffering; we did this to
ourselves. Furthermore, as Johnson-DeBaufre notes, if the earliest form of the
prophet persecution motif preserved in the Gospels is understood as an explanation for a situation of national calamity, one need not assume that behind
every instance of the motif in the Gospels lies an actual historical experience of
nonbelieving Jews killing Jesus believers.

This *self*-blame is lost in the redaction of Q, both in Matthew and the Third
Gospel, when the prophet killers are inscribed as those opposed to the
Matthean and Lukan communities. The historical question of whether these
invocations of the prophet persecution motif necessarily point to *Jewish*
persecution of Jesus believers is equally lost beneath the unexamined assumption that it must.[61] Acts underscores the Gospel accusation of prophet persecutor as *other* in even bolder lines by offering Stephen up as the embodiment
of the persecuted prophet, while aligning his murderers with ancestors he
does not share.

THE CONCLUSION OF THE SPEECH: THE ACCUSATION PROVED. Stephen's prophet
persecution accusation in direct address is followed immediately by narrative
confirmation of its veracity, as the prophet persecutors drag him out to be
stoned. This instance of persecution shares a close intertextual relationship to
Q oracles of prophet persecution preserved in Luke (Luke/Q 11.49–50, 13.34–
35) and, through these oracles, with the story of the murder of Zechariah, son
of Jehoiada, recorded in 2 Chronicles 24.17–25.

According to the chronicler, Zechariah is persecuted because of his words
indicting King Joash and the people of Judah for transgressions relating to law
and temple. The people conspire, at the bidding of the king, to stone the prophet
in the court of the temple. As he is stoned, Zechariah cries out for vengeance.[62]
Vengeance does come quickly, for in the next episode Jerusalem is destroyed,
while King Joash is defeated by enemy armies and ultimately murdered by his
servants. The Q tradition of prophet persecution draws on this Zechariah

tradition, as Dale Allison has demonstrated.[63] This is most clear from the explicit invoking of Zechariah at Luke/Q 11.49–50:

> Therefore also the Sophia of God said, "I will send them prophets
> and apostles, some of whom they will kill and persecute," so that this
> generation may be charged with the blood of all the prophets since
> the foundation of the world, from the blood of Abel to the blood of
> Zechariah, who perished between the altar and the sanctuary. Yes, I
> tell you, it will be charged against this generation. (Luke/Q 11.49–50)

Allusions to the Zechariah tradition in this oracle and Luke/Q 13.34–35 include mention of prophets sent by God (Luke/Q 11.49; 2 Chron. 24.19); focus on the blood of Zechariah (Luke/Q 11.51; 2 Chron. 24.25), which needs requiting (Luke/Q 11.50, 11.51; 2 Chron. 24.22); death by stoning (Luke/Q 13.34; 2 Chron. 24.21); judgment upon Jerusalem (Luke/Q 13.35; 2 Chron. 24.23–24); and the forsakenness of the "house"/temple (Luke/Q 13.35; 2 Chron. 24.18). These verbal and thematic parallels lead Allison to observe that Q "moves the historic language of Chronicles to the eschatological time of Jesus."[64]

That the narrative method of Luke-Acts is to situate not only Jesus but also Stephen within the line of persecuted prophets embodied in this tradition of the blood of Zechariah is clear from the verbal connections between the prophet persecution oracle of Luke 11 and the Stephen narrative. In phrasing not shared by Matthew, the Lukan Jesus introduces the persecution oracle of 11.49–50 by linking his audience to prophet persecutors of old: "Woe to you! For you build the tombs of the prophets whom your ancestors killed. So you are *witnesses* [μάρτυρες] and *approve* [συνευδοκεῖτε] of the deeds of your ancestors" (11.47–48). This word combination "witness" and "approve" appears again in Luke-Acts only once more, in relation to Saul's role in Stephen's death: ". . . and the *witnesses* [οἱ μάρτυρες] laid their coats at the feet of a young man named Saul. . . . And Saul *approved* [ἦν συνευδοκῶν] of their killing him" (Acts 7.58–8.1; cf. 22.19). In this way, the unconverted Saul is marked as the living embodiment of those who stand accused by Jesus, the descendents of those murdering the prophets from Abel through Zechariah. Stephen's execution *by stoning* (Acts 7.59: καὶ ἐλιθοβόλουν τὸν Στέφανον) is a further tie between his death, the fate of Zechariah (2 Chron. 24.21 LXX: καὶ ἐλιθοβόλησαν αὐτὸν), and the accusation of Jesus (Luke 13.34: λιθοβολοῦσα τοὺς ἀπεσταλμένους).[65]

The Import of Trial and Fate of Stephen as it is Linked to Jesus and Paul.

The interdependence of the trials and fates of Jesus, Stephen, and Paul is well established.[66] In broad general terms, the lives of all three persons conform to the Deuteronomistic pattern of the suffering prophet noted above. All three are sent by God to deliver prophetic oracles, all are rejected by Israel, and all suffer persecution in Jerusalem.

Like Jesus, Stephen is brought before the Sanhedrin (Luke 22.26; cf. Acts 6.12); both Jesus and Stephen speak of the eschatological Son of Man at the right hand of God (Luke 22.69; cf. Acts 7.56); and as Jesus commends his spirit to God on the cross (Luke 23.46), so Stephen prays to the Lord Jesus to receive his spirit at death (Acts 7.59).[67] Overlap between the passion narratives of Mark and Matthew and the Stephen narrative also suggest that Jesus' passion is a model for the death of Stephen. The charge common to Mark and Matthew concerning the destruction of the temple is not leveled against Jesus in the Third Gospel; rather, the author of Luke-Acts reserves this accusation for the trial of Stephen (Mark 14.58; Matt. 26.61; Acts 6.14; not in Luke). This is also true of the charge of blasphemy (Mark 14.64; Matt. 26.65; Acts 6.11; not in Luke) and the characterization of the accusers as false witnesses (Mark 14.56–57; Matt. 26.60–61; Acts 6.13; not in Luke).

The linkage between Stephen and Paul in Acts is explicit. In an interjection devoid of subtlety, Luke introduces Paul at the moment of Stephen's death: "And dragging him outside of the city, they stoned him; laying their garments at the feet of a youth named Saul" (7.58); "And Saul approved of their killing him" (8.1a). Again in Paul's defense speech on the steps of the temple, Luke underscores the connection between Paul's own mission and Stephen's death. Note the complex narrative construction in Paul's speech concerning a past conversation between himself and the Lord, in which the Lord had urged him to leave Jerusalem and go to the Gentiles.[68] Paul recalls how, within this conversation, he reminded the Lord specifically of those details implicating him in the death of Stephen that are first mentioned in 7.58 and 8.1:

> After I had returned to Jerusalem and while I was praying in the temple, I fell into a trance and saw Jesus. . . . And I said, "Lord, they themselves know that I imprisoned and beat in the synagogues those believing in you, and when the blood of Stephen your martyr was shed I myself was standing by, approving and keeping the coats of those who killed him." (22.17–21)

Stephen is also linked to Paul by the nearly identical wording of the charges leveled against them. In Acts 6.13, Stephen is accused of defying the temple: "This man never stops saying things against this holy place and the law," words mirrored in the accusation against Paul in Acts 21.28: "This is the man who is teaching everyone everywhere against our people, our law, and this place [the temple]."

These connecting links demonstrate the coherence and continuity that extends from Gospel to Acts. Theophilus may rest assured that Paul is prefigured by Stephen who is prefigured by Jesus. But for purposes of understanding Stephen's perfect rhetorical fittingness, no less significant than the narrative details binding these three heroes, are the details reserved for Stephen's death alone. Narrative details unique to Stephen's martyrdom provide the author of Luke-Acts with the means to clarify and underscore the murderousness and barbarity of unbelieving Jews in ways that the constraints of his narratives of Jesus and Paul do not allow.

STEPHEN AND THE IGNORANCE MOTIF. Key to Luke's defense of a movement whose founder suffered the humiliation of Roman crucifixion is the strong emphasis on the conformity of that death with the plan of God.[69] Concomitant with emphasis on divinely willed and foreordained crucifixion is focus on human misperception and ignorance. Thus, a Pauline speech links the foreordained nature of Jesus' death with Jewish misperception of prophetic Scripture at 13.27. In at least one instance, at Acts 3.17–19, it is suggested that ignorance is a mitigating factor in Jewish responsibility for Jesus' crucifixion, for which repentance and forgiveness are available.[70] But Acts also makes clear—especially at 17.30–31—that the excuse of ignorance no longer holds after Jesus' resurrection demonstrates his identity as the Messiah. The mitigating factor of ignorance, then, does not apply to the Jews who stone Stephen. As Charles Talbert has phrased it, "what could be attributed to ignorance the first time . . . is clearly deliberate the second."[71] Unlike Jesus' crucifiers, the Jews murdering Stephen are without the ignorance excuse and hence fully culpable.[72]

STEPHEN AND IMPERIAL SOCIOLOGY. Finally, and crucially, it should be noted that Jewish agency in Stephen's death stands apart from Jewish agency in both the death of Jesus and the arrest and trial of Paul in that it is free from the mitigating circumstance of the involvement of Roman authorities. While the author of Luke-Acts minimizes the involvement of Roman soldiers in Jesus passion and has Pilate declare Jesus' innocence threefold, he does not avoid entirely the tradition that Romans were involved in Jesus' crucifixion, particularly in the Third Gospel.[73] Likewise, while Acts does not narrate the death of Paul at the hands of Gentiles and characterizes the Roman arrest of Paul as a benevolent attempt to *rescue* Paul from the Jews, he does not ignore the tradition that Paul was arrested by Romans and held in Roman custody. In contrast, the stoning of Stephen is a purely Jewish affair. The first martyr for Christ is executed by a Jewish mob completely outside of Roman view. As such, it is a key passage in Luke's multipronged program of distinguishing Jews from Christians, while seeking security for the latter within the Roman state.

The rhetorical method of denigrating *Ioudaioi* in Acts does not include heaping disapprobation on Jewish ritual practice, as illustrated by depictions of Paul, the ideal "Jew," circumcising Timothy, taking a Nazarite vow, and praying in the temple. The realm of derision is, rather, within Jewish juridical process and social behavior. Erika Heusler has underscored the tendency to denigrate Jewish legal procedure in the two-volume work by noting that the author's redaction of Mark's passion narrative presents the juridical processes of the Romans as fair and that of Jews as unfair.[74] Lawrence Wills demonstrates how Acts' depiction of Jews conforms to the "imperial sociology" of elite Romanized authors who depict the masses, whom they fear and despise, as easily incited by base and dishonest compatriots to acts of violent rebellion.[75]

Recognizing Luke's dual interests in denigrating Jewish legal processes and depicting Jews as fomenters of violence helps to unravel a long-standing interpretative problem in Stephen's death narrative: the fact that it contains both elements of a formal legal proceeding—a trial before a council (*synedrion*) at 6.12, interrogation before a high priest at 7.1, and formal witnesses at 6.9–11—and indications of mob behavior at 6.12 and 7.58b. These disparate elements are commonly accounted for as signs of rupture and struggle between source and redactor. In Ernst Haenchen's vivid rendering of this struggle, Luke is imagined as trying desperately to tame an unwieldy and historical lynching story by cloaking it in a methodic legal procedure:

> Now the pack is unleashed to hunt Stephen out of the city and stone him. Probably here a part of the older Martyrdom emerges, and *it threatens to destroy the framework which Luke has so ingeniously, painstakingly constructed*: that of ostensibly legal proceedings before the High Council. . . . Hence Luke, by mentioning witnesses . . . *attempts to steer his account back into the paths of juridical procedure.*[76]

I argue instead that Luke is quite in control of his narrative and the easy flow from legal procedure to mob violence is precisely the point: Jewish juridical process is so base that it cannot but result in riotous behavior.

It has been noted above that the method of execution, stoning by a mob, aligns the death of Stephen with that of the persecuted prophets from Jewish Scripture. From the perspective of imperial sociology, death by stoning also serves to mark the martyrdom as barbarous/un-Roman. Romans in authority did not stone people, a fact that might be accounted for by their aversion to such a "democratic" form of execution.[77] Theodor Mommsen's encyclopedic survey of Roman imperial discipline—*Römisches Strafrecht*—includes no entry on stoning.[78] In Roman and Romanized literary sources, stoning is the resort of trouble-making crowds. Josephus speaks of the practice of stoning as "savagery" (ὠμότης; *Ant.* 14.2); Virgil's conjures a stoning mob early in the *Aeneid*:

> When rioting breaks out in a great city,
> And the rampaging rabble goes so far
> That stones fly, and incendiary brands—
> For anger [*furor*] can supply that kind of weapon—
> (*Aen.* 1.201–210 [Fitzgerald])[79]

From the perspective of Roman imperial sociology adopted by Acts, only the mobs of *Ioudaioi*, as fomenters of *stasis*, fling stones.

Conclusion

In contrast with the fates of the Lukan Jesus and the Paul of Acts, the martyrdom of Stephen functions perfectly as a means both to vilify the Jews as barbaric and murderous enemies of the Roman order and to bracket Romans out of the originary violence that creates the first martyred Jesus follower and marks the church's first great persecution and expansion. Aside from the brief mention of the death of James by the sword at 12.2, there are no more martyr tales narrated in Acts. In the rhetorical method of Luke-Acts, no more such tales need to be told. Stephen is the prototype for the Christian martyr. While Acts does not use the term "martyr" in what will become its technical sense in early Christian literature—as a term reserved only for those whose evangelistic confession is sealed by death—the late scribal tradition that has substituted "πρωτομάρτυρος" (first martyr) for "μάρτυρος" (martyr) as epithet for Stephen at 22.20 has captured the symbolic import of the Stephen story.[80] In Acts' story, Stephen is the originary martyr. The particular details of the deaths of all the other apostolic martyrs—including Paul, Peter, and James the brother of Jesus—need no elaboration; they are all superceded by/folded into the type. Key to the prototype's identity is his geographic location and the identity of the executioner. In Acts' view, and in stark contrast to other legendary tales concerning both Peter and Paul, the perfect martyr dies not in Rome but in Jerusalem; not at the hands of the emperor but at the will of a barbaric Jewish mob.

Eusebius also identifies Stephen as the perfect martyr, though not for any of the reasons outlined here. For Eusebius, Stephen merits the epithet because as he dies, his last gasping prayer is for the forgiveness of his tormentors. He mentions Stephen in connection with his narrative of the deaths of the martyrs at Vienne and Lyon, who "prayed for those who had inflicted torture, even as did Stephen, the perfect martyr [Στέφανος ὁ τέλειος μάρτυς], 'Lord, do not stand this sin against them'" (*Hist. eccl.* 5.2.5). That is, Eusebius holds up Stephen as a perfect model because he prays mercy upon his enemies. This chapter has come to something of an opposite conclusion—that the Stephen story is not a "merciful story" but rather a story that enacts a sort of rhetorical violence against the Jews by vilifying them as originary murderers of Christians. In my final chapter, I explore Stephen's prayer for forgiveness, and related Christian prayers for enemies, in an attempt to tease out the relationship between the depiction of enemies, prayers for mercy, and acts of vilification in early Christian texts. But first, I turn to disrupting the perfect coherence of Acts' Stephen narrative through consideration of related stories concerning the death of James, the brother of Jesus.

3

Disrupting Acts

*Reading Stephen alongside James, the
Brother of Jesus*

This chapter is an exercise in disrupting the coherence of the Acts
narrative as *the* history of the postresurrection *ekklēsia* and its first
martyr. The two-volume narrative provided by Luke for his elite
patron/ideal reader, Theophilus, possesses a relatively strong
coherence, both thematically and structurally. This coherence owes to
a series of assertions of divine providence and prophecy fulfillment,
as well as to a tightly woven sequence of thematic doublets and
parallels within and across the two volumes.[1] This feature of the Acts
narrative, along with its status as *the* single narrative of the
postresurrection events among Jesus believers canonized as
Scripture, has resulted in a pervasive tendency to read its version of
events as the obvious and true account of early Christian history.

The previous chapter has demonstrated the pivotal role of the
Stephen episode in the construction of this coherent narrative,
inasmuch as the episode links the fates of Jesus and Paul and
facilitates the constitution of those who follow "the Way" as a social/
religious group distinct from "the Jews." It is this martyrdom of
Stephen at the hands of a riotous mob of Jews that has taken pride of
place among the events narrated in Acts that stand among the
"obvious" and the "true"; it is this event that reflected for F. C. Baur
the first instance of an "indubitable reality" in Acts, which has been
affirmed, with near unanimity, by Acts scholars since Baur's time.[2]
The argument here attempts to dislodge the Stephen episode from its
privileged place as the single true account of the first Christian

martyr by situating it within a multivoiced narrative of violence among Jews and Christians under empire.

Since I am framing questions of history in terms of rhetoric and ethics, rather than as a process of retrieving kernels of historical truth, I note at the outset that to call into question this "indubitable" reality is not to insist, in an equally positivistic sense, that the Stephen named in Acts did not exist. It is possible that among the thousands of Jews in Judea who met their deaths violently under Roman occupation was a follower of Jesus whose name was Stephen. Perhaps he was filled with the Holy Spirit. Perhaps he died in a fight. Perhaps that fight was an instance of violence turned inward—a case of fraternal violence, Jew against Jew, owing to his vision of Jesus as the Son of Man, standing at the right hand of God. My analysis here is not in the service of denying the historical possibility that a Jewish Jesus believer named Stephen could have been killed by Jews who did not so believe, but in the significance with which that story has been imbued, first by Luke's hand and subsequently by its canonization as sacred Scripture and sacred history. In Acts' telescopic narrative of early Christian history, only one death beyond the death of Jesus merits significant and sympathetic treatment—the murder of Stephen by "the Jews" outside of Roman agency, with the effect of severing Christianity from those rabid Jewish persecutors. Considering that one death narrative *alongside* others is one way to resist that telescopic focus and its detrimental effects. The argument proceeds in the following two steps.

First, I introduce as a companion to the Stephen story the story of the martyrdom of James as preserved in Hegesippus. A comparison of these two texts will demonstrate that they are both variations on a single trope; both narratives are grappling with the issue of how to speak of Jesus believers as distinct from "Jews," and both arrive at remarkably similar solutions. Drawing attention to the common service to which these two martyrs are put for their authors will make clear that both Stephen and James, as crafted by Acts and Hegesippus, are symbolic characters, used by their authors to think through the parting.

A widely held working assumption among scholars of early Christianity is that late first- and early second-century narratives tend to thematize their own social and ideological concerns through projecting those concerns onto characters—whether fictional or historical[3]—depicted in earlier first-century settings. In reading of Thecla and the Apostle Paul in *The Acts of Thecla*, for instance, one learns about the increasing valorization of asceticism in the second century, and not about the actual historical dialogues, adventures, and mishaps of these two heroes in the middle of the first. Likewise, the Gospel of Mary is studied for what it reveals of a late first- or early second-century struggle for women's authority to speak for Jesus, without any suggestion that the quarrel depicted between Mary and Peter in this text is based on historical reminiscence and preserves actual words exchanged by them. By considering Stephen next to Hegesippus' James, a character so obviously constructed in the service of this sort of thematizing project, I support my argument that the narrative concerns of Acts lie elsewhere than in the faithful preservation of the *realia* of first-century violence among Jesus believers and other Jews.

Second, I consider two additional related narratives of violence among Jesus believers and other Jews: the violent encounter between James and "the enemy," Paul, preserved in the Pseudo-Clementine *Recognitions* 1.27–71; and the narrative of the death of James as preserved by Josephus in the *Antiquities*. These two texts, like Acts and Hegesippus, speak about violence and division among nonbelieving Jews and the earliest followers of Jesus. But each of these texts has a different "social center" and hence emplots that violence differently, using a different set of proper names and charting a different web of relationships among those named parties.[4] Through this analysis, it will become apparent that Acts' narrative of the death of Stephen and of this death's role in effecting the parting between Jews and Christians is neither as inevitable nor as natural as this book's canonical status and well-ordered structure have made it seem. By introducing this multivoiced narrative, my aim is to complicate the story of the "parting" and provide a more useful way to imagine the workings of violence, and of solidarity, among Jews and Christians in the early centuries.[5]

The Death of James, Brother of Jesus, according to Hegesippus

In Hegesippus' telling, preserved by Eusebius (*Hist. eccl.* 2.23.4–18), James is the direct successor of Jesus, put in charge of the Jerusalem church. Marked as holy already "from his mother's womb," he is singularly pious, taking on the role of intercession in the temple reserved for the high priest alone. Because of James' testimony that Jesus is the messiah, many among the people and their leaders come to belief in Jesus. This leads to an uproar among the "Jews, scribes, and the Pharisees." When the opposition compels James to stand on the pinnacle of the temple and cry out his renunciation of Jesus, he does not renounce. Instead, as a good martyr should, Hegesippus' James dies for his confession (*martyria*), shouting from the pinnacle that Jesus is the Son of Man, "sitting in heaven at the right hand of the great power" (*Hist. eccl.* 2.23.13). Immediately after he gives his testimony, James is thrown down from the temple, stoned, and finally clubbed to death. As in the stories of Jesus and Stephen, the brutality of his tormentors serves as a foil for his own merciful dying prayer of forgiveness. Before his death, he utters the prayer offered by his brother on the cross in the Third Gospel, "Father, forgive them, for they know not what they do" (*Hist. eccl.* 2.23.16). As with the dying prayers of Jesus and Stephen for mercy upon their tormentors, this prayer has no merciful effect. The final form of the narrative asserts that the murder of James by the children of Israel has imminent dire theological and political consequences. It is because of his execution that God abandons Jerusalem to the Roman armies who will eventually destroy it: "and so James suffered martyrdom. . . . He became a true witness both to Jews and to Greeks that Jesus is the Christ. And immediately Vespasian besieged them" (2.23.18).[6]

Hegesippus' account of the death of James contains a number of peculiarities that have long puzzled. James is marked as both a Nazarite and a high priest ("He drank no wine or strong drink, nor did he eat flesh; no razor went upon his head. . . . He alone was allowed to enter into the sanctuary, for he did not wear wool but linen, and he used to enter alone into the temple and be found kneeling and praying for forgiveness for the people . . ." *Hist. eccl.* 2.23.5 [Lake, LCL]). In addition to the epithet associated with him in other sources as well—James the Just—he is also named by a puzzling Greek term ὠβλίας, which the text translates as "rampart": "He was called the Just and Oblias, that is in Greek, 'Rampart of the people and righteousness'" (ἐκαλεῖτο ὁ δίκαιος καὶ ὠβλίας, ὅ ἐστιν Ἑλληνιστὶ περιοχὴ τοῦ λαοῦ, καὶ δικαιοσύνη; *Hist. eccl.* 2.23.7). James is interrogated specifically concerning the "door of Jesus" (ἡ θύρα τοῦ Ἰησοῦ; *Hist. eccl.* 2.23.8). His death entails three methods of execution—being thrown from the pinnacle of the temple, a stoning, and, finally, a beating from a fuller's club. Appearing from nowhere to intercede on James' behalf as he is stoned is "one of the priests of the sons of Rechab, the son of Rechabim, to whom Jeremiah the prophet bore witness" (*Hist. eccl.* 2.23.17). Accounting for these peculiarities requires some consideration of the nature of the text and the process by which it was composed.

Questions of Dating, Dependency, and Method of Composition

Eusebius is our only source of information on Hegesippus, and he appears not to have tampered much with the fragments of the *Hypomnemata* that he preserves, including Hegesippus' account of the death of James. Hegesippus' work is generally dated to "the episcopate of Eleutherus," ca. 180 CE. Common tropes, including the tracking of true tradition through lists of bishops (*Hist. eccl.* 4.22.1–3, 2.23.1, 3.32.1–2), and depicting the church in its origins as a virgin defiled by later heretics (*Hist. eccl.* 4.22.4–5) suggest that the work is a heresiology.[7] While the question of the relationship of the *Hypomnemata* to Eusebius' *Ecclesiastical History* is relatively straightforward, the place of this James narrative within the *Stemma* of early Christian accounts of the death of James is more complex and controverted. It is clear that Hegesippus' text evinces knowledge of Gospel traditions of Jesus' death on which the James' martyrdom is modeled and also shares resonance with the death of Stephen. Yet, whether Hegesippus knows Acts' Stephen narrative or Josephus' report of the death of James is less certain.[8] Further and even more complex questions concern the relationship of Hegesippus' version of the death to the multiple early Christian accounts of the death of James preserved in Clement of Alexandria, the Pseudo-Clementine *Recognitions*, Epiphanius, and the Nag Hammadi *Apocalypses of James.*[9]

F. Stanley Jones has argued that Hegesippus is the first to pen an early Christian version of the martyrdom of James (ca. 180 CE) and that all other early Christian versions of James' death derive from the written text preserved in the *Hypomnemata.* Jones proposes further that Hegesippus' written text owes to an oral response given to him by a visiting Palestinian bishop during Hegesippus' investigative inquiry concerning ecclesiastical leadership in the region of Palestine.[10] A more persuasive accounting for the Hegesippus narrative, however, is that Hegesippus himself works with a preexisting written source. The hypothesis that some sort of *Grundschrift* pre-dates Hegesippus' writing better accounts for the many details of the James' narrative that are irrelevant to his heresiological interest, as Wilhelm Pratscher has noted.[11] Moreover, and most importantly, understanding the written text as the result of complex and overlapping methods of scribal exegesis of Scripture, and not as the product of an oral interview, better explains the many textual peculiarities noted above.

Here, the work of Richard Bauckham in identifying the exegetical principles that propel the narrative is foundational and compelling. As Bauckham has argued, references to James as "rampart of the people" and to the "gate of Jesus" are best understood within the context of early Christian self-understanding that its people embodied various architectural features of the eschatological temple foretold in the Prophets and Psalms. For example, individual Christians are the "stones" of this temple (1 Pet. 2.5); James, Peter, and John, the "pillars" (Gal. 2.9); the apostles and prophets, the "foundation"; and Christ, the "cornerstone" (Eph. 2.20).[12] Having argued first for this metaphorical association between Christians and the eschatological temple, Bauckham then demonstrates that the Hegesippus legend participates in a common form of ancient storytelling, in which biographical incidents are generated through a process of literalizing metaphorical references (as, for instance, when the wild beasts of Paul's hyperbole [I Cor. 15.32] morph into a corporeal lion sent to combat Paul in an Ephesian arena [*Acts of Paul* 7; cf. 2 Tim. 4.17]).[13] Owing to this process of literalizing the metaphorical, "old traditions about James and the Jerusalem church imagined as the eschatological Temple, gave rise, through appropriate biblical exegesis, to an account in which the physical Temple building in Jerusalem plays a major role in James story."[14] Thus, the close metaphorical association of James with the eschatological temple, and with Jesus, the messianic cornerstone of that temple, translates into a story in which James has priestly[15] access to the literal temple and is ultimately killed by being thrown down from its pinnacle ($\tau\grave{o}$ $\pi\tau\epsilon\rho\acute{v}\gamma\iota ov$; cf. Matt. 4.5; Luke 4.9).[16] A final exegetical principle that serves to explain peculiarities of the James narrative, one that is also utilized in rabbinic and Qumran exegesis, is *gezerâ šawâ*, according to which scriptural passages containing common phrases, or "catchwords," are used to interpret each other. Thus, for example, the *"tents of righteousness"* of Psalm 118.15, generate a narrative of James "the righteous," while also prompting an association with the *"tents of the Rechabites"* (Jer. 35.7, 35.10), who are also righteous. Recognizing this series of catchword associations clarifies what might otherwise appear as the inexplicable appearance of a Rechabite interceding on James' behalf at his death. Further catchword associations may also explain the Nazarite references and the death by fuller's club.[17] In short, the James narrative preserved in Hegesippus owes to exegetical processes much like those that have generated the canonical narratives of the passion of Jesus. In both instances, the narratives owe not to faithful transmission of eyewitness testimony but rather to eyes trained on Scriptures, searching those Scriptures for details that can be "historicized."[18]

Owing to the murkiness of the waters when one plunges beneath the textual surface in search of a nonexistent *Grundschrift*, especially in cases where textual relationships are as knotty as they are in the James tradition, it is difficult to make strong claims concerning the precise form and dating of such a preexisting text. Therefore, while convinced that Hegesippus' James narrative owes considerably more to the workings of scribal exegesis than to oral interview, I otherwise refrain from weighing in on the numerous possibilities for emplotting a martyrdom of James *Stemma*.

My primary concern is to underscore the common rhetorical strategies of Hegesippus' James narrative and the narrative of Stephen in Acts, especially the means by which they etiologize the split between Jews who believe in Jesus and Jews who do not. As noted above, some scholars have accounted for common motifs in these two accounts by arguing that Hegesippus knows Acts chapter 7. Others, including Karlman Beyschlag, have made a strong case that the Stephen pericope is derived from an *Ur*-martyrdom of James;[19] and others

still, that familiarity with the Gospel passion narratives, along with indepen-
dent access to a number of common martyrdom motifs in circulation, provide
a sufficient explanation for the similarities between Acts' Stephen and
Hegesippus' James. For my purposes, it is not necessary to explain how to
account for the common perspective—whether or not one account derives
from the other—but only to underscore their common rhetorical assertions
and to consider the effects of this rhetoric.

Thinking with Stephen and James

If, as Daniel Boyarin has argued, the discourse of martyrdom is a crucial site
for the construction of early Jewish and Christian identity, and this identity
construction has an oppositional component—Judaism as not-Christianity,
Christianity as not-Judaism—then the deaths of Stephen and James constitute
relatively early attempts at this construction, from the side of Jesus believers/
proto-Christians. Both are struggling to mark the split between Jews who
believe in Jesus and those who do not, and both etiologize that split at the point
of a violent death.

To be sure, neither attempt has produced a "full-blown" martyrology, at
least according to the templates proposed in recent scholarship to distinguish
martyrdoms from other types of death narratives in the second century.[20] One
reason for this is that Stephen in Acts and James in the *Hypomnemata* face
execution from what may be considered an "internal enemy," rather than from
foreign administrators of the occupying state—in these texts there is neither a
Nebuchadnezzar nor an Antiochus, no Nero or Trajan. In some sense then,
Stephen and James, like the Zechariah of 2 Chronicles, fall under the category
of persecuted prophets, and not martyrs.[21] But these death narratives cannot be
satisfyingly categorized solely within the rubrics of "internal" violence because
of the markers in each text suggesting that victims and persecutors belong to
different social groups. I suggest that Acts' Stephen and Hegesippus' James are
located at the interstices of two kinds of violent death narratives, that of the
persecuted prophet killed by his own people and of the martyr killed by the
external enemy.[22] Consider the common means by which Stephen and James
are constructed against "the Jews" who oppose them.

THE TEMPLE AS LOCUS OF CONFLICT. For both Stephen and James, the temple
is at the heart of the conflict. In the Stephen narrative, this conflict takes shape
in an accusation that Stephen speaks against the temple (Acts 6.13–14) and in
a speech that is interpreted in just that way, raising the ire of the crowd. James'
link with the temple is more heavily underscored, beginning before his birth

and extending after his death. According to Hegesippus, James is set apart for temple service from his mother's womb and intercedes in the temple as high priest. He gives testimony from the pinnacle of the temple and is thrown down from that pinnacle to his death.[23]

CONFESSION OF THE "SON OF MAN" AS THE TIPPING POINT. In both Hegesippus and Acts, the violent mob action follows immediately upon the martyr's testimony concerning the Son of Man. Having already enraged his audience with words against the temple, Stephen's subsequent announcement that he sees "the Son of Man standing at the right hand of God" provokes them to drag him out and begin the stoning (Acts 7.56–58). Hegesippus' James martyrdom is structured likewise, so that his acclamation of the Son of Man "sitting in heaven on the right hand of the great power" prompts the scribes and Pharisees to throw him from the temple's pinnacle (Hist. eccl. 2.23.13–14).[24]

MOCK TRIAL; LYNCH JUSTICE. As demonstrated in the previous chapter, the rhetorical effect of Acts' depiction of the prosecution of Stephen, in which a formal judicial process collapses into riotous and deadly mob behavior, is to confirm the barbarous nature of "the Jews." According to Hegesippus, James' death is also ignited by an "uproarious crowd" of "Jews, Scribes and Pharisees" (ἦν θόρυβος τῶν Ἰουδαίων καὶ γραμματέων καὶ φαρισαίων; Hist. eccl. 2.23.10). James is subjected by this group to an investigative inquiry at the pinnacle of the temple, but as in the case of Stephen, the death of James is not the result of a formal judicial process ending with the formal pronouncement of the death penalty as his deserved reward. Rather, it is the outcome of a series of impulsive violent actions, which, when taken together, evoke a scene of chaos—the throwing down; the stoning, which continues over the cry of the interceding Rechabite; and the clubbing by the fuller.[25]

THE HYPER-MERCIFUL VICTIM. As in the case of Stephen's death, the riotous and deadly behavior of the mob in Hegesippus' James narrative is juxtaposed with the merciful response of the martyr who prays forgiveness on his tormentors as he dies. Because such forgiveness is so obviously undeserved, this plea comes to be understood in some early Christian quarters as a radical challenge to cosmic frameworks of justice, by which the unrepentant wicked are not forgiven but punished. Accounting for the extreme radicality of these dying forgiveness prayers is the subject of my next chapter. Here, I note that the exceptional mercy of the Jesus believer is underscored even more strongly in Hegesippus than in Acts, for James' dying prayer of mercy is but an extension of his lifelong intercession on behalf of the Jews: "He used to enter alone into the temple and be found kneeling and praying for the forgiveness of the people [αἰτούμενος ὑπὲρ τοῦ λαοῦ ἄφεσιν], so that his knees grew hard like a camel's because of his constant worship of God, kneeling and asking forgiveness for the people [αἰτεῖσθαι ἄφεσιν τῷ λαῷ]" (Hist. eccl. 2.23.6 [Lake, LCL]). The dying forgiveness prayer receives further emphasis in the James narrative by the Rechabite who draws attention to it as James is being stoned ("Stop! What are you doing [τί ποιεῖτε]? The just is praying for you" [Hist. eccl. 2.23.17]).[26]

JEWISH REJECTION LEADING TO COSMIC VINDICATION. One distinction between the narratives of Luke-Acts and Hegesippus is that in the former it is the killing of Jesus that causes the destruction of Jerusalem, while for Hegesippus, Jerusalem's demise owes to the death of James, the brother. In the Third Gospel, Jesus weeps at the impending destruction of the city and attributes it to the fact that Jerusalem did not recognize the time of its "visitation from God" (Luke 19.44). Hegesippus (or possibly the redactor) makes the consequences of the killing of James both swift and clear in his summary sentences: "He became a true witness both to Jews and to Greeks that Jesus is the Christ, and at once Vespasian began to besiege them" (μάρτυς οὗτος ἀληθὴς Ἰουδαίοις τε καὶ Ἕλλησιν γεγένηται ὅτι Ἰησοῦς ὁ Χριστός ἐστιν. Καὶ εὐθὺς Οὐεσπασιανὸς πολιορκεῖ αὐτούς; Hist. eccl. 2.23.18 [Lake, LCL]). These two narratives share affinity in both conceding that Rome is the ultimate agent of God's retribution, while depicting that imperial violence as a "background issue." The central conflict is the murderous attack on the innocent martyr by Jews who reject messianic claims for Jesus.

"AGAINST THE RACE OF JUDAH AND THE CHRIST": TRUE JEWS, HOSTILE JEWS, AND THE CONFUSION OF CATEGORIES. Finally, consider the issue of category confusion, common to both the final form of Hegesippus' Hypomnemata and the book of Acts. The question of Acts' depiction of Jews and Judaism remains controverted primarily because the author of Acts is not equipped with the semantic toolbox that would enable him to distinguish between Christians and Jews as two distinct social groups.[27] This not only results in a measure of category confusion, by which Acts can attach to its protagonists the term Ioudaios as a badge of honor, but also depicts those individual Jewish protagonists as confounding or utterly refuting (διακατελέγχομαι) the corporate body of "the Jews"/hoi Ioudaioi. The author of Acts knows of, but does not embrace, the category "Christian," for his group. A likely explanation for this author's avoidance of the term "Christian," as recently suggested by Richard Pervo, is that Luke fears its potentially sectarian connotations. The author does not see his social group—"the Christians"—as one among many factions within Judaism, merely standing alongside the Pharisees and the Sadducees, but rather as "true" Judaism, or true Israel itself.

This struggle to categorize Jesus believers as "true Jews," as opposed to factional or sectarian Jews, is also evident in Hegesippus' *Hypomnemata*. Like the author of Acts, Hegesippus is still groping for the proper names of the groups whose split he etiologizes. In the view of Hegesippus, the "sects" αἱρέσις have their origin among the Jews (*Hist. eccl.* 4.22.5).[28] In a creative throwback to the terminology of the divided kingdom under Solomon, Hegesippus folds the seven-sect schema into the designation for the northern tribes of the divided kingdom. The enemy/other is marked as "those with different opinions among the circumcision, among the sons of Israel [ἦσαν δὲ γνῶμαι διάφοροι ἐν τῇ περιτομῇ ἐν υἱοῖς Ἰσραηλιτῶν]. . . . Essenes, Galileans, Hemerobaptists, Masbothei, Samaritans, Sadducees and Pharisees." These "sons of Israel"—the tribes of the northern kingdom—stand against his own group, which he marks as the southern kingdom—the tribe of Judah and the Messiah (τῆς φυλῆς Ἰούδα καὶ τοῦ Χριστοῦ; *Hist. eccl.* 4.22.7). Thus, those who believe in Jesus as the Christ are truly the "race" of the Judeans.[29]

Like the text of Acts, Hegesippus' text contains a measure of category confusion, such that in some instances, it is the sectarian sons of Israel, those who stand "against the race of Judah and the Christ," who instigate persecution against the relatives of Jesus.[30] In the James narrative itself, however, the sectarians hold a mixed view concerning Jesus as "the Way." Only the "sect of the Pharisees," along with the scribes and *the Jews*, collude in James' death. From this interstitial place, before the category of the Christian martyr is securely established, Hegesippus and Acts both engage in awkward attempts to assert themselves as *true* Jews/Judeans while also inscribing their enemy/other as nonbelieving persecutory *Jews*.[31]

CONCLUSION. The comparisons made above are not intended to mask the differences in detail that the narratives of James and Stephen contain. Hegesippus' James tradition situates this conflict more centrally within "Judaism" itself. The brother of Jesus is also a Nazarite and a high priest, interceding life long for "the people" within the Jerusalem temple. Before his death, the entirety of the people accedes that James is righteous and fair-minded (ἡμεῖς γάρ μαρτυροῦμέν σοι καὶ πᾶς ὁ λαὸς ὅτι δίκαιος εἶ καὶ ὅτι πρόσωπον οὐ λαμβάνεις; *Hist. eccl.* 2.23.10). It is the death of James himself, rather than the death of Jesus, that is said to result in the destruction of Jerusalem. In contrast, the Greek-named *Stephanos* associated with "Hellenists" and Diaspora Jews already stands some distance from the temple when the conflict between himself and supporters of the temple breaks out. While this death coincides with the end of the association of "the Jews" as "the people" of God in Acts,[32] it is not regarded by the author of Luke-Acts as the cause of the destruction of Jerusalem. But regardless of their respective locations within "Jewish Christianity," on the one hand, and "Pauline Christianity," on the other, the stories bear remarkable similarities. Both imagine that the split between their group and "the Jews" owes to a murder of the "true Jew"—the Jesus prophet—by "the Jews" who reject him. Belief in Jesus brings one necessarily in conflict with the temple; the high Christology inherent in acclamations of Jesus as Son of Man provokes the execution; the accusers engage in mob behavior and lynch justice; the Jesus prophet/martyr responds to the barbaric crime with a prayer of extreme (undeserved) mercy; and the outcome is the devastation of the Jews, whose suffering is explained, not as a consequence of imperial occupation per se but as owing directly to their violent rejection of Jesus and his witnesses. Though Hegesippus' martyrdom account is extracanonical, and though much has been made of the differing view of the so-called Jewish Christians, on the one hand, and Pauline Christian, on the other, he does not depart significantly from the structure of the canonical narrative. I turn now to extracanonical versions that parse the James narrative quite differently.

Persecution in the Pseudo-Clementine *Recognitions* 1.27–71

Embedded in the Pseudo-Clementine *Recognitions* at 1.27–71 is another narrative of the conflict between Jews who believe in Jesus and other Jews, along with a murderous raging "enemy" as the cause of the great rift between them. While untangling the various traditions knotted together in the Pseudo-Clementine literature might be considered the "mother" of all literary-critical problems, scholars of this literature who agree on little else find consensus in acknowledging that *Recognitions* 1.27–71 contains a discrete source. No consensus exists on a precise date, but the range of proposed dates fall roughly within a half century, between 150 and 200 CE.[33] As with my discussion of Hegesippus' James, I am sidestepping much of this larger source-critical debate to focus on the rhetoric of *Recognitions* 1.27–71 as it stands, and especially on how various groupings of Jews are positioned within it.

After a recitation of history from creation to the death of the "prophet like Moses," on the cross, the narrative turns to the matter of conflict between those among the people who believe that Jesus is the prophet like Moses and those who do not. The company of believers meet at the temple steps to debate the high priest and other "sectarian" opponents, with the disciples rebuffing various accusations concerning Jesus and their movement in turn. After the first day of debate, James the bishop ascends to the temple and assumes the role of chief advocate for the view that Jesus is the Christ. At the end of seven full days of forceful persuasion by James, the entirety of the people is persuaded to be baptized. But at that very moment, the "enemy" (Paul) enters, instigates a violent riot and kills a number of the believers, leaving James the bishop himself for dead.[34] The believers flee to Jericho, and the text ends with a menacing Paul who, with the blessing of Caiaphas, turns to seeking out more believers to destroy.

Affinities between Recognitions 1.27–71 and Acts

Numerous intersections exist between *Recognitions* 1.27–71 and the book of Acts, including similar depictions of Gamaliel as defender of the Jesus group and similar threats of dire consequences for those who refuse the "prophet like Moses." Many of these intersections concern details that, in Acts, directly connect to the story of Stephen and his martyrdom. While the historical overview of *Recognitions* 1.27–71 is larger in scope, when it reaches the time of Moses, it begins to overlap considerably with sentiments expressed in Stephen's historiographical speech of Acts 7.2–50.[35] Both speeches dwell at considerable length on the story of Moses and the Exodus; both underscore the scriptural promise that God will raise up another prophet "like Moses" and point to Jesus as that prophet. A further common element shared between these two recitations of history is the view that temple worship is somehow a departure from the proper worship of God (cf. Acts 7.44–50 with *Rec.* 1.36.1, 1.38.5). As with the conflict scenes between Stephen and his audience in Acts 7, the hostile opponents of the Jesus believers in the *Recognitions* are depicted as "teeth gnashers" shouting at the protagonists (cf. Acts 7.54 with *Rec.* 1.53.1, 1.65.2, 1.65.5; Acts 7.57 with *Rec.* 1.70.1). Confrontation takes place at the point of the temple (in Acts, expressed in charges concerning the temple; in the *Recognitions*, expressed through the place of the disputation, the temple steps). Saul/Paul, the one who "breathes threats and murder" in Acts, and at whose feet the coats of the stoners of Stephen are laid, is not only threatening such things in the *Recognitions* but is also directly implicated as instigating the violent slaughter of Jesus followers subsequent to James' testimony (cf. Acts 8.1, 8.3, 22.19–20; *Rec.* 1.70–71). Similar to the pattern in Acts' Stephen episode of death, burial, and the scattering of witnesses (Acts 8.1–2), the denouement of the conflict in the later text involves burying two brothers (1.71.5) and displacement of large numbers of believers from Jerusalem to Jericho.[36]

Alternate Ideology

But however much *Recognitions* 1.27–71 shares with Acts, its tone concerning nonbelieving Jews is less polemical. Stephen's speech in Acts 7 stresses the ancestors' misunderstanding, disobedience, and idolatry. These vices are viewed as congenital and closely linked to the people's propensity to murder the prophets, as Stephen's culminating accusation reveals:

> You stiff-necked people, uncircumcised in heart and ears, you are
> forever opposing the Holy Spirit, just as your ancestors used to do.
> Which of the prophets did your ancestors not persecute? They killed
> those who foretold the coming of the Righteous One, and now you
> have become his betrayers and murderers. You are the ones that
> received the law as ordained by angels, and yet you have not kept it.
> (Acts 7.51–53)

In contrast, while the *Recognitions* includes acknowledgement of the people's idolatry, it accounts for this sin in less hostile tones. The narrator is at pains to note that the people sin not because of their congenitally stiff-necked nature but owing to their long association with Egyptian customs (cf. *Rec.* 1.35.1–1.36.1).[37]

The *Recognitions* does include a sampling of the divisive rhetoric that will come to dominate the *Adversus Iudaeos* literature. In the disputation between the believers and "the sectarians," the charge is leveled by Lebbaeus that the entire people had responded to Christ's compassion by killing him.[38] In an exegetical tradition shared with Acts, the *Recognitions* warns that those who do not heed the "prophet like Moses" are subject to banishment/death.[39] But this particular version of the Christ-killing charge, along with this assertion of exclusivistic salvation, stands next to passages in which relations between Jewish believers and nonbelievers are cast in more conciliatory language.

In *Recognitions'* recitation of history, the Christ-killing charge is attributed not to the whole people but to a subset—the wicked or impious (1.41.2). Moreover, the *Recognitions'* historical recitation does not culminate in the charge of Christ-killing, nor does it characterize the people as congenital prophet persecutors. Jesus believers are regarded as law observant, and stress is repeatedly laid on the fact that the only difference separating believers from nonbelievers is the question of whether or not Jesus is the messiah (*Rec.* 1.43.2, 1.50.5, 1.44.2, 1.60, 1.62.4).

A notable expression of the hope among the Jesus-believing group that they might achieve a small measure of common agreement with nonbelievers concerning Jesus comes in the plea of Barabbas to nonbelieving Jews that they at least refrain from "hating" Jesus:

... Barabbas ... who was elected apostle in the place of Judas, began
to warn the people not to hate Jesus or blaspheme him. "For it is
much more proper even for the one who does not know Jesus or is in
doubt about him to love him rather than to hate [him] for God has
established a reward for love, but a punishment for hate." (1.60.5–6;
Latin version [Jones]).[40]

In suggesting that God has an eschatological reward for those who have
doubts about Jesus, or even those who do not know him, so long as they show
him love rather than hate, Barabbas offers a soteriology that does not hinge
exclusivistically on Christ belief.

Stephen's Absence

As noted above, a number of thematic and verbal affinities between Acts and
the *Recognitions* concern materials that, in Acts, bear directly on the Stephen
pericope. Yet in the *Recognitions*, the violence among, as well as the subsequent
division of, believers and nonbelievers is narrated without any mention of
Stephen whatsoever. This is particularly remarkable in view of the common
materials concerning the violence of the pre-conversion Paul these narratives share.

In both Acts and the *Recognitions*, Paul receives permission from the High
Priest Caiaphas to carry out a mission of persecution against the church (cf.
Acts 9.1–2, 22.4–5, 26.10–12; *Rec.* 1.71.3–4). In the *Recognitions*, this collabora-
tion comes after "the enemy"/Paul has been depicted at the forefront of a
group of aggressors, instigating the slaughter of numerous believers and
raising forceful weapons to kill the Bishop James himself. Acts contains a
more muted depiction of Saul/Paul as a persecutor. Saul/Paul is marked as
"breathing threats and murder" (ἐμπνέων ἀπειλῆς καὶ φόνου; 9.1) but is never
depicted as drawing a weapon or throwing a stone. The closest that the
Acts narrative comes to specifying Saul/Paul's role in the persecution of
Christians—that is, the closest place of conformity between the murdering
enemy of the *Recognitions* and the protagonist of Acts—is the reference to the
mob that lays their coats at Saul's feet while stoning Stephen.[41] Yet, this death
by which Acts depicts the Apostle Paul as complicit in the death of a Jesus
believer receives no mention in the *Recognitions'* depiction of Paul as the principal murderer of those who confess Jesus as messiah. In spite of the pivotal
role of Stephen in the narrative method of Acts, in spite of the primacy Stephen
will come to have in Christian tradition as first martyr, and in spite of the
indubitable reality with which this story of Stephen will come to be imbued by
generations of Christian biblical scholars, Acts' Stephen does not exist in the

narrative world of the *Recognitions* even at the point where these two texts so closely converge.

Josephus on the Killing of John the Baptist and James the Brother of Jesus

Given the import the notion of Jews as the font of persecution was to have in the Christian West, it is no small irony that Josephus—our only first-century author standing outside of the Jesus movement who remarks on the execution of those linked to it—reports substantial Jewish opposition to two of these killings. Consider first, as a preface to my analysis of the Josephan account of the death of James, his report on the death of John the Baptist.[42] This report of the execution of John both opens and closes with Jews assessing Antipas' subsequent misfortune as divinely merited punishment for a wicked deed: "But to some of the Jews it seemed that the destruction of Herod's army by God was a just punishment because of what he had done to John who was called the Baptist" (*Ant.* 18.116); "It seemed to the Jews that the destruction of Herod's army was a vindication [of John], God wishing to do this evil to Herod" (*Ant.* 18.119).[43]

Second, and at greater length, consider Josephus' version of the death of James the brother of Jesus.[44] This version of James' death is part of a story Josephus tells to illustrate the ruthlessness of a Sadducean when given the opportunity to render verdicts in legal proceedings.[45] In the Roman power vacuum created by the procurator Festus's death, Ananus, a high priest of the Sadducean school, convenes a council that delivers James up to be stoned (ὁ Ἄνανος . . . καθίζει συνέδριον κριτῶν καὶ παραγαγὼν εἰς αὐτὸ τὸν ἀδελφὸν Ἰησοῦ τοῦ λεγομένου Χριστοῦ, Ἰάκωβος ὄνομα αὐτῷ, καί τινας ἑτέρους, ὡς παρανομησάντων κατηγορίαν ποιησάμενος παρέδωκε λευσθησομένους; *Ant.* 20.200). The narrative, while tantalizing, lacks detail. Those who are executed with James remain nameless, characterized only as "certain others." Perhaps we are to imagine that these are also persons linked with James, and through James to Jesus, but this is not clearly stated, and the Greek ἕτεροι could well designate persons caught up in Ananus' savagery for other reasons. Aside from the general designation of transgressing the law—παρανομησάντος—the crime that leads to the stoning is also unspecified.

Most remarkable is the sense of outrage and solidarity Josephus conjures among those inhabitants of the city who were considered to be both fairminded and strict observers of the law (ὅσοι δὲ ἐδόκουν ἐπιεικέστατοι τῶν κατὰ τὴν πόλιν εἶναι καὶ περὶ τοὺς νόμους ἀκριβεῖς; *Ant.* 20.201).[46] This group is "offended"—or, as Steve Mason translates, "burdened with grief"—over this (βαρέως ἤνεγκαν ἐπὶ τούτῳ; Ant. 20.201).[47] They successfully plead their case with both Agrippa II and the incoming Roman procurator Albinus to have Ananus deposed for his reckless use of power.

These two reports on John the Baptist and James would be remarkable on internal grounds alone since Josephus' predilection, even in the Antiquities, is to view the executions of both religious upstarts and political rebels with a certain satisfaction. Certain branches of historical Jesus scholarship have placed John the Baptist and Jesus in the company of the Jewish sign prophets Theudas (Ant. 20.97–99) and "the Egyptian" (Ant. 20.168–172) since all evoke Exodus imagery and all attract crowds hungry in one way or another for "tokens of deliverance."[48] Such placement helpfully elucidates the potentially anti-Roman edge of the ministry of John and Jesus, an edge that is much less pointed when the Gospels are read apart from Josephus. And yet, however similar the movements of Theudas, the Egyptian, and leaders of the early Jesus movement might be, it must be noted that Josephus himself does not regard them as cut of the same cloth. Theudas is a "magician" (γόης) who reaps the fruit of his foolishness (ἀφροσύνη; Ant. 20.97, 20.98); the Egyptian is likewise numbered among magicians and charlatans (Ant. 20.168); and both of these men are justly hunted down by Roman procurators.[49] In contrast, John is said to preach virtues of righteousness and piety, James' death is mourned by the reasonable and law observant, and Josephus regards both of these executions as transgressions rather than vindications.

Conclusion

In this chapter, I have challenged the univocity of the Acts narrative, its story of the first Christian martyr, and its construction of Jews and Christians at the point of Stephen's death. One method of resisting this text's univocity has been to note that both Acts' Stephen and Hegesippus' James tell virtually the same story. As demonstrated above, while neither text employs the firmly fixed identity terms "Jew" and "Christian," both still narrate a break at the point of death between two distinct groups, one that persecutes and one that is persecuted. The polarization of these two groups is underscored through the juxtaposition of the barbaric persecutors with the hyper-merciful response of the persecuted protagonist. In both of these texts, the presence of the colonial occupier is muted and the violence explained as owing to the barbarity of the "Jewish" others in their rejection of Jesus. A second strategy for disrupting this narrative has been to consider related texts that provide alternate ways to imagine Judeo-Christian relationships under empire in the first century and beyond.

Pseudo-Clementine Recognitions *1.27–71*

The Pseudo-Clementine *Recognitions* radically reshuffles the cards in the game of identity construction, through its designation of ally and enemy. Against the grain of Acts' depiction of "the Jews" as the hostile opponents of the Jesus believers, both Jewish and Gentile, *Recognitions* 1.27–71 suggests that Paul, and not the Jewish people, is the real enemy. Though *Recognitions* 1.27–71 also acknowledges a border between Jesus believers and nonbelieving Jews, it prefers one without the injurious barbed wire spilling over the top, one low enough that it can be talked across. Because the commonalities underscored in *Recognitions* 1.27–71 are not those that Jewish Jesus followers share with Pauline Christians but rather with the broader Jewish community, Annette Yoshiko Reed has argued convincingly that the text could appropriately be classified as a Jewish text.[50]

To be sure, the ideology of this text is also problematic. While the text spares the Jewish nation from the accusation of killing the true Jesus prophet/ martyr, it nevertheless reinscribes an etiology of the parting as caused by the murder of the innocent victim by the hostile enemy. As with Acts and Hegesippus, the violence here owes exclusively to internal theological quarrels and is utterly divorced from any question of imperial violence.[51] Furthermore, in its efforts to underscore that Jewish idolatry is not congenital, the text reinscribes an ethnocentric bias present in much early Christian literature, marking the Egyptian other as the source of an infectious and evil idolatry.[52]

Yet, reading this text against the Acts narrative serves the useful function of reminding us that, in spite of what Acts suggests, relations between believing and nonbelieving Jews could sometimes be irenic, and ties between these groups were not so quickly severed. The text disrupts the seeming inevitability of the linear progression emplotted in Acts, from the Jews to the Gentiles, from Jerusalem to Rome. As a text dated roughly to the turn of the third century, embedded in a mid-fourth-century document, which also expresses positive sentiments toward Jesus believers who embrace Jewish practices, it further calls into question the long-standing scholarly paradigm dating the demise of "Jewish Christianity" to the second century.

I also suggest that setting the narrative of the murder (or near murder)[53] of James by Paul next to the stoning of Stephen by the Jews illustrates again that these death narratives function primarily as a means to think through the parting and that they are by and large divorced from specific concern to represent the *realia* of first-century violence. Given the nature of our sources on James, including Paul's own references to James in his Epistle to the Galatians, an argument that the depiction in *Recognitions* 11.27–71 of the pre-conversion Paul raising his hand to murder James corresponds to an actual historical event would be widely—perhaps universally—rejected by scholars. In light of the generic similarities between *Recognitions* 1.27–71 and Acts, the same assessment could be made regarding the stoning of Stephen episode.

Antiquities 20.199–203

As the earliest to record a narrative of James' death, and as a Jew who is not a follower of Jesus, Josephus is generally regarded as the most reliable source for ascertaining what really happened to James. My own view is that the Josephus account is indeed a useful source for reconstructing a first-century narrative of violence among Jesus believers and other Jews. Though, I do not argue on the traditional grounds of historical reliability—that Josephus contains sure and certain data—but rather because the way he frames his story evokes a more complex, and hence richer, historical reconstruction.

But before turning to the complexities of the narrative, I note first its relative lack of detail. Because Josephus provides no speeches, no trial proceedings, no specific outline of what laws were transgressed, and no means of accounting for the relationship between James and "certain others," this account exposes the fragmentary nature of our sources, the gaps and fissures that exist in narrative accountings of the past, and the role that is left to historical imagination in filling those gaps. When the paucity of detail is not conceded, and the story is analyzed through the lens of a master narrative that posits "Jews" as killers of "Christians," it can be read as a typical instance of a Christian (James) being persecuted by "the Jews," or, more narrowly, the "Jewish establishment."[54] Once this step is taken, imagination can fill in the gaps with a religious crime at the heart of the execution, so that James is understood to have been charged with a ritual violation, or the crime of blasphemy owing to his Christ belief.[55]

But Josephus himself does not use the dichotomous set of proper names, violent Jew–victimized Christian, in emplotting this narrative. The proper names Josephus uses and the relationships he emplots among them evoke multiple subject positions and alliances in Judea under first-century Roman Empire. Instead of framing the story within the opposition dying-Christian–murdering-Jew as the Acts narrative does, Josephus presents us with a larger and more complex cast of characters: (1) a Jewish high priest hostile to (2) James, the brother of Jesus, who is executed, along with

(3) certain other Jews (who may or may not be followers of Jesus);[56] (4) a prominent non-Christian Jewish group sympathetic to and politically motivated on behalf of the executed; (5) the Jewish client king; and (6) the Roman overlord.

This more complex set of subject positions makes possible a considerably richer historical narrative than the book of Acts, standing alone, allows. In making mention of the intricate dance of power between high priest and Roman procurator, Josephus' story of James, like the Gospel stories of the crucifixion of Jesus and unlike the story of Stephen, provides at least some hint of the machinery of the imperial system at work. Moreover, the fact that Josephus does not refer to James dying either *as* a Christian or *because* of his Christianity reminds us that in this first generation after Jesus, it is not necessary to assume that one's belief in Jesus was the central fact of one's identity and the sole explanation for one's suffering. Furthermore, that James dies with "certain others," who are not identified as having any connection to Jesus, evokes a situation of common suffering across a spectrum of religious orientations.[57] Finally, Josephus provides a precious character sketch, one so incongruous with mainstream biblical scholarship that it is seldom contemplated: that of leading law-observant Jews (Pharisees?) first disturbed by the death of a leader in the Jesus movement and then engaging in political action to requite it.

To repeat, this narrative of James is not a preferred source for constructing a first-century narrative of violence in Judea because it can be said that Josephus, unlike Acts or the Pseudo-Clementines, has reliably transmitted a historical kernel of truth or that the specific events he emplots can be proven to have taken place. Rather, it is because this narrative does better justice to the kinds of situations in which early Jesus believers in Judea would have found themselves, to the possible common suffering of Jews—Jesus believers or not—under empire and to the possible alliances among Jews—Jesus believers or not—in solidarity and resistance.

4

"Father, Forgive Them"

The Place of the Perfect Prayer in the Construction of Christian Identity

Stephen's final gesture before dying is prayer on behalf of those who stone him. In a clear allusion to the dying forgiveness prayer of the Lukan Jesus from the cross, Stephen prays, "Lord, do not hold this sin against them [κύριε, μὴ στήσῃς αὐτοῖς ταύτην τὴν ἁμαρτίαν]" (Acts 7.60; cf. Luke 23.34a). The prayer puzzles on a number of levels. Unlike many other forgiveness prayers preserved in Christian tradition, it is "freestanding"—detached from the expected conditional clause tying this forgiveness to repentance on the part of the persecutors. Therefore, on a fundamental level, it challenges the widely held talionic framework of cosmic justice in which unrepentant evildoers ultimately meet their requisite punishment. Furthermore and ironically, because the prayer is woven into a narrative in which the Jewish persecutors of Stephen are condemned, the prayer for forgiveness is rendered inefficacious by the author who preserves it. Stephen, *the character*, may pray for mercy upon his tormentors, but Luke, *the author*, makes clear that Stephen's prayer has no consequence for those tormentors. Especially in view of Acts' construction of unbelieving Jews as villainous and savage, the assertion of this merciful response to his Jewish persecutors by the protagonist Stephen stands jarringly at odds with the author's own depictions of them.

How one accounts for these puzzles, or whether one recognizes them in the first place, has great import for how one situates Luke-Acts within discourses concerning emerging early Jewish and

Christian identities. If one contemplates the merciful prayers solely in relation to the martyr's cry for vengeance, one might embrace a marcionite
reading of Luke-Acts, affirming the victory of Jesus and Stephen's God of love
over the hateful God of the Maccabees.[1] Should one argue that the prayer
does not communicate a radically new sentiment but stands well within traditional Jewish expressions of intercession and mercy, Luke-Acts can be read
as fully continuous with such forms of Judaism.[2] If one sees the prayer
as reflective of the author's own perspective and ideals, one could argue
that through it the author of Luke-Acts demonstrates compassion toward
the Jews.[3]

This chapter argues, instead, that the conundrum of Stephen's dying
forgiveness prayer is best explained as part of Luke-Acts' attempt at a
much more complicated rhetorical balancing act. After situating Stephen's
prayer in relation to its direct antecedent, the dying forgiveness prayer of
the Lukan Jesus from the cross (Luke 23.34a), I will demonstrate that
these prayers function as assertions of radical discontinuity between
Judaism and Christianity. The dying forgiveness prayer is a dramatic overturning of the martyr's cry for vengeance. As expressions of self-mastery and
the ability to refrain from retaliating in the face of undeserved violence
inflicted by Jews, the prayers embody the dominical teachings on enemy love
and non-retaliation, and assert the ethical superiority of Christianity over
Judaism.

As assertions of Christianity's novelty on the grounds of mercy in the face
of Jewish violence, they also have something of a marcionite flavor. Yet, Luke-
Acts avoids the marcionite position that aligns teachings of extreme mercy with
the existence of a Father God who does not judge, by securing the prayers
within narratives that underscore their futility. Thus, for this author, the prayers
have a distinctive grammar, the grammar of intransitivity, whereby they serve
to celebrate the perfection of the one who prays forgiveness, without affecting
those for whom the prayers are offered.

This chapter also considers traces of an alternate transitive reading strategy,
in which the possibility that the prayers might effect forgiveness upon those for
whom they are offered is entertained. It is clear that some early Christians were
disturbed about this possibility, for such undeserved forgiveness would be a
breach of justice. An inappropriate use of the dying forgiveness prayers conjures an eschatological moment in which evildoers do not receive the divine
punishment that is their due. In this regard, the dying forgiveness prayers
prompted more anxiety than the dominical teachings on enemy love and non-
retaliation, for the latter could be more easily contained within preexisting
frameworks of just retribution.

Luke 23.34a

Crucial to the significance of Stephen's dying forgiveness prayer is its direct antecedent, the prayer of Jesus from Luke's passion narrative at Lk 23.34a. While the significance of Stephen's death is the central focus of this book, the privileged place of the dominical form of the forgiveness prayer in reception history, along with the common issues binding these two iterations of the forgiveness prayer, require that they be considered in tandem.

The Text-Critical Problem

The dying prayer of Jesus at Luke 23.34a is absent from several significant textual witnesses, including P^{75}, as well as B and D*. The weak manuscript attestation leads some scholars to argue that the text is not originally Lukan.[4] This argument against Lukan originality has been traditionally buttressed by the protest that no scribe could willfully excise such a significant dominical prayer from a biblical manuscript.[5] The stronger case, however, rests with those who argue for the originality of the prayer.[6] While absent from significant manuscript traditions, the words are found in textual witnesses as important as ℵ* and A. The patristic evidence for the prayer in the Third Gospel is also substantial. The presence of the tradition in Irenaeus (*Haer.* 3.16.9, 3.18.5) and verbatim matches with the prayer in Hegesippus and Tatian's *Diatessaron* seem best explained as evidence that such a prayer was contained in Luke rather than drawn from another source.[7]

Internal considerations also point in the direction of Lukan originality. As many have noted, a close interlocking structure knits the death of Stephen to the death of Jesus across the two volumes.[8] Before his death, the persecuted Stephen speaks three times in front of the murderous mob. In the two instances in which the manuscript tradition is secure, his words are modeled closely, though not precisely, on the words of the persecuted Jesus. Compare Jesus before the council in Luke 22.69, "But from now on the Son of Man will be seated at the right hand of the power of God," with Stephen before the mob in Acts 7.56, "Look, I see the heavens opened and the Son of Man standing at the right hand of God!"; and Luke 23.46, "Father into your hands I commend my spirit," with Acts 7.59, "Lord Jesus, receive my spirit." Those who argue against Lukan originality and for later scribal interpolation of 23.34a must presume the unlikely scenario by which the author of Luke-Acts modeled two of Stephen's dying utterances on words of Jesus, then scripted for Stephen a third saying, an original forgiveness prayer, that was later modified and retrojected into the Gospel of Luke.[9] The careful parallels in the first two instances of Stephen's speech suggest, to the contrary, that this third and final utterance concerning forgiveness in Acts 7.60 is not a detail Luke introduces here for the first time but that once again he draws from a model saying in the Third Gospel, that is, an original prayer for forgiveness attributed to Jesus in Luke 23.34a.

A further internal consideration is the explanatory clause "for they know not what they do," which conforms to the teleology of Luke-Acts regarding the relation of sin and ignorance. The characterization of Jesus' persecutors as acting against him "in ignorance" in Luke 23.34a is consistent with apostolic preaching in Acts that the Jews acted in ignorance when they crucified Jesus. Hence, Peter's speech: "But you rejected the Holy and Righteous One and asked to have a murderer given to you, and you killed the Author of life. . . . And now, friends, I know that you acted in ignorance, as did your rulers" (Acts 3.14–17); and Paul's: "Because the residents of Jerusalem and their leaders did not recognize him or understand the words of the prophets that are read every Sabbath, they fulfilled those words by condemning him" (Acts 13.27). In short, Luke 23.34a, in which Jesus makes excuse for those who crucify on account of their ignorance, anticipates precisely the apostolic preaching concerning the ignorance of Jesus' tormentors.

Finally, the traditional means of clinching the case against Lukan originality—the suggestion that such a powerful dominical saying simply could not be excised by a scribe—now loses its force as scholars of text criticism situate early Christian scribal activity within its social, religious, and ideological contexts.[10] The scribes who transmitted the manuscripts of the New Testament struggled to make theological/ideological sense of them. Processes of excision, interpolation, and other forms of amending the manuscripts that lay before them were part and parcel of this struggle. It appears that, at least in some ancient scribal quarter, the forgiveness prayer did not make sense. Those who have argued this view most recently, including Eldon Epp, Bart Ehrman, and Kim Haines-Eitzen, have stressed the non-sense of the prayer in terms of increasing anti-Judaism.[11] A Jesus prayer for forgiveness *of Jews* strains credulity in the second century and beyond, in view of increasing anti-Jewish sentiment in Christian communities and especially in view of the Christian reading of the destruction of Jerusalem as sure sign of God's vengeance on the crucifiers. While concurring that anti-Judaism is one likely motivation for scribal excision of the prayer, I note further that the ideological challenge of the prayer is not only that Jesus prays for the forgiveness of *Jews* but also that Jesus prays for the forgiveness of *undeserving and unrepentant* Jews. As I will underscore below, the forgiveness prayers can be read as a radical disruption of the talionic framework of divine justice. This double-edged concern of the emerging church to carve out a position that was both anti-Jewish and pro-talionic (which is to say, the position of anti-marcionite, proto-orthodox Christianity) provides a fuller explanation for the scribal excision of the dominical forgiveness prayer from the Gospel of Luke.

The Expiring Excuse Clause

While this dominical prayer from the cross in the Third Gospel has understandably received more scrutiny than the successive prayer of Stephen, both by early and modern readers, it is possible to read Jesus' prayer as creating less theological dissonance than Stephen's. Though the prayer is "freestanding" in the sense that it does not explicitly offer forgiveness on the condition of repentance, it at least offers the ignorance excuse—for they know not what they do—as an explanatory clause. Key to the teleology of the sin/ignorance motif in Luke-Acts is the assertion that the ignorance excuse is not valid in perpetuity but expires after the postresurrection apostolic preaching, for both Jews and Gentiles. Consider especially Acts 17.30–31: "While God has overlooked the times of human ignorance, now he commands all people everywhere to repent, because he has fixed a day on which he will have the world judged in righteousness by a man whom he has appointed, and of this he has given assurance to all by raising him from the dead." The merciful prayer of Stephen, "Lord, do not hold this sin against them," is a starker disruption of talionic justice than that of Jesus due to its postresurrection setting. Unlike those who crucify Jesus then, Stephen's killers are without excuse. They *do* know what they do, and even yet Stephen prays mercy upon them. Moreover, if one understands this Lukan teleology of ignorance to be linked to the distinction between forgivable sins against the Son of Man and unforgivable sins against the Holy Spirit (cf. Luke 12.10–12), the contrast between the two prayers is further underscored. Since Stephen at the moment of his death is "filled with the Holy Spirit" (πλήρης πνεύματος ἁγίου; Acts 7.55), he is asking that his persecutors be forgiven for a resistance to the Holy Spirit that Luke's Jesus has pronounced unforgivable.[12]

The Question of the Prayer's Object

The merciful prayer in the Third Gospel might also be considered less dissonant with the overarching theme of vengeance against *Ioudaioi* if the object of forgiveness is read as Roman rather than Jewish. The antecedent of αὐτοῖς at Luke 23.34a is not clearly specified. For whom, precisely, does Jesus ask forgiveness?

It has been argued that the objects of the prayer are those driving the nails in 23.33, who are presumably Roman soldiers, even though they are not specifically so named.[13] Or, it may be the Jewish agents of the crucifixion—the chief priests, the leaders, and the people—who are the last-mentioned antecedent at 23.13.[14] If Jesus is understood to be forgiving the Romans here, then the promised vengeance spoken by him does not contradict the merciful prayer, for these conflicting messages are aimed at different recipients. In this reading, Jesus' turn from the Jews whom he condemns, and toward the Romans whom he forgives, anticipates the same movement of Paul in Acts, and ultimately of the Gentile church in subsequent Christian centuries.[15] Alternately, if Jesus' plea for mercy is read as pertaining to the Jews,[16] then the prayer of Jesus aligns perfectly with the prayers of Stephen in Acts and James in Hegesippus and bespeaks the same contradiction—a hero's plea for mercy upon Jews contained within a broader narrative condemning them. In contrast to the Third Gospel, there is no ambiguity concerning the intended object of Stephen's forgiveness prayer. As I have underscored in chapter 2, Stephen's martyrdom owes exclusively to the agency of the Jewish mob. No Romans are at the scene of this barbarian stoning. The objects of Stephen's prayer are undoubtedly the *Ioudaioi* whom the author of Acts condemns.

Echoes of Scripture in Luke 23.34a/Acts 7.60

Early Christian exegetical traditions making connections between the Lukan forgiveness prayers and texts from Hebrew Scripture are few and relatively late. A recent cluster of modern scholarship, however, attempts to situate the forgiveness prayers securely within Jewish Scriptures to conclude that the prayer has a "thoroughly Jewish background" or—even more strongly—that "Luke has not given up on the Jews."[17] Because my own position, to the contrary, is that through these dying forgiveness prayers Luke attempts to construct a break between Jews and Christians, I consider here the merits of those who argue that these prayers are closely modeled on Jewish Scriptures and who then conclude that the author of Luke-Acts stresses continuity more than rupture.

The Intercessions of Named Biblical Prophets

Matthias Blum, in his effort to underscore that Luke's depiction of the dying Jesus at prayer stands within a thoroughly Jewish scriptural frame, has suggested that Jesus' prayer of intercession on behalf of the Jews at 23.34a positions him in a line with Abraham (Gen. 17), Moses (Exod. 32), and Samuel (1 Sam.

12.19) as a prophet who prays/pleads for God's mercy on behalf of sinful people.[18] But any possible parallels between the various intercessions of these Biblical prophets and the prayer of Jesus from the cross are too general to prove instructive. Abraham, Moses, and Samuel do make intercessions on behalf of peoples, but both the situations in which they pray and the content of their prayers are dramatically different from those in Luke-Acts.

Atonement for Inadvertent Sins

More sustained arguments have been put forth that particularly because of the explanatory clause "for they know not what they do," the forgiveness prayer of Jesus invokes atonement ceremonies elaborated in the Torah pertaining to inadvertent sins of the congregation (Num. 15.22–31; cf. also Lev. 4).[19] But any connection between the forgiveness prayer and provisions for the atonement of inadvertent sins seems at best a faint echo rather than a clear literary allusion. While Jesus is indeed asking here for the forgiveness of unwitting sin, the situation in which he does so is far removed from the provisions imagined by the authors of the Pentateuchal legislation. The primary role for performing rites of atonement for inadvertent sins in these Scriptures is assigned to the priest, and while Luke casts Jesus in the mold of the Old Testament "prophet like Moses,"[20] he makes no explicit connection between Jesus' life and death and any priestly function.[21] Furthermore, and differently from Luke, in the provisions from Torah, the congregation is presumed to be cooperating in the process of making amends, for they are instructed to aid in preparation for the priestly intercession by presenting the sacrificial animal to the priest. A related and most obvious difference is that the Torah provisions do not imagine that the priest is facing imminent death at the hands of an angry mob for whom he is authorized to make atonement.

Isaiah 53.12c

Isaiah 53, which concerns the mission and death of the suffering servant becomes a veritable minefield for early Christian exegetes seeking to demonstrate that the ignominious circumstances of Jesus' execution were foretold by the prophets. The humility of Jesus' crucifixion is explained as fulfilling the prophecy of the servant who is "like a lamb that is led to the slaughter" (Isa. 53.7). Of particular service to the Gospel authors and the fathers in verse 12 of this chapter were the phrases, "he was numbered with the transgressors" and "he bore the sins of many." The last line of this verse from Isaiah is sometimes pointed to as the prophetic inspiration for Luke's (and later Stephen's and James') insertion of a prayer of forgiveness at the point of death.[22] As the NRSV translates from the Hebrew, while he poured out himself to death: "[he] made intercession for the transgressors" (מֵעֲשְׁפֵלֹ יַפְגִּיעַ). Unlike the previous textual models discussed, the Isaiah passage in Hebrew at least shares with the Lukan passion the detail of intercession in the context of persecution. Moreover, it is clear that Luke has Isaiah 53.12 readily at hand—albeit in LXX form—for he incorporates the prophecy of Isaiah 53.12b, "and he was counted among the lawless" into his passion narrative at 22.37. A key difficulty with seeing the verse as direct model for Luke, however, is that the Septuagint—the translation of the Hebrew Scriptures Luke depends upon throughout his work—does not contain the notion of intercession for transgressors at 53.12c. The verse in the Greek Bible concludes, rather, "He bore the sins of many *and was handed over because of their transgressions* (καὶ διὰ τὰς ἀνομίας αὐτῶν παρεδόθη). Hence, those who argue that the intercessory prayer of Jesus at Luke 23.34a owes to Luke's reliance on Isaiah 53.12 must argue that Luke somehow has some access to a Hebrew text, or to an unattested Greek variant.[23]

Wisdom of Solomon

Brian Beck has suggested that the response of Jesus from the cross can be illuminated by the close parallels between it and the situation of the suffering righteous, especially as found in the Wisdom of Solomon at 1.16–3.9. Noting that one of the crucial issues faced by the righteous sufferer is whether "he can sustain insult and torture without moral collapse," he argues that the prayer for enemies at Luke 23.34 "brings out the bearing of Jesus under testing, and illustrates his consistency of character." Like the righteous man suffering unjust persecution in Wisdom of Solomon (cf. esp. 2.19), Jesus also demonstrates gentleness (ἐπιείκεια) and the ability to bear evil without resentment (ἀνεξικακία).[24] While the depictions of Jesus and the righteous man in the Wisdom of Solomon do share these character traits, there is a crucial difference in their response to persecution. The righteous man does not pray for the forgiveness of his enemies but suffers in silence. Differently from Jesus who prays forgiveness upon his tormentors, the silence of the righteous sufferer (Wis. 2) enables him to exhibit the virtue of gentleness and self-mastery without contravening the overarching framework of the text that affirms that the righteous will be rewarded and the persecutors, judged (Wis. 3).

Evaluation

For purposes of my own argument, it is not necessary to suggest that Luke's narrative world was totally divorced from the conceptual precedents considered

above. It is possible that readers of Luke might hear echoes of atonement provisions or affirmations of the suffering servant's gentleness in these prayers.
Origen provides a relatively early instance of one who connects Levitical provisions for inadvertent sins and the dominical clause, "for they know not what
they do."[25] Eventually, commentators do link Luke 23.34a and Isaiah 53.12c as
an instance of prophecy and fulfillment. My chief objection to arguments that
have cited these passages as conceptual precedents for the forgiveness prayers
is how they attempt to minimize the radicality of Luke's project by suggesting
that if a Jewish precedent can be found for Luke's prayer, then Luke still stands
within Judaism, does not attempt to severe Christianity from Judaism, and
cannot be understood as anti-Jewish.

A first principle, however, in both the study of literary allusion and in the
more diffuse study of literary echo is that allusion and echo always supply
the original text with new meaning. Heinrich Plett's observation in regards to
the study of quotation—that every quotation provokes conflict or interference
between the material quoted and its new context—also applies to other forms
of allusion.[26] Richard Hayes, for instance, in his study of literary echoes in
Paul's Letters, speaks of the revisionary power of allusive echo to generate new
figuration. He notes that a key task of criticism attuned to the rhetorical effect
of literary echoes is "to give an account of the distortions and new figuration
that [echoes] generate."[27] While the arguments above focus on the possible allusions to Scripture and wisdom literature that the prayers for mercy activate,
they fail to note the "revisionary power," "interference, or conflict" that Luke's
use of the allusion entails. While Luke does not invent, but rather invokes,
traditions of merciful prayers for sinners and gentleness in the face of persecution, he also exerts a considerable amount of revisionary power by placing those
prayers of mercy on the lips of martyrs on behalf of their executioners. Here
precisely lies Lukan originality, Lukan departure from Jewish literary precedent. To appreciate this revisionary power, it is instructive to compare these
dying prayers with those of other martyrs.

Vengeance Overturned: Reading Luke's Prayers against the Martyr's Cry

In the literature of the suffering righteous and persecuted prophets, as well as in
martyrdom texts proper, belief that God will ultimately vindicate the righteous
and judge their tormentors pervades. God's ultimate justice, in the form of vengeance against tormentors, is a bedrock solution to the problem of theodicy, the
question of God's presence in the midst of suffering. As noted in the instance of

Wisdom of Solomon, while the righteous sufferer may endure in gentleness and forbearance (ἐπιείκεια καὶ ἀνεξικακία; 2.19–20), the poet offers confident assurance that their tormentors will ultimately be punished; the ungodly die without hope (3.10–19). The tormented may endure in silence—compare again Wisdom of Solomon 2, as well as the depiction of the suffering servant in Isaiah 53, which draws explicit attention to the closed mouth of the persecuted (v. 7). But for the martyr, at least as typical as silent resistance are last words expressing conviction in the tormentor's ultimate punishment.[28] In the Maccabean literature, confident and spiteful predictions of vengeance are delivered by the tormented directly to the persecuting tyrant. Four of the seven martyred brothers in 2 Maccabees proclaim vengeance on their tormentor in their last speeches.[29] In 4 Maccabees, the brothers' convictions concerning ultimate vengeance are foregrounded in a unison chorus: "For we shall have the prize of virtue; but you because of your blood thirstyness will deservedly undergo from the divine justice eternal torment by fire" (9.9). The conviction of ultimate vengeance is then repeated at each of the seven deaths, thereby taking on the quality of a liturgical refrain (9.24, 9.32, 10.11, 10.21, 11.3, 12.12, 12.18; cf. 18.5, 18.22.[30]

While the question of whether or not Luke-Acts has direct familiarity with this Maccabean martyrdom tradition is not clear, the pericope concerning Stephen's death does have a close intertextual relationship with the murder of Zechariah, son of Jehoiada recorded in 2 Chronicles 24.17–25, as noted in chapter 2. Here, I consider specifically the import of Zechariah's final dying plea, "May YHWH see and avenge!" (2 Chr. 24.22), and its subsequent elaborations in rabbinic and early Christian literature. This story of Zechariah's violent fate and its link to a forsaken Jerusalem becomes a touchstone in rabbinic and other Hellenistic Jewish sources for meditations on prophet persecution, blood vengeance, and communal blame for the destruction of the city in 70 CE.[31] In these traditions, Zechariah's cry for vengeance is not silenced by his death, for after his murder his blood continues to signal the need for requital. According to the Babylonian Talmud (b. Git. 57b), Zechariah's blood "boils" on the temple floor for 250 years, until it is requited by Nebuchadnezzar. In Midrash Numbers 30.15, the blood is said to splash on the temple wall.[32] This tradition of Zechariah's blood seething in the temple as a means to communicate the need for its requital is also echoed in the legend preserved in the Protevangelium of James.[33] In this version of the story, Zechariah son of Jehoiada has been conflated with the father of John the Baptist. The first to enter the sanctuary in search of Zechariah views his dried blood next to the altar and hears a voice explaining, "Zechariah has been murdered! His blood will not be cleaned up until his avenger appears" (Prot. Jas. 24.4–5). Subsequently, the priests discover that Zechariah's blood has turned to stone (Prot. Jas. 24.9).

While it is impossible to date with precision when each of these traditions originates, the reference in Q 11.50–51 to the requital of Zechariah's blood by "this generation" demonstrates that Luke-Acts taps into some version of it. Especially, in view of these graphic traditions of Zechariah's blood seething—or splashing or congealing—as a signal of the urgent need for its requital, the divergence of the dying prayers of Zechariah and Stephen is dramatic. With his dying words, "Lord, do not stand this sin against them," Stephen seems to offer a counter discourse—a New Testament if you will—a deliberate refutation of the vengefully expressed desire of the dying Zechariah, "Behold Lord, and judge."

Reading the Lucan Prayers alongside Hegesippus' James

As I have suggested in a previous chapter, the martyrdoms of Stephen in Acts and James in Hegesippus serve near-identical functions in constructing a break between Jews, on the one hand, and Christians, on the other. The importance of the forgiveness prayer itself in marking the ideal Christian martyr as distinct from the vengeful Jew is clear in the James narrative, for even more so than in the case of Luke's Stephen, the extreme mercy of Hegesippus' James is featured. James is characterized as praying habitually for the forgiveness of the people before his martyrdom. Furthermore, at the point when he prays for the forgiveness of his killers, the Rechabite rushes forward to draw attention to that prayer.[34]

It is also the case that the story of James in Hegesippus serves as an instance in which, on the one hand, Jewish Scriptures influence the narrative of the idealized Jesus follower, but on the other, expressions of aggression against enemies in those Scriptures are replaced by prayers for forgiveness. As noted in a previous chapter, the narrative of James standing at the pinnacle of the actual Jerusalem temple owes to a method of scriptural exegesis that literalizes the metaphorical association of James with the eschatological temple. As R. Bauckham has convincingly shown, scribal exegesis of Psalm 118 [LXX 117] serves as a generating influence for Hegesippus' account. For instance, the cry concerning the "the gates/tents of righteousness" (Ps. 118.15, 118.19 [LXX 117.15, 117.19]) and the lament that the Psalmist is "pushed and shaken that he might fall" (Ps. 118.13 [LXX 117.13]) become elements in Hegesippus' martyrdom: James is associated with righteousness, interrogated concerning Jesus, the "gate," and is pushed so that he falls from the temple's pinnacle.[35] Yet, much in the way that Luke alters the Chronicler's story of the dying Zechariah, substituting mercy for vengeance, so the author of this James legend, generated through an exegesis of Psalm 118 [LXX 117], omits the aggressive response toward persecutors expressed in the Psalm. The voice of the persecuted Psalmist does not pray forgiveness upon tormentors, but rather proclaims a threefold hostile response:

> all the nations encircled me, but in the name of the Lord I repulsed them [ἠμυνάμην αὐτούς]. They encircled me completely, but in the name of the Lord I repulsed them [ἠμυνάμην αὐτούς]. They encircled me as bees do a honeycomb. . . but in the name of the Lord I repulsed them [ἠμυνάμην αὐτούς]. (LXX Ps 117.10–12)[36]

The writer of the Hegesippus narrative mines the Psalm for imagery of righteousness and the eschatological temple but not for the Psalmist's aversion to the encircling enemy. Instead, in the midst of his enemies, Hegesippus' James prays so incessantly for forgiveness that his knees become "as calloused as a camel's" and invokes forgiveness upon them again in his very last breath.

To summarize up to this point, the dying forgiveness prayer of Jesus signals a dramatic turn from the cry of vengeance expected as the martyr's last word. The radicality of the Jesus prayer is taken to an even greater extreme by Stephen, who does not append an explanatory clause and who prays forgiveness after the time of allowance for ignorance has expired. Hegesippus also stresses the extreme nature of the martyr's mercy by depicting his commitment to such mercy as a lifelong (high) priestly practice. While neither the author of Luke-Acts nor Hegesippus has fully embraced the term Christian for the social group they represent, in both cases the "Father, forgive them" functions much like the declaration "Christianos sum" in later martyrdom literature—the utterance is performative, constructing the followers of the Way as a new type. The new type embodies a distinctively superior ethic against the foil of murderous Jews. The dying declaration indelibly inscribes followers of the Way as radically forgiving, in stark contrast with the barbarous *Ioudaioi* who are radically unforgivable.

While the assertion of novelty on the grounds of mercy in the face of violence has a marcionite flavor, the narratives make clear that the extremely merciful prayers are not directed to a new God who does not judge. In spite of the prayers of Jesus and Stephen, the Third Gospel underscores that the temple's destruction owes to Jewish refusal to embrace Jesus, and Acts closes by emphasizing God's rejection of non-believing Jews. In a similar rhetorical construction in Hegesippus, James may be depicted as desiring God to forgive his tormentors, but the troops of Vespasian evoked by the author (or possibly the redactor) to encircle the city of Jerusalem immediately after his death (καὶ εὐθὺς Οὐεσπασιανός πολιορκεῖ αὐτούς; *Hist. eccl.* 2.23.18) ensure that James' request for mercy does not prevent his killers from receiving their due punishment. For both authors, the hero may offer a prayer for mercy, but the narrative directs this prayer to a God who has refused to heed it.

To better underscore the function of this prayer in the construction of early Christian identity, I turn now to consider the teachings attributed to Jesus in the Sermon on the Mount/Sermon on the Plain.[37] Observing that the dying forgiveness prayers in Luke-Acts are an assertion of a Christian *novum* might be understood as nothing more than an acknowledgment that these prayers are embodiments of the teachings attributed to Jesus in the SM/SP since the sermon itself is widely regarded as *the* distinguishing feature of Christian ethical teaching. In what follows, I first take up instances in which the forgiveness prayers do indeed seem to function similarly to Jesus' ethical teaching on enemy love and non-retaliation from the SM/SP. But I close the chapter by demonstrating the distinctive radicality of the forgiveness prayer that sets it apart even from this body of ethical teaching.

The Relation of the Dying Forgiveness Prayers to the Sermon on the Mount/Sermon on the Plain

As many modern commentators have noted, the depiction of Jesus, Stephen, and James praying forgiveness on their tormentors at the time of their deaths can be read as deliberate and exemplary enactments of Jesus' teaching to love enemies and pray for—rather than retaliate against—those who persecute. In both Matthew's Sermon on the Mount (5.38–48) and Luke's Sermon on the Plain (6.29–36), enemies are those who do violence to the community;[38] and one way in which the command to love enemies is concretized is through the exhortation to pray for them.[39] Such love and prayers are understood to be an overturning of the principle of retaliation, as is suggested structurally in Matthew where the antithesis concerning enemy love (5.43–48) follows immediately upon that concerning non-retaliation (5.38–42). In Luke, the principles of enemy love and non-retaliation are woven together even more seamlessly, with the exhortation to turn the other cheek along with other forms of nonreciprocal behavior supplied as specific instances of enemy love. As Luke 6.27–30 reads:

> But I say to you that listen, Love your enemies, do good to those who hate you, bless those who curse you, pray for those who abuse you. If anyone strikes you on the cheek offer the other also; and from anyone who takes away your coat do not withhold even your shirt. Give to everyone who begs from you; and if anyone takes away your goods, do not ask for them again.

In view of these ethical exhortations, Jesus' prayer from the cross for his tormentors to be forgiven can be understood as a concrete demonstration of his greatest ethical teaching on enemy love. When Stephen prays likewise at his martyrdom, he is engaging in a supreme exercise of *imitatio Christi*. That at least some early Christian readers connected the dying forgiveness prayers of Jesus and Stephen directly to the ethical teaching on enemy love and prayers for persecutors in the SM/SP is evident from the writings of Irenaeus:

> That he exclaimed upon the cross, "Father forgive them for they know not what they do," [exhibits] the long-suffering patience, compassion and goodness of Christ. . . . For the word of God who said to us, "love your enemies, pray for those who hate you," himself did this very thing upon the cross. (*Haer.* 3.185 [Roberts–Donaldson])

and Cyprian:

> How will you love your enemies and pray for your adversaries and persecutors? We see what happened in the case of Stephen. When he was being killed by the violence and stones of the Jews, he did not ask for vengeance but forgiveness for his murderers, saying, "O Lord, do not lay this sin against them." (*Pat.* 16 [Wallis])

On the question of whether early Christians regarded the enemy love teaching as novel, the rhetorical markers are conflicted. As Helmut Koester has noted, in the early church the enemy love teaching is the most frequently transmitted of all the synoptic logia.[40] Yet, it is also the case that Christians transmit the saying for divergent purposes.

In writings in which the enemy love saying is considered within Greco-Roman cultural norms, there are frequent assertions of enemy love as a Christian *proprium*. As early as Clement of Rome, enemy love is regarded as a distinctive teaching causing the Gentiles to marvel (2 *Clem.* 13.4); and Justin Martyr also asserts the teaching of enemy love as something new (*Apol.* 1.15.9). A most explicit insistence on the distinctiveness of Christian enemy love in which the inscribed reader is Gentile is Tertullian's *Ad Scapulam* 1, in which he asserts, "To love friends is the custom for all people, but to love enemies is customary only for Christians." Tertullian's rhetoric here has convinced W. C. van Unnik, who points to this statement as a key indication of the contrast between Gentile and Christian ethics, indeed the point at which "Christianity separates itself from Antiquity."[41]

It is also the case, however, that second- and third-century Christians sometimes positioned these teachings as corresponding to non-Christian views, rather than insisting upon their radicality. That is, many early Christians were concerned to argue for the inclusion of Christians within the cultural norm and did so by explaining how Christians shared the dominant ethical framework and/or improved upon it, rather than by arguing for Christian superiority based upon their ethical *differences* from Greco-Roman norms. This is seen especially in arguments working to underscore that Christian teaching dovetails with the leading philosophy of the day in its heralding of virtues such as philanthropy, and the ability to restrain rage. Consider, for example, Clement of Alexandria's crediting to Homer a prophetic understanding of the principle of generosity toward enemies (*Strom.* 2.19), or Origen's concession to Celsus that Jesus' teaching to turn the other cheek is merely a "coarser" restatement of what Socrates had already taught in Plato's *Crito* (*Cels.* 7.58–59). It is this rhetorical move of aligning the teachings of Jesus with—rather than distancing them from—those of the ancient Greeks that has caused John Whittaker to argue, in explicit opposition to van Unnik, that Jesus' teaching on enemy love and non-retaliation merely echoes a commonplace of Hellenistic morality.[42]

Within the myriad of issues raised by early Christian transmission of the enemy love saying, the question of most relevance to my analysis of the Stephen pericope is how enemy love figures in relation to debates concerning the nature and degree of continuity versus rupture between Christians and Jews. Under what circumstances is this saying, like the dying forgiveness prayers, asserted as a Christian *novum* diametrically opposed to Judaism, and when is it read otherwise? I will address these questions in the following way. I first take up two early Christian authors who do not quote the dying forgiveness prayers but who do assert Christian novelty in relation to the dominical sayings on enemy love and non-retaliation, Marcion and Justin Martyr. I then turn to an exploration of the grammar of the prayers, and the analogous grammar of the Roman discourse of clemency, as a means to explicate more fully how it was possible for some early Christians to celebrate enemy love and forgiveness as distinctive components of their ethic, all the while engaging in the uncharitable practice of vilifying Jews. Next, traces of transitive readings are identified, that is, indications that some early Christians thought through the possibility that a prayer for the forgiveness of the undeserving might actually effect such forgiveness. Finally, I take note of readers who regarded the exhortation on enemy love from the SM/SP as an extension, rather than an overturning, of the *lex talionis* from the Old Testament. This analysis demonstrates how the dying forgiveness prayers were potentially more radical than Jesus' ethical teaching on enemy love and non-retaliation since the former constitute a challenge to the framework of cosmic justice, which the latter need not.

The Marcionite Antithesis

The rupture asserted between Christianity and Judaism in marcionite thinking has received considerable attention in chapter 1, and only a few elements of that thinking need be underscored here. First, we have strong indication of the centrality of the dominical sayings on enemy love and non-retaliation to this asserted rupture, owing especially to Tertullian's concern to refute Marcion's reading. In marcionite thinking, the teachings on enemy love and non-retaliation from the SM/SP are essential to the new and distinctive Christian revelation. They stand in clear antithesis to the *lex talionis* of the vengeful creator God (cf. Exod. 21.23–35; Lev. 24.19–20; Deut. 19.21).[43]

Second, though according to Tertullian, Marcion does not abandon the notion of a final judgment, he does assign the duty to the lesser, creator god, thereby disassociating it from the Father God. As Tertullian, in his characteristically biting sarcasm, describes Marcion's new judgment-free god: "a better god has been discovered, one who is neither offended nor angry nor inflicts punishment, who has no fire warming up in hell, and no outer darkness wherein there is shuddering and gnashing of teeth: he is merely kind" (*Marc.* 1.27.2 [Evans]).[44] Because the Father God does not judge, the tensions I have underscored in Luke-Acts and Hegesippus, whereby heroes offer prayers for mercy to a God who does not heed them, are mollified, if not erased, in marcionite logic.

Third, while marcionite logic asserts rupture between Christianity and Judaism through association of love, mercy, and forgiveness with the former, and hatred and vengeance with the latter, we have no indications from our heresiologists that Marcion accuses contemporary Jews of engaging in violence against Christians. Rather, his assertion of Christian novelty in diametric opposition to Judaism appears to be confined to the realms of theology (two distinct Gods) and Scripture (Old vs. New Testament). As will be shown next, a contemporary of Marcion, Justin Martyr, shuffles the puzzle pieces differently.

Justin Martyr on Enemy Love

In his *Dialogue with Trypho*, Justin is also deeply engaged in the project of defining Christianity as a category distinct from Judaism, and, like Marcion, he employs the dominical teachings on enemy love and prayer for persecutors to make that distinction.[45] But unlike Marcion, and quite similarly to Luke-Acts and Hegesippus, Justin fixes that distinction in the realm of the social.

It is well known that in *Trypho*, Justin repeatedly charges the Jews with the quintessential act of prophet persecution—killing the Christ. He also accuses Jews of multiple acts of violence toward Christians themselves. Frequently, the charges relate to verbal violence, including the cursing of Christ in the synagogue and the sending of messengers to blaspheme Christians. The charges also rise to holding Jews responsible, through their cursing, for the murders of Christians at the hands of the Gentiles (96) and for enacting the actual murders themselves, "so often as [they] have the power to do so" (133.6). The question of the relationship of these accusations of Jewish violence against Christians to actual historical violence has received considerable scholarly attention. Much of it has focused on the issue of whether Justin's accusations that Jews curse Christ proves that the *Birkat Ha-Minim*—a Hellenistic Jewish malediction composed for liturgical use in the synagogue as a means of excluding heretics—was aimed directly at Christians and prevented them from participating in synagogue life.[46]

Less attention has been drawn to the rhetorical strategy, employed repeatedly by Justin in *Trypho*, of pairing these accusations with assertions of extreme Christian mercy, through reference to the SM/SP. Consider three passages that are most often scrutinized with respect to the Christ-cursing charge. In the first, Justin makes explicit juxtaposition between the practice of Jewish cursing that leads to death and the dominical saying on enemy love that shapes Christian response to that persecution:

> For, in your synagogues you curse all those who through him are
> called Christians, and the Gentiles put into effect your curse by
> killing all those who merely admit that they are Christians. To all
> our persecutors we say: "You are our brothers. . . ." *Furthermore, we*
> *pray for you that you might experience the mercy of Christ; for he*
> *instructed us to pray even for our enemies, when he said: "Be kind and*
> *merciful, even as your heavenly Father is merciful."* (*Trypho* 96.2–3
> [Falls], emphasis added)

In the second, Justin links the destruction of Judea to Jewish refusal to repent/(convert) and then notes again that Christians respond to this cursing with practices of enemy love and prayer for persecutors:

> And, in addition to this, even now, after your city has been seized and
> your whole country ravaged, you not only refuse to repent, but you
> defiantly curse him and all his followers. But, as far as we Christians
> are concerned, *we do not hate you,* nor those who believed the wicked
> rumors you have spread against us; on the contrary, *we pray that even*

now you may mend your ways and find mercy from God. (*Trypho* 108.3
[Falls], emphasis added)

In the final reference to Christ-cursing in *Trypho*, the accusation that Jewish cursing is linked to Jewish murder is most explicit. Once again, Jewish
murder is met with the Christian response of enemy love and prayer for persecutors, through direct reference to the teachings of Jesus:

> Indeed, your hand is still raised to do evil, because, although you
> have slain Christ, you do not repent; on the contrary, you hate and,
> whenever you have the power, kill us who through him believe in
> God. . . . And you cease not to curse him and those who belong to
> him, though we pray for you and for all men, as we were instructed
> by Christ, our Lord. *For he taught us to pray even for our enemies, and to
> love those that hate us, and to bless those that curse us.* (*Trypho* 133.6
> [Falls], emphasis added)[47]

Justin makes reference to Jesus' teaching on enemy love and non-
retaliation in his First Apology as well, for which the inscribed audience is
Gentile (cf. *Apol.* 1.14, 1.15, 1.16).[48] But it is only in his dialogue with the Jew
Trypho, in which Justin's focus is on distinguishing Jews from Christians,
that he marshals Christian prayers for enemies as the merciful response to
what he casts as a situation of persecution for which the Jews are ultimately
to blame.

Finally, it should be noted that while Justin never cites the forgiveness
prayer of Jesus in Luke 23.34a, nor does he know of the Stephen tradition
and the dying prayer associated with it, *Trypho* essentially replicates in the
genre of a dialogue the rhetorical strategy employed in Luke-Acts through
the genre of narrative—the dying prayers of Jesus and Stephen embody the
assertions of Justin: contemporary Jews breathe threats and murder, and
carry out those murders whenever it is in their power to do so; Christians
respond in love and prayers of mercy for these persecutors. In short, as we
have seen in the case of Luke-Acts and Hegesippus, Justin asserts Christian
novelty on the grounds of extreme mercy without embracing the marcionite
position that aligns this novelty with the revelation of a Father God who does
not judge.

As a means of accounting more fully for the logic of this widely held, proto-
orthodox understanding both that Christian distinctiveness is predicated upon
their merciful prayers for undeserving Jews, and that these Jews are condemned
by the Father God who judges, I turn now to consider the grammar of these
affirmations.

Grammatical Intransitivity: The Perfect Subject of Christian
Enemy Love and Forgiveness

In an important early twentieth-century review of the early Christian transmission of the enemy love saying, Walter Bauer observes that the rhetoric of enemy
love and non-retaliation functions primarily in terms of identity assertion, and
not as a program for ethical action. Bauer supports his argument by noting the
paucity of early Christian texts in which these ethical exhortations are translated into deed of mercy and charity toward enemies.[49] One obvious explanation for the relative lack of textual material suggesting that the principle of
enemy love should translate into regular demonstrations of such love is that
this principle loses out to the more urgently held conviction to hate the devil,
and by extension the devil's servants, which the enemies of Christians most
obviously were.[50] The anti-marcionite *Dialogue of Admantius* articulates this
sentiment explicitly by pointing to the example of Jesus himself. *Admantius*
cites the dominical exhortation for evildoers to flee (Matt. 7.23; Luke 13.27) as
an instance in which Jesus has decided that the need to resist evil trumps the
practice of enemy love (*Admantius* 813A).

Another way to account for the dissonance between the assertion of the
enemy love principle and the practice of enemy vilification is to consider the
logic of their grammar. In many assertions of the Christian principle of enemy
love, the grammatical force of the injunction is intransitive, serving to idealize
the subject who so prays, without articulating any expectation of what this love
and these prayers could do for their objects. Consider this intransitivity as it is
demonstrated in the dying forgiveness prayers. The forgiveness prayers
are invoked to idealize the subject who so prays as one who is "wonderful" or
"perfect." Eusebius cites Stephen at prayer before his death as the model of perfection imitated by the martyrs of Vienne and Lyon (*Hist. eccl.* 5.2.5); Epiphanius
refers to James' recitation of the forgiveness prayer as "wonderful" (*Pan.* 78.14.6);
Irenaeus cites Luke 23.34a as example of Jesus' compassion: "That he exclaimed
upon the cross, 'Father forgive them for they know not what they do,' [exhibits]
the long-suffering patience, compassion and goodness of Christ. . . ." (*Haer.*
3.18.5 [Roberts–Donaldson), and Acts 7.60 to prove that the prayer of Stephen is
in conformity to the prayer of Jesus, and works to effect his perfection: "and thus
did [Stephen] fulfill the perfect doctrine, copying in every respect the Leader of
martyrdom, and praying for those who were slaying him, in these words: 'Lord,
lay not this sin to their charge.' Thus were they perfected [τελειόω] who knew
one and the same God . . ." (*Haer.* 3.12.13 [Roberts–Donaldson]; cf. *Haer.* 3.16.9).
Perfection of the subject is the driving force behind Polycarp's exhortation to

pray for enemies as well: "Pray also for kings and magistrates and rulers, as well as for those who persecute and hate you and for the enemies of the cross, that your fruit may be manifest to all and *you may be perfected in him* [*ut sitis in illo perfecti*]" (*Phil.* 12.3 [Ehrman, LCL], emphasis added). In all these instances, the acclamations and exhortations direct the reader toward the subject, the one who so prays, and not toward the object, the enemies themselves.

That the dying forgiveness prayers can be extolled as a sign of the praying subject's perfection without any concession that these prayers have consequence for persecutors has been noted in the instances of the Lukan Jesus, Acts' Stephen, and Hegesippus' James. It is also readily seen in the writings of Irenaeus, whose praise in passages noted above for Jesus' compassionate prayer from the cross affects not his strong confidence that Jews who fastened Christ to this cross are condemned. In book 4 of *Against Heresies*, he likens Jewish Exodus through Egyptian destruction to Christian salvation through Jewish condemnation:

> Unless, then the Jews had become the slayers of the Lord (which did, indeed, take eternal life away from them) . . . we could not have been saved. For as they were saved [during the Exodus] by means of the blindness of the Egyptians, so are we, too, by that of the Jews; if, indeed, the death of the Lord is the condemnation of those who fastened him to the cross, and who did not believe in his advent, but the salvation of those who believe in Him. (*Haer.* 4.28.4 [Roberts–Donaldson])

Irenaeus, then, apparently without awareness of the irony, is able to affirm both the compassion of Jesus praying for his crucifiers and the certainty that those crucifiers receive no compassion as a result of the prayer.[51]

The impulse to read the prayers intransitively can be more fully understood when this phenomenon is considered alongside the Roman discourse of clemency, wherein the subject's beneficence is also celebrated, without corresponding attention to the objects of that beneficence. That early Christian writers operate in a world that celebrates the granting of pardon primarily in terms of the emperor's power and virtue, rather than in terms of the captives' plight, helps to make sense of the function of enemy love and forgiveness in their writings.

Clemency as an Analogue for Intransitive Readings of the Dying Forgiveness Prayers

Clemency is a peculiarly Roman virtue embodying a particular sort of mercy. Inasmuch as the virtue bespeaks the ability to control rage against enemies, and to refrain from avenging all but the most serious of injuries, it is closely allied with the Greek virtue of self-mastery, the control of the passions. There are resonances between *clementia* and Greek virtues such as self-control and gentleness (σωφροσύνη, ἐγκράτεια, πραότης). Yet, *clementia* is not the equivalent of self-mastery, as is made clear through consideration of how these various virtues are employed in discourses of power and authority. In comparison to *clementia*, self-mastery might be considered as having something of a "populist" bent since, as embodied in Stoic/Cynic philosophy, self-mastery is a virtue that all would do well to cultivate. In particular circumstances, even a woman or a slave might be said to possess this virtue. Moreover, in certain instances, self-mastery may be employed as a weapon in the politics of dissent and resistance. Consider, for example, 4 Maccabees, where the self-mastery of the entire Maccabean family enables them to defy the colonizing tyrant, and even the Maccabean mother proves under threat of torture that she too can "take it like a man."[52]

In contrast, clemency is a virtue that has a more firmly fixed and vertical power dynamic. Only one in a position to exact revenge, through his legal and practical authority, may chose instead to exercise leniency. It is not the virtue someone of lesser status might grant to someone with greater, nor is it invoked as a means of resisting tyranny—for it is always the possession of the one with superior social standing. "A slave, a snake, or an arrow may slay even a king," notes Seneca in his essay on clemency, "but no one has saved a life who was not greater than the one whom he saved [*servavit quidem nemo nisi maior eo, quem servabat*]" (*Clem.* 1.21.1 [Basore, LCL]). As he spins out elaborate and complex definitions of the virtue, Seneca underscores that clemency "means restraining the mind from vengeance when it has the power to take it, or the leniency of a superior towards an inferior in fixing punishment (*Clem.* 2.3.1 [Basore, LCL])."[53]

In the period of concern to us, the Roman imperial period in which the author of Luke-Acts writes, the emperor is, of course, the supreme wielder of the virtue of clemency. And while the arena of clemency includes the law court as well as the battlefield, for purposes of situating Luke-Acts, battlefield clemency holds particular interest. Numerous artistic representations of the emperor pardoning barbarians after their conquest survive from the imperial period, including several images on the massive column of Trajan erected in Rome to commemorate his defeat of the Dacians in the first decade of the second century. Here, for instance, Trajan is depicted gesturing magnanimously to a group of Dacian women, guiding them to the boat that will deport them from their defeated homeland. In this image, the women are resigned but not horrified. Their modesty remains in tact—they are fully clothed and protected captives of war, not disheveled victims of rape and other brutalities.[54] Such depictions of captives with serene—and sometimes even joyful—countenance at the prospect of incorporation into the beneficent empire are common to the discourse of clemency. As Melissa Dowling notes in her interpretation of one of these images, preserved on an altar base from the Villa Albani:

> Each man carries the arms of his own peoples; each represents a different conquered group; each marches with freedom and almost an expression of joy. The struggles and horrors of battle are ignored; all we see celebrated are the happy new additions to the Roman world. The extant Augustan victory reliefs emphasize conquered men joyous in the clemency they have received, not agonized over their losses, not in the act of being executed. . . . The presentation of happy captives links together the disparate ideas of victory, clemency, justice, and piety. . . . The victory attests to the *virtus* of the conqueror. . . . Piety is present in the form of the dedication, an offering to the gods in thanks for victory. Justice appears in the barbarians' cheerful acceptance of the clement treatment.[55]

The exercise of clemency is, then, an exercise of power. The precondition of *clementia* is submission; in situations of conquest, clemency signals victory so complete that the vanquished may be pardoned. The subjectivity of the vanquished is not a topic of concern.

Inasmuch as clemency is an imperial virtue, I suggest that the forgiveness prayers in Luke-Acts are part of this author's distinct way of merging Roman discourse about the emperor with Christian discourse about Jesus. Joel Marcus has recently argued that crucifixion in the Roman world was regarded *among the crucifiers themselves* as a sort of parodic exaltation, "Crucifixion was intended to unmask, in a deliberately grotesque manner, the pretension and arrogance of those who had exalted themselves beyond their station. . . ."[56] Marcus observes that the danger of such parody is the difficulty in the end of discerning who is mocking whom, such that "the height of the cross might undergo a transvaluation and be seen to point toward the spiritual eminence rather than the arrogance of the victim."[57] By the time that Luke-Acts is written, this transvaluation of the meaning of crucifixion is well under way. That Jesus is emperor-like in Luke's passion is clear from the total control of emotions he exhibits throughout the story. There is no grief in Gethsemane or no cry of dereliction from the cross.[58] His forgiveness of the condemned criminal on the cross (Luke 23.41–43) as well as his prayer for the forgiveness of his crucifiers are additional means by which Luke elevates Jesus' status, marking him as true emperor—the one who has the power to pardon.[59]

To be sure, the discourse of clemency is not a precise analogue to the dying forgiveness prayers in early Christian literature. Jesus in the Third Gospel and Stephen in Acts appeal to a deity to grant forgiveness, an act of deference to a higher power that the emperor need not make since he alone authorizes the pardon. Furthermore, from a Roman perspective, the *Ioudaioi* whom Luke depicts in his narrative, whether those who assent to Jesus' crucifixion or those casting stones at Stephen, would not be considered worthy candidates for clement treatment. Even for a reader steeped in the logic of clemency, a prayer for the forgiveness of the undeserving would still puzzle. Moreover, and of course, Luke is not himself an agent of the colonizing power, but rather writes under colonial rule. The violence I identify here is rhetorical violence within a textual tradition.

But clemency is a useful discourse for illuminating the function of the forgiveness prayers in Luke-Acts for the following reasons: First, the power dynamics of clemency make clear that the prayers for mercy need not signal passivity, humility, submission, or deference on the part of the one who so prays. Instead, the prayers for forgiveness can be understood as an assertion of power over those inscribed as persecutors. Second, the discourse of clemency inscribes imperial conquest as beneficence, skirting the issue of brute force that is the precondition of the clement treatment. Luke is not himself an agent of the colonizing power. Yet, he appropriates something of the colonizer's logic by celebrating the beneficence his heroes extend toward the Jews, while concomitantly affirming that the violent destruction of Jerusalem by the Romans is a deserved punishment and that unrepentant *Ioudaioi* are cut off from salvation. Finally, inasmuch as the celebration of clemency is primarily a celebration of the emperor's virtue, which is not concerned to convey the true plight of the objects of the emperor's clemency, it serves to clarify the practice of reading the forgiveness prayers only in terms of their subjects.

In short, the prayers for forgiveness are an instance in which Luke-Acts has absorbed something of Roman imperial outlooks and aims. Their likeness to Roman clemency serves as a reminder that caution needs to be exercised in assessing assertions of beneficence in early Christian literature. Such claims are not always innocent. In the telling of Luke-Acts, the merciful teachings of early Christians share some space with the discourse of the *Pax Romana*—inscribing violence as peace, conquest as beneficence, and cruelty and clemency. This is not to deny that certain strands of Jesus movement embodied values of merciful treatment toward enemies and passivity in the face of hostility. It is also not to insist that all early Christian readers understood the prayers only terms of their subjects. I turn now to consider alternate readings of the prayers.

Reading Transitively

In spite of the frequency with which it is invoked in imperial discourse, it must also be noted that clemency is not an uncomplicated virtue in the Roman world.

Reading Seneca's treatise on clemency with some suspicion, one may observe that simmering very near to the surface of these pages addressed to the Emperor Nero is Seneca's anxiety that the virtuous and "manly" exercise of pardon known as *clementia* might be confused with something much more fragile and feminine. According to Seneca, *clementia* separates the elite, self-mastered male from women and wild beasts: "[T]he peculiar marks of a lofty spirit are mildness and composure, and the lofty disregard of injustice and wrongs. It is for woman to rage in anger, for wild beasts . . . to bite and worry their prostrate victims." (*Clem.* 1.5.5 [Basore, LCL]).[60] But what if disregard for injustice and wrong owes not to a lofty spirit but to something more visceral? What if one chooses to refrain from inflicting a violent punishment because he is disturbed by the prospect of suffering? Such a one is not exercising clemency but is rather under the sway of a womanish emotion, *misericordia*.[61] To preclude the possibility that one might mistake clemency for something weaker and more undisciplined, Seneca underscores that the opposite of clemency is not severity (*severitas*) but cruelty (*crudelitas*). Severity is necessary and like clemency is also a virtue (*Clem.* 2.4.1). There is also the problem that *clementia*—pardon in accordance with what is fair and good—lies very near to *venia* and *ignoscere*—the execution of a pardon that is an unjust remittance of punishment that ought to be extracted (2.7.1–4). Between the idea of a just pardon and an unjust pardon, a rational act and an emotional disturbance, stands only a thin line.

We might understand early Christian concerns with marcionite claims of an all-merciful "Father" God as infused with this same anxious concern about gender and justice, appropriate and inappropriate pardon. Tertullian is at great pains to assert that any kindness of God is a virile kindness, for, like Seneca, he cements *clementia* to *severitas* as twin expressions of masculine virtue. Tertullian's God is revealed both as Father and as Lord: "as Father in clemency, as Lord in discipline: as Father in kindly authority, as Lord in that which is stern" (*Marc.* 2.13.5 [Evans]).[62] Behind these strong assertions of masculinity lie the suggestion that the chief injury inflicted by Marcion is that his merciful god is an emasculated god, one who is too weak to administer proper justice.[63]

In this section, I bring together texts suggesting that some early Christians feared that the dying forgiveness prayers of Jesus and Stephen, standing alone and without clarification, might signal an inappropriate pardon of undeserving sinners. While those who read the freestanding petitions for forgiveness intransitively need not have been disturbed by them, there are also indications of early Christians thinking through another possibility: these prayers might actually have an effect, and quite possibly an unjust effect, on those for whom they were offered. Traces of these transitive readings come solely from negative evidence, from those who either deny the possibility of such forgiveness or refuse to acknowledge the prayer. But these denials and refusals suggest the presence of alternate readings.

One clear indication of a reader who has thought through the possibility of a transitive reading of Stephen's forgiveness prayer and has come to the conclusion that such a prayer would constitute a breach of justice is Asterius of Amasea (ca. 330–420). [64] In Asterius' homily on the stoning of Stephen, he lays out quite explicitly the theological problem that comes from a transitive reading of Stephen's prayer:

> But let us also consider the words of [Stephen's] prayer, to what aim he says, "Lord, do not hold their sin against them." He prays not, as some incorrectly presume, that the sin of his enemies should remain unavenged and guiltless. That would make him opposing Divine intention: he would seem to rectify the righteous judgment and the legislation which would give the murderers what they deserved.
> (*Homily on Stephen* 10.1 [Dehandschutter])

He, then, presses Stephen's words into conformity with a view of God's justice that makes forgiveness contingent upon repentance, and conversion:

> But what does he say? "Lord, do not hold their sin against them" that is, "Give them fear because of compunction; bring them to regret what they dared, let them not die away in circumcision, draw them through repentance to knowledge about you, kindle in their hearts the flame of the Spirit. If they repent in that way, it will be manifest that you hold not that sin against them, but by the bath of grace they will wash away your and my blood and be free of any charge."
> (*Homily on Stephen* 10.2 [Dehandschutter])

Asterius, then, rewrites the forgiveness prayer to underscore that forgiveness and repentance must be anchored together. But reading against the grain, one sees that he has thought through another reading of the prayer—some might suppose the "enemies" to be inappropriately pardoned, such that their sin lies unavenged.

Asterius was not the first to anchor the prayer to the insistence that forgiveness is granted only to those who repent. This remedy is seen in one legend preserved in Jerome, where—in an act of creative imagination rivaling even Mel Gibson's recent film portrayal of the passion of Christ—thousands of Jews are supposed to have gathered around the cross to witness Jesus' death. They convert en masse subsequent to Jesus' prayer:

> The Lord so loved Jerusalem that he wept and lamented over the city. And as he hung on the cross he said, "Father forgive them for they

know not what they do." And he brought about what he prayed for, and immediately several thousand Jews became faithful, and until the 42nd year, time was given for them to repent.[65]

It is also stressed by Cyprian in his third-century treatise on patience, who inserts a conditional clause into his reading of Jesus' prayer from the cross:

> And after all these things [suffered upon the cross], He still receives his murderers, *if they will be converted and come to him*; and with a saving patience, He who is benignant to preserve, closes His Church to none. Those adversaries, those blasphemers, those who were always enemies to his name, *if they repent of their sin, if they acknowledge the crime committed*, He receives, not only to the pardon of their sin, but to the reward of the heavenly kingdom. (*Pat.* 8 [Wallis], emphasis added)

A turn away from the freestanding forgiveness prayer to a dying prayer more securely within the bounds of appropriate pardon may also be traced in early Christian martyrdom narratives. Consider the example of the martyr Potamiaena preserved by Eusebius. As the day of her execution draws near, Potamiaena prays for Basilides, the soldier who leads her away to death. But the narrative makes clear that the soldier deserves such prayers, for when the crowd had harried Potamiaena, Basilides demonstrated the most mercy and kindness (πλεῖστον ἔλεον καὶ φιλανθροπίαν). Potamiaena prays then, not that Basilides be forgiven his sin but that he be "requited" (ἀποτίνω), that is, be given a just reward. The narrative ends with Basilides openly proclaiming his Christianity, a faith he embraces thanks to a vision of Potamiaena after her death (*Hist. eccl.* 6.5.1–7). The prayer for Basilides, then, is not for undeserved mercy but rather for justice.[66]

Alongside readings that stress that repentance must precede pardon stands a reading preserved in the third-century *Didascalia* containing the hint that, as the tradition of the dying forgiveness prayer was transmitted, some came to question the prayer's efficacy altogether. At both paragraphs 6 and 25 of the *Didascalia*, a modified version of the forgiveness prayer includes the conditional plea also affixed to Jesus' prayer for the cup to be removed from him in Gethsemane: "For our Savior himself also was pleading with his Father for sinners, as it is written in the Gospel: My Father, they know not what they do, neither what they speak: *but if it be possible*, forgive them" (cf. Luke 23.34a; Matt. 26.39; 1 Tim. 1.7; emphasis added). The Gospel tradition makes clear that it was not possible for God to grant Jesus' Gethsemane prayer. Just as that prayer did not prevent Jesus' arrest and execution, so here the prayer for forgiveness of his persecutors, merged with the same conditional clause—"if it be possible"— also suggests that it might be impossible for the pardon to be granted.

Returning to the text-critical question introduced early in this chapter, I suggest again that striking the dominical saying from the text of the Third Gospel is another mechanism for suppressing the notion that Jesus might forgive unrepentant sinners. The force of the ideological repugnance required to prompt a scribe to excise a phrase from the Gospels attributed to the Lord himself from the cross demonstrates the high stakes of this controversy in some quarters. That the theological stakes were higher for the forgiveness prayer than for the exhortations on enemy love and non-retaliation is made clear by considering readers who were able to situate the latter within the cosmic frame of retributive justice. To this analysis, I now turn.

Patience in Expectation of Vengeance

In this final section I trace a line of thinking, most fully reflected in the writings of Tertullian, which could account for the enemy love teaching but not for the forgiveness prayer, within the framework of talionic justice. While the readings considered below counsel merciful treatment of enemies, clear limits on the extent of that mercy are also established. In them, humans are encouraged to refrain from retaliating against tormentors, not because such behaviors models that of an all-merciful God, rather because vengeance, a necessary response to tormentors, is best reserved for God alone.

As Gordon Zerbe has documented for both early Jewish and New Testament texts, confidence in God's ultimate vengeance frequently becomes rationale for passivity, non-retaliation, and even merciful behavior in the face of persecution.[67] The idea that human restraint will be followed by God's vengeance occurs in texts traditionally categorized as Wisdom Literature (e.g., Prov. 20.22: "Do not say, 'I will repay evil'; wait for the Lord, and he will help you"); as well as within apocalyptic literature (e.g., 1QS X, 19–20: "To no man shall I return evil for evil, I shall pursue a man only for good; for with God resides the judgment of all the living, and He shall pay each man his recompense" [trans. Wise et al.]).[68] The Apostle Paul argues similarly for restraint and performance of good deeds toward enemies in light of God's ultimate vengeance in Romans 12.17–19: "Do not repay anyone evil for evil, but take thought for what is noble in the sight of all . . . never avenge yourselves, but leave room for the wrath of God; for it is written, 'Vengeance is mine, I will repay, says the Lord.' No, if your enemies are hungry feed them; if they are thirsty, give them something to drink; for by doing this you will heap burning coals on their heads."[69]

On occasion scholars have suggested that the rationale of deferring vengeance to God lies behind exhortations to enemy love and non-retaliation even

within the Sermon on the Mount/Sermon on the Plain. After concluding that
Paul is motivated by deference to God's impending vengeance in Romans
12.19–21, Krister Stendahl makes the closing observation that it would also be
"reasonable to find that the command about turning the other cheek . . . [Matt.
5.39] and the logion about not judging [7.1] have as their basis the trust in the
ultimate judgment of God."[70] In Zerbe's recent study of the question, he concludes that within the earliest strand of the enemy love exhortation associated
with Jesus preserved in Q, "non-retaliation and good deeds in response to persecutors . . . are grounded in the hope of eschatological vindication and
judgment."[71] Both Stendahl and Zerbe temper the implications of their analyses
by noting that the message regarding the extension of mercy toward enemies
in the Sermon on the Mount/Sermon on the Plain is somewhat mixed and
includes elements that transcend an interpretation predicated solely on God's
vengeance. This may indeed be so. But it is the case that at least one early third-
century reader of the Sermon on the Plain found the rationale for non-retaliation
and enemy love in God's ultimate justice: Tertullian of Carthage, whose understanding of Jesus' teaching on enemy love and non-retaliation does not
transcend the rationale of God's ultimate vindictiveness but rather is predicated squarely upon it.

Tertullian's exegesis of Luke in his five-volume work, *Against Marcion*, provides us with a relatively early and extensive interpretation of Jesus' teachings
on non-retaliation and enemy love. His interpretation of these teachings, in
which he stresses continuity over discontinuity, comes in response to Marcion's
assertion of rupture.[72]

He counters Marcion's dualism by noting that Christ in this teaching is not
exhorting the forgiveness of wrong but rather forbearance in the face of wrongdoing. The overarching principle guiding Tertullian's argument here should be
familiar from the discussion above: Christ exhorts this forbearance not because
the assault should go unpunished but because vengeance is ideally extracted by
God, rather than humans. Throughout Tertullian's rebuttal of Marcion, the
essential function of God's judgment and punishment of wrongdoing are highlighted; without this threat, humans have no motivation to refrain from
violence. His articulation of this sentiment in the discussion of turning the
other cheek is representative of his thinking on this point:

> So then if I look for [Christ's] actual reason for enjoining forbear-
> ance so full and complete, it can only be convincing if it appertains
> to that Creator who promises vengeance and presents himself as
> judge. Otherwise if such a burden of forbearance . . . is imposed
> upon me by one who is not going to be my defender, in vain does he

enjoin forbearance: for he sets before me no reward for [following] his injunction, I mean, no fruit of my endurance: and this is the revenge which he ought to have left in my discretion if he himself does not provide it, or else, if he was not leaving it to me, he ought to provide it for me: because it is in the interest of good conduct, that injury should be avenged. For it is by fear of vengeance that all iniquity is kept in check. But for that, if indiscriminate liberty is accorded, iniquity will get the mastery, so as to pluck out both eyes, and knock out all the teeth, because it is convinced of impunity. (*Marc.* 4.16.6–7 [Evans])

To underscore that Christ's teaching on forbearance is consistent with, rather than opposed to, the teaching of the Old Testament, he argues that the meaning implicit in "turn the other cheek" is identical to that behind the Creator's speech in Deuteronomy 32.35, "Vengeance is mine and I will avenge" (*Marc.* 4.16.4; see also 2.18.1). He notes further that the prophets, in a manner similar to Christ, inculcated forbearance by exhorting their listeners to forget malice against brother and refrain from plotting evil against neighbor (*Marc.* 4.16.3–4).

In short, Tertullian sees Christ's exhortation to turn the other cheek as continuous with, rather than antithetical to, the *lex talionis* of the Old Testament. It is not a new revelation that persecutors should remain guiltless, but an exhortation to patience, in expectation of vengeance (*patientiam docet vindicate expectatricem*; *Marc.* 4.16.4). Ultimately, punishment will be delivered; Jesus' followers only need to refrain from inflicting it themselves. In Tertullian's reasoning, the intent of both the *lex talionis* and the injunction to "turn the other cheek" is to restrain violent human behavior. To be sure, Tertullian is a Christian supersessionist, but unlike the marcionites, he ultimately situates that religious superiority in the realm of epistemology and not ethics. The New Testament does not disrupt the talionic ethical framework of the Old Testament but rather offers a superior understanding, a more certain conviction of God's coming vengeance.[73]

In his lengthy commentary on the Third Gospel, Tertullian himself makes no reference to Luke 23.34a. It is impossible to know whether the text of the Gospel he reads has already been purged of this text, or whether he himself knows, but suppresses this prayer.[74] In any case, for those early Christians who, like Tertullian, understand Jesus' teaching on enemy love and non-retaliation within the framework of God's ultimate vengeance, prayers for God to forgive those undeserving enemies, rather than to judge them, would be read as confounding that framework. Whether Tertullian has suppressed the forgiveness prayer or it has already been suppressed for him, the impulse to do so is understandable in view of the prayer's radical assertion of divine mercy over justice. That is, it was possible to insist that the teachings on enemy love and non-retaliation were continuous with Old Testament teachings and did not disrupt the talionic framework of the cosmos. The same case could not be readily made for the dying forgiveness prayer.

Conclusion

Through comparison of the dying forgiveness prayers of Jesus, Stephen, and James to models for proper comportment of the suffering righteous in biblical and extrabiblical literature, a rhetorical strategy may be traced. The author of Luke-Acts, like Hegesippus, seems to be testing a means of asserting Christian difference from Jews through demonstrating the triumph of love and mercy over hate and vengeance. By depicting Jesus, Stephen, and James in this novel, hyper-merciful way—as petitioning God to extend forgiveness to persecuting enemies who are absolutely undeserving—these authors are apparently inspired by the dominical sayings on enemy love, non-retaliation, and prayer for persecutors to think through a most extreme embodiment of those teachings.[75] The prayer radically challenges both the stoic silence of the suffering righteous one, who is confident in God's ultimate vengeance, and the martyr whose dying cry to God is that vengeance be done. This unprecedented plea for mercy upon those tormentors is the assertion of a "new testament" for a new social group.

The radical assertion of the superlative nature of Christian forgiveness does not lead to the "marcionite" conclusion that the Father God refrains from enacting vengeance against unrepentant evildoers (= nonbelieving Jews) in either Luke's or Hegesippus' composition because both of these authors read the prayers intransitively. The prayers idealize the heroes in these texts—they are perfected through these acts of mercy—but these texts also underscore that the prayers have no effect upon the Jews for whom the prayers are offered. In their intransitivity, the dying prayers for forgiveness share rhetorical space with the virile and distinctively Roman discourse of imperial clemency.

Yet, the assertion of superiority on the basis of mercy, or clemency, entails a complicated balancing act. Hovering over every instance of extremely generous pardon is the question of the appropriateness of that pardon: Does the pardon owe to the self-restraint of a lofty spirit, or to the weakness of a womanish self, prone to irrationality, injustice, and aversion to the administration of necessary suffering? This, then, is the tightrope that the proto-orthodox anti-marcionite attempts to walk to assert extreme mercy as distinctively Christian and diametrically opposed to Judaism without falling into the "marcionite" logic that assigns this novel expression of mercy and love to the effeminate impulse of a newly revealed God who does not execute judgment.

Some early Christians secured the assertion of extreme mercy from the threat of injustice by rewriting the prayers to underscore repentance as the precondition for mercy. Others suppressed the prayer altogether. Contemplating the scribal suppression of the prayer and reading these rewritten prayers against the grain, it is possible, perhaps, to hear a faint echo of an irenic sentiment extended by some Christians toward some Jews. The scribe who excised the prayer at Luke 23.34 may have done so in the knowledge of Christians using the verse to argue the case that "the Jews" should be treated mercifully. Asterius insists that Stephen prays, "not *as some incorrectly presume*, that the sin of his enemies should remain unavenged and guiltless" (my emphasis). Perhaps his insistence that such a reading is incorrect suggests that he knows of Christians who do indeed believe that the "enemies" of Stephen should stand "unavenged and guiltless." Perhaps this belief is not held in the abstract but comes from regard for non-Christian Jews in communities where those holding this belief live. Yet, it is difficult to sustain this imaginative exercise, in view of the paucity of traces of this perspective contained in our sources.

That the dying forgiveness prayer posed a more serious threat to talionic notions of divine justice than the dominical exhortation merely to love enemies is indicated by early Christians who read the latter as conforming to, rather than overturning, the *lex talionis* of the Old Testament. Teachings on enemy love did not necessarily oppose affirmations of divine severity. This distinguishes them from prayers asking for divine severity to be set aside.

The violent effects of this rhetorical strategy of Christian identity construction are manifold, if largely veiled. Through it, Jews are depicted in Luke-Acts as murderers of Jesus and Stephen; in Hegesippus, of James; and in Justin Martyr, of Christians in general, "so often as they have the power to do so." The rhetorical power of these depictions forecloses possibilities for imagining non-Christian Jews of the first century in other subject positions: as common allies with Christian Jews in striving for the *basileia* of God; as resisting, rather than perpetrating, violence; or—perhaps most importantly in view of the situation on the ground in late first-century Judea—as a social group that has experienced the trauma of Roman conquest. Judith Lieu has observed that because suffering is central to Justin Martyr's construction of Christianity, he not only repeatedly depicts Jews as persecutors but also delegitimizes Jewish suffering itself.[76] This observation may be applied more widely to early Christian literature of the second century.

Rhetorical violence is heaped upon rhetorical violence through the laying upon these constructed murderous Jews a particular kind of repentance as the sole means to forgiveness and restoration. Asterius of Amasea expresses this sentiment most succinctly by translating Stephen's forgiveness prayer as a plea to "let them not die away in circumcision" but to "draw them through repentance to knowledge." This easy equation of Stephen's killers with the circumcised and of repentance with the move away from circumcision collapses any distinction between the sinful deed and the very state of being "Jewish," as well as any distinction between atonement for sin and the conversion to Christianity. Thus, the fourth-century Asterius, through the vehicle of Stephen's martyrdom, exemplifies the conundrum most recently articulated by Susannah Heschel with respect to the Christ-killing charge: "The religion of mercy and forgiveness came into being through a sin that Christian culture considered unforgivable, the Jews' act of deicide. No repentance is possible, since the Jews cannot acknowledge the act of deicide without acknowledging Jesus as Christ, itself an act of conversion, not atonement."[77] The nearly invisible nature of this rhetorical violence owes, in part, to the frequency with which depictions of "Jews" as killers of "Christians" are read positivistically as transcriptions of actual violence, rather than as rhetorically constructed stereotypes employing problematic proper nouns. It owes also to the fact that Christian readers, directed by rhetorical markers to identify with the merciful martyr who loves and prays for his persecutors, generally do not notice that this charitable subject is drawn against an uncharitably constructed foil. Thus, in a veiled and paradoxical manner, the edifice of Christianity as a religion of extreme mercy is constructed upon a scaffolding of Jew vilification.

Epilogue

I have argued that the Stephen pericope plays a crucial role in Acts' early second-century project of constructing Christians as a legitimate social–religious group distinct from Jews. In addition to clarifying the significance of the ancient appraisal of Stephen as perfect martyr owing to his merciful dying prayer, I have demonstrated how Stephen functions as the perfect martyr in terms of rhetorical fittingness. The pericope perfectly suits the overarching rhetorical aims of Luke-Acts, which include (1) securing a place for its author's social group within the Roman Empire by appropriating Jewish prestige markers, while simultaneously denigrating actual Jews (insofar as they refuse to accept Jesus as messiah) as subversive and murderous subjects of empire; (2) engaging in the daunting task of demonstrating that followers of the Way are innocent of any charges of subversion they face and that Rome's preferred stance toward these followers is to do them no harm. He does this in the face of widespread traditions of Roman involvement in the crucifixion of Jesus and the execution of Paul, to say nothing of the devastation of Judea as a consequence of Roman military conquest,[1] (3) negotiating complex issues of "marcionite" identity by affirming Christians as distinctive in their ethical practice of enemy love, while denying that this practice upsets the cosmic framework of justice and the notion of divine severity.

In view of Stephen's prototypical function as first martyr in Acts, one could, with justification, argue that the story, from beginning

to end, is the fictional creation of its author. This author's propensity for symbolic characters and the significance attached to a first Christian martyr named
"Crown," the lack of attestation of a martyr tradition for Stephen outside of
Acts before Irenaeus, and the fact that crucial details of this pericope align
squarely with those of Hegesippus' narrative of the martyrdom of James
strongly support such a conclusion.

Yet, my concern in this book has not been to insist on this conclusion. The
problem animating my argument has not been whether or not an early Jesus
follower named Stephen "really" existed or whether other Jews "really" killed
him. It is rather how Luke's telescopic narrative of one significant death beyond
the crucifixion of Jesus—that of a merciful Jesus follower by merciless Jews—
has found its place in the cannon of Christian Scriptures, and subsequently in
the deep structures of Christian consciousness, as an originary event. The first
Christian martyr is killed by "the Jews" in a way that tars all Jews as murderous,
while veiling both the magnitude and the imperial circumstance of first-century
bloodshed in this region of the ancient Mediterranean. It is this particular
emplotment of proper names and the relations between them that I challenge.

As a means of suggesting an alternate multivoiced narrative of violence
among Jews under empire in the first century, I have set the Stephen pericope
alongside related death narratives of James, the brother of Jesus. While Hegesippus' James narratives conforms to Acts' narrative of Stephen, both the earlier
version of James' execution penned by Josephus and the later version of James'
"near-death" experience in the Pseudo-Clementine *Recognitions* plot violence and
allegiance differently. These two texts evoke alternate webs of relationships, suggesting that not every interaction among Jews who confessed Jesus as messiah,
and Jews who did not, conformed to the mold of the Acts' narrative. In Josephus,
we see strict observers of the Jewish law "burdened with grief," at the death of
James, the brother of Jesus—a far cry from "the Jews" who gnash their teeth at
Stephen (Acts 7.54) or take pleasure in Herod's killing of James, the brother of
John (Acts 12.1). In the case of the *Recognitions*, which depends on Acts while radically altering the story line, we see an instance of an ancient resistant reading—
one that refuses to accept the starkness of Acts' line dividing all Jesus believers
from other Jews and that removes Stephen from the story altogether.

In setting the Stephen pericope alongside Hegesippus' narrative of the
martyrdom of James and mapping out their common logic, this book has also
aimed to add to the number of primary texts surveyed under the rubric of martyrdom and identity construction. Neither Stephen nor Hegesippus' James are
"Christian martyrs" in the sense that others will be so named in literature
asserting clear and impermeable boundaries between Christians and Jews.
They instead offer a glimpse of the process of boundary formation *in media*

res. Both Acts and Hegesippus are located in an interstitial place, constructing death narratives that incorporate some features of the trope of the persecuted prophet (an in-group phenomenon), along with some features linked to the trope of martyrdom (death at the hands of an external enemy). Neither has landed on the terminology that will come to distinguish two separate social groups. One employs the categories of an Israel divided into two kingdoms—"the sons of Israel" standing against "the race of Judeans and the Christ"; the other singles out a prominent "Jew" to "utterly refute the Jews." Neither has completed his death narrative with the confession that will become firmly fixed with the death of a Christian martyr—*Christianos sum.* Each employs instead a version of the petition for divine pardon of the persecutors. I suggest that from this interstitial place, both Acts and Hegesippus offer up the dying forgiveness petition as an experimental speech act, influenced by marcionite debate, to produce group identity and self-definition on the axis of extreme mercy. That these dying words, "Father, forgive them," give way to the *Christianos sum* in later Christian martyr traditions owes, in part, to the potentially disturbing implications of such a merciful prayer.[2]

While underscoring the rhetorical violence inscribed in the book of Acts, I do not insist that this violence necessarily owes to malicious intentions held by its author. Though my evaluation of this rhetoric has been largely negative, it is not meant to preclude a sympathetic imagining of this author's situation. Luke's own position within the ancient Roman Empire was undoubtedly precarious. He may well have known of instances in which not only Romans and other "Gentiles" but also Jews who did not confess faith in Jesus acted violently toward Jesus followers. Moreover, he could not have envisioned the full effects his conjured rabid Jews would have once Christianity achieved its privileged place in that empire and had the power to impose physical violence upon its hated *others.*[3]

In arguing that the dying forgiveness prayers in the Lukan narrative also, if ironically, effect a sort of rhetorical violence, I do not mean to suggest that every invocation of the Christian ethic of enemy love and forgiveness necessarily involves such violence. A study of the reception history of the forgiveness prayers in the early church indicates that this specific saying, along with the more general dominical teachings on enemy love and non-retaliation, provoked multiple and various reactions. Practices of nonviolence and enemy love were surely prompted by these teachings. Yet, without denying the potential of early Christian teaching on enemy love and non-retaliation to effect ethical practices of a peaceful, merciful, and conciliatory nature, I challenge the notion that every invocation of this beneficent rhetoric was innocent of violence. This challenge is raised in the interest of a fuller accounting of how early Christian rhetoric of beneficence is both enmeshed with Roman imperial rhetoric of beneficence and also implicated in that rhetoric's violent subtext. Yet, my interest is not "simply" historical. This project is undertaken also with a view to contemporary Christian ethical teaching and practice. It is fueled by the conviction that the language of enemy love, non-retaliation, and forgiveness, so closely identified with Christianity, cannot be fully exploited for peaceful ends, unless those who identify with and/or are sympathetic to this religious tradition acknowledge the violent ends this language may also serve.

The arguments set forth in this work, then, challenge both traditional historical assessments of Acts and pervasive assumptions concerning Christian identity. They stand against a broad and deep consensus, both in popular and in scholarly communities, that Acts transmits a narrative of the early postresurrection community that has a basic historical reliability, and an even deeper and broader consensus on the indubitable historical reality of Stephen's violent death. Furthermore, they call into question a basic fundament of Christian identity—the broadly assumed, if often unarticulated, premise that Christian ethics, inspired by New Testament teachings, cannot be implicated in violence. This latter assumption, of course, shades into marcionism, and I claim no originality in observing that while marcionites lost the battle in defining Christian orthodoxy, they nevertheless won the war in terms of the long-lasting imprint of their idea that the Christian God with His Scriptures, as distinct from the God of the Old Testament, exudes only love and mercy. Yet, especially because this assumption remains both unarticulated and pervasive, and also bears closely on Luke-Acts scholarship, I close this book with one last look at Marcion, his enduring influence, and one of his earliest and most vociferous adversaries.

Marcion and His Influence

Those who work in marcionite studies are familiar with Adolf Harnack's advocacy for a particular tenant of marcionite thought: the refutation of the Old Testament. Less than a hundred years ago, Harnack ended his monograph on Marcion and his "alien" God with a challenge to the Protestant church to strip from the Old Testament its canonical status. His thesis, succinctly stated:

> The rejection of the Old Testament in the second century was a
> mistake which the great church rightly avoided; to maintain it in the
> sixteenth century was a fate from which the Reformation was not yet
> able to escape; but still to preserve it in Protestantism as a canonical
> document since the nineteenth century is the consequence of a
> religious and ecclesiastical paralysis.[4]

From a twenty-first-century perch, one might wish to relegate Harnack's seemingly bald-faced rejection of the Old Testament as Scripture to a bygone era.[5] And yet, particularly as far as questions of biblical violence are concerned, Marcion's schema of violent Judaism and peaceful Christianity is still embraced with startling regularity. Contributions to the question of religion and violence as disparate as the philosopher René Girard's and the depth psychologist Eugen Drewermann's have embraced the Christian God of peace against the legalistic "coils" of a violent Judaism.[6]

Slavoj Žižek has noted that an ideology has achieved its most potent success "when even the facts which at first sight contradict it start to function as arguments in its favor."[7] We have seen this phenomenon in chapter 1, where two scholars who are perceptive enough to recognize the scope of the violent rhetoric with which the first two chapters of Luke are imbued, proceed unwittingly to read this violence in a marcionite way: assigning it to the realm of the Old Testament and arguing that the Third Gospel aims ultimately to refute it.[8] That this exegetical move reflects a more systemic tendency to misread early Christian anti-marcionite texts is indicated by considering it alongside Eric Osborn's recent monograph on Tertullian's anti-marcionite polemic.[9]

When Osborn criticizes Tertullian's affirmation of a God who smites, kills, and creates evil, he attributes this unsavory God-view solely to Tertullian's affirmation of the Old Testament. Noting that Tertullian insists that God inflicts punishments (*mala poenae*) he observes, "this is Tertullian's most unconvincing argument. He accepts without qualification the avenging God *of the Deuteronomist*" [emphasis added]. While he attributes the advance to one God, rather than two, Osborn, like Marcion, sees in the New Testament *a significant moral advance*, in which violence is eschewed for peace:

> There was a dispensation of the creator and there is now a dispensation of Christ; the two orders differ in language, moral precepts and the law. But these differences are part of the plan of one God who planned and predicted a radical change; cruelty would be replaced by goodness; swords would become ploughshares.[10]

In a formulation that borders on a marcionite divine dualism, Osborn invokes the image of a merciful Christ standing in opposition to, and as a corrective for, the vengeful Old Testament God:

> Tertullian cannot renounce scripture or rule. He refuses to see that the jealous vindictive God of the Deuteronomist is not the helpless, compassionate figure on the cross, and he could never disown the later. He could not say, with William Blake, "Thinking as I do that the

Creator of this world is a very cruel being, and being a worshipper of
Christ, I cannot help saying, "The Son, O how unlike the Father."
First God almighty comes with a thump on the head. Then Jesus
Christ comes with a balm to heal it.[11]

By categorizing violence as solely an Old Testament concept, the explanation for Christian atrocities lies in their fateful decision to canonize the Scripture of the Jews:

None will deny that Tertullian's validation of the Old Testament has
been of influence in Christian thought, and few will deny its harmful
effects in promoting the fear of God and mutual destruction of
humans.[12]

In an exegetical twist that directs blame toward the victims, Osborn suggests that if it had not been for the Christian decision to retain the Old Testament, Christians might have forgiven, rather than condemned, their Jewish
enemies:

Tertullian is utterly subordinate to the text of scripture and will not
allow any ground for Marcion's objections. Old Testament barbarity
has to be defended. He is no longer, as were New Testament writers
and Justin, afraid of the Jews, because *he cites to them the judgment of
their own scriptures*. The failure of Christian forgiveness, *derived from
the unity of scripture*, was to have serious consequences.[13]

Ironically, then, the Tertullian scholar Osborn, like Marcion himself, sees
language about God and ethics in the New Testament as radically distinct from
and superior to that found in the Old and then faults Tertullian for remaining
stuck within the Old Testament's ethical framework. Tertullian's own logic,
however, as he argues for the unity and consistency of Old and New Testaments, is much more clear-eyed than this.

The Savage God and His Angry Christ: Reading
the Third Gospel with Tertullian

One of Tertullian's primary tasks in the *Adversus Marcionem* is to argue that
both severity and mercy belong to one and the same God. To be sure, Tertullian
is thus obligated to acknowledge passages from the Old Testament in which
God demonstrates himself to be merciful and compassionate.[14] But the fear for
Tertullian is not really that Christians might forget that the God of the Old

Testament loves and forgives people but rather that Christians under Marcion's influence might altogether disregard the judging God who punishes sin. Therefore, the passion driving his argument, and also the point where Tertullian evidences his most pointed wit and sarcasm, lies in his insistence that God in Marcion's own Gospel is savage (*saevitas*) and avenging.[15]

This, then, is what brings Tertullian to argue that the exhortation to love enemies in the Sermon on the Plain is predicated on vengeance, not mercy. It also enables him to see what scholars such as Eric Osborn may not. Namely, that divine violence and vengeance are presumed in the Third Gospel, the *New Testament*. Tertullian revels at this Gospel's promise of violently disciplined bodies. On the parable of the unfaithful slave, in which the worst slave is punished through dismemberment and the other slaves receive beatings in proportion to the severity of their sin (Luke 12.39–49), Tertullian comments, "And whom else shall I understand by him who beats the servants with few or with many stripes, and requires from them in proportion as he has entrusted to them, if not a God who repays?" (*Marc.* 4.29.12 [Evans]). He is quick to point to the multiple instances in which Jesus pronounces judgment and woe (e.g., *Marc.* 4.15.3, 4.17.9–11, 4.27.1). He reads apocalyptic passages of Luke 21 and 22, for evidence of the unity between the Gospel and prophets on the impending "shatterings" (*concussiones*) facing the peoples of the earth (*Marc.* 4.39–40). The multiple references to beatings, curses, shatterings, and judgment in his version of the Third Gospel prompt Tertullian's final triumphant observation at the close of book 4: "I am sorry for you Marcion: your labor has been in vain. Even in your gospel Christ Jesus is mine" *Marc.* 4.43.9[Evans].[16]

Through this juxtaposition of Osborn's marcionite reading of Tertullian, with Tertullian's own anti-marcionite reading of the Third Gospel, a key tension point in Christian identity construction is exposed. The allure of the marcionite assertion of Christian ethical superiority on the axis of love, mercy, and non-retaliation is so pervasive that Osborn marshals "facts which at first sight contradict it" as arguments in its favor. Tertullian himself resists that allure, through his enthusiastic embrace of the savage God and his angry Christ, whom he finds within the Third Gospel. In spite of the violence of Tertullian's theology, which is not to be commended, he does for modern readers a useful service. Through his unabashed embrace of the violence of this Gospel, he reminds us of its place in the Lukan narrative.

Notes

INTRODUCTION

1. To invoke but two of these events: in Judea following the riots at the death of Herod the Great in 4 BCE, Josephus puts the number of crosses raised in retribution at two thousand (*Ant.* 17.295); both Tacitus and Josephus put the casualties from the Judean War of 66–70 CE at six hundred thousand.

2. *Dying for God: Martyrdom and the Making of Christianity and Judaism* (Figurae; Stanford: Stanford University Press, 1999), 94–95.

3. Elizabeth Castelli, *Martyrdom and Memory: Early Christian Culture Making* (Gender, Theory and Religion; New York: Columbia University Press, 2004). Judith Perkins, *The Suffering Self: Pain and Narrative Representation in the Early Christian Era* (London: Routledge, 1995).

4. Jan Willem van Henten, *The Maccabean Martyrs as Saviours of the Jewish People: A Study of 2 and 4 Maccabees* (JSPSup 57; Leiden: Brill, 1997); Judith Lieu, *Image and Reality: The Jews in the World of the Christians in the Second Century* (Edinburgh: T&T Clark, 1996), 57–102; idem, *Neither Jew Nor Greek?: Constructing Early Christianity* (London: T&T Clark, 2002), 211–31.

5. Denise K. Buell, *Why This New Race: Ethnic Reasoning in Early Christianity* (New York: Columbia University Press, 2005), 52–59.

6. As Beth Berkowitz argues in *Execution and Invention: Death Penalty Discourse in Early Rabbinic and Christian Cultures* (New York: Oxford University Press, 2006), 198–204, esp. 200: "We have [in Ignatius] martyrdom on top of martyrdom on top of martyrdom: Ignatius martyrs himself for those church members who in turn 'martyr' themselves for the bishop, all of whom imitate the originary martyrdom of Christ for God. Yet Ignatius also demands obedience as a bishop: He is both the subject of suffering and the object for whom one suffers."

7. Boyarin, *Dying for God*; idem, *Borderlines: The Partition of Judaeo-Christianity* (Divinations: Rereading Late Ancient Religion; Philadelphia: University of Pennsylvania Press, 2004); see also Lieu, n. 4 above.

8. van Henten has identified a typology of Jewish and Christian martyrdom containing the following five elements: "1) The point of departure for the narrative is formed by an enactment issued by the (pagan) authorities, often in a situation of oppression. Transgression of this law results in the death penalty. 2) The enforcement of the law brings Jews or Christians into a loyalty conflict, since Jews cannot stay faithful to their God, the Law and their Jewish way of life if they comply with the enactment and Christians in similar circumstances have to make concessions to their religious convictions. 3) When Christians or Jews are forced to decide between complying with the law of the government or remaining faithful to their religion and practices, they choose to die rather than obey the authorities. 4) This becomes obvious during the examination, often accompanied by torture, by the ruler or other officials. 5) The execution is described." See his, "Jewish and Christian Martyrs," in *Holy Persons in Judaism and Christianity* (ed. Marcel Poorthuis and Joshua Schwartz; Leiden: Brill, 2004), 163–81, esp. 166–67; cf. also idem, *Maccabean Martyrs as Saviours*, 8.

While not refuting any of the elements in van Henten's typology, which are present in both early and late martyrdom texts, Boyarin has argued more specifically for a distinctive turn in the discourse of martyrdom in the second century, a turn that was part and parcel of the process by which Christianity came to be constructed as a distinct entity, a "religion" over and against Judaism. The elements he identifies as new and distinct to the project of late antique martyrdom, and common both in Jewish and Christian martyrdom narratives, are (1) a performative speech act associated with statement of pure essence—for Christians, the *Christianos sum*; for Jews, the proclamation, "God is one"; (2) an understanding of martyrdom as the fulfilling of a religious mandate, rather than an act of resistance/defiance; a "yes" over a "no"—that is, "dying for God," rather than dying to resist the order to break the law; and (3) the inclusion of powerful erotic elements, including visionary experiences. See *Dying for God*, 95–96. Compare the further development of the argument concerning the process by which Christianity is constructed as a religion against both Judaism and heresy in Boyarin, *Borderlines*.

9. For fullest argumentation, see Richard Pervo, *Dating Acts: Between the Evangelists and the Apologists* (Santa Rosa, Calif.: Polebridge, 2006); cf. the similar arguments of Joseph Tyson in *Marcion and Luke-Acts: A Defining Struggle* (Columbia: South Carolina University Press, 2006). Tyson revisits and expands the early twentieth-century arguments of John Knox that Acts, along with the final form of Luke, is written as a response to Marcion, arguments that I shall consider in greater detail below. Other arguments that position Acts as a text of the second century include Christopher Mount, *Pauline Christianity: Luke-Acts and the Legacy of Paul* (NovTSup 104; Leiden: Brill, 2002); and Rose Mary D'Angelo, "The ANHP Question in Luke-Acts: Imperial Masculinity and the Deployment of Women in the Early Second Century," in *A Feminist Companion to Luke* (ed. Amy-Jill Levine; FCNTECW 3; Sheffield: Sheffield Academic Press, 2002), 44–69.

Though he does not argue for a late date himself, Andrew Gregory's conclusions concerning the reception of Luke in the second century also support a second-century date. See his *The Reception of Luke and Acts in the Period before Irenaeus: Looking for Luke in the Second Century* (Tübingen: Mohr, 2003), 353.

10. Pervo, *Dating Acts*, argues for dependence on both the *Antiquities* and the Pauline Corpus. For Josephus and Acts, see also Steve Mason, *Josephus and the New Testament* (Peabody, Mass.: Hendrickson, 1992), 185–225.

11. Pervo, *Dating Acts*, explicitly proposes a date for Acts of ca. 115 CE, though many of his own arguments suggest 120–30 CE as more likely. While it is reasonable to assume that Acts was written before the *Epistula Apostolorum* and the *Acts of Paul* (both emerging ca. 150–75 CE and both drawing on Acts as a source), by Pervo's own reckoning the possibility that Polycarp of Smyrna, writing ca. 130 CE, supplies the outer limits of the possible range hangs by the thread of one common phrase (cf. Pol. *Phil.* 1.2; Acts 2.24; and *Dating Acts*, 17–20).

Situating Acts in the third rather than second decade of the second century better explains the "marcionite" influence bearing on the final form of Luke-Acts, an influence proposed recently by Joseph Tyson, for which I shall make supporting arguments in a subsequent chapter. Furthermore, Acts' particular animosity toward "the Jews" as a social group need not be explained as part of the hostility toward this social group fomenting *before* the revolts under Trajan (115–17 CE), as Pervo suggests. It is as readily accounted for as a response to that violence, or even as reflecting the perception of Jews as instigators of *stasis* that would have flowered again in events leading up to the Bar Kochba rebellion of 132–35 CE.

12. For similarity of arguments between Acts and Justin, see J. C. O'Neill, *The Theology of Acts in Its Historical Setting* (2d ed.; London: SPCK, 1970), 1–58; Oskar Skarsaune, *The Proof from Prophecy: A Study in Justin Martyr's Proof-Text Tradition: Text-Type, Provenance, Theological Profile* (NovTSup 56; Leiden: Brill, 1987), 257–59; Mogens Müller, "The Reception of the Old Testament in Matthew and Luke-Acts: From Interpretation to Proof from Scripture," *NovT* 43 (2001): 315–30.

13. On the dating and provenance of 4 Maccabees, see Henten, *Maccabean Martyrs as Saviours*, 73–81. On links between the Martyrdom of Polycarp and the Maccabean literature, see Lieu, *Image and Reality*, 79–82.

14. Hence, in their programmatic essay, Elizabeth Castelli and Hal Taussig call for "the study of Christian beginnings [to] focus on patterns of emergence rather than a single point of origin," and to "imagine that which is studied [to be] characterized by development and process rather than by miracle or revolution" ("Drawing Large and Startling Figures: Reimagining Christian Origins by Painting Like Picasso," in *Reimagining Christian Origins: A Colloquium Honoring Burton L. Mack* (ed. Elisabeth A. Castelli and Hal Taussig; Valley Forge, Penn.: Trinity, 1996), 3–20. Cf. also Buell, *Why This New Race*, 25–29.

15. See Boyarin, *Dying for God*, 1–19; idem, *Borderlines*, 1–33.

16. Therefore, while I am in agreement with both Lawrence Wills ("Depiction of Jews in Acts," *JBL* 110 [1991]: 631–54) and Richard Pervo (*Dating Acts*, 324–27) on the basic tenor of Acts' view of Jews, unlike them, I prefer to speak of Acts as engaged in

boundary construction, rather than boundary maintenance. If we understand the job description of Acts as boundary maintenance, the rewriting of Acts' etiology of the Gentile mission in the Pseudo-Clementine *Recognitions* 1.27–71 alone would require that he receive a failing performance review. However carefully Luke was laying and/or policing the bricks, both the *Acts of Paul* and the *Recognitions* 1.27–71 make clear that others stole those bricks for use in different construction projects.

17. A related instance of an author concerned to distinguish Christians from Jews, but who also exhibits a measure of category confusion, is Hegesippus. Because of the strong connections between Hegesippus' martyrdom of James and Acts' martyrdom of Stephen, this text is a major focus of chap. 3.

18. Richard Pervo seems to have pegged the issue correctly here by suggesting that the author of Acts avoids the term "Christian" because it suggests for him factionalism and/or sectarianism. Acts does not wish to cast the movement as merely a sect (*hairesis*) within Judaism—alongside the parties of the Pharisees and Sadducees—but rather as something all encompassing, "true Israel," as opposed to "false Israel." See *Dating Acts*, 168–69.

19. In speaking of Acts as anti-Jewish, I note at the outset that I am focusing on the rhetoric of the text, and the effects of that rhetoric, rather than the issue of authorial intention. Because it is impossible to do so, I do not propose to clarify the motives of the author of Acts for inscribing Jews and Jesus followers as he does, nor do I suggest that this author is conscious of the violent effects of this inscription.

20. Wayne A. Meeks and Robert L. Wilken, *Jews and Christians in Antioch in the First Four Centuries of the Common Era* (SBL Sources for Biblical Study 13; Missoula, Mont.: Scholars Press, 1978).

21. E. Leigh Gibson, "Jewish Antagonism or Christian Polemic: The Case of the *Martyrdom of Pionius*," *JECS* 9 (2001): 339–58, esp. 353.

22. Boyarin, *Dying for God*, 22–41.

23. Annette Yoshiko Reed, "'Jewish Christianity' after the 'Parting of the Ways': Approaches to Historiography and Self-definition in the Pseudo-Clementines" in *The Ways That Never Parted* (ed. Adam H. Becker and Annette Yoshiko Reed; TSAJ 95; Tübingen: Mohr, 2003), 189.

24. Though Eusebius does follow Acts in his assessment of the significance of Stephen's martyrdom, his assessment of Acts' merit as a precursor to his own history is uneven. Rather than granting to Acts the status as the pathbreaking "history" upon which subsequent church historians might build, Eusebius crafts himself as the pioneer in writing such history: "the first to enter on the undertaking, as travelers on some desolate and untrodden way for nowhere can we find even the bare footsteps of men who have preceded us in the same path" (Eusebius, *Hist. eccl.* 1.1.3 [Lake, LCL]). For Eusebius, Acts counts merely among the flowers from the literary meadows that he has plucked to incorporate into his unified historical treatment.

25. "St. Paul and the Three" (originally published in 1865 in *Dissertations on the Apostolic Age* and reprinted [in the second and subsequent editions]) in pages 292–374 of *Saint Paul's Epistle to the Galatians* (7th ed.; London: MacMillan, 1881), esp. 298.

26. Adele Reinhartz notes a similar polarity in the Fourth Gospel, see "Love, Hate, and Violence in the Gospel of John," in *Violence in the New Testament* (ed. E. Leigh Gibson and Shelly Matthews; London: T&T Clark, 2005), 109–23.

27. Adolf von Harnack, *The Mission and Expansion of Christianity in the First Three Centuries* (trans. James Moffatt; 1908; repr., New York: Harper & Row, 1961), 58; W. H. C. Frend, *Martyrdom and Persecution in the Early Church: A Study of a Conflict from the Maccabees to Donatus* (New York: New York University Press, 1967), 138–40, 146–47, 187, 194, 200–201, 215, 252–53.

28. H. W. Tajra, *The Martyrdom of St. Paul: Historical and Judicial Context, Traditions, and Legends* (WUNT 2/67; Tübingen: Mohr, 1994). A quotation from this work illustrates the general tenor of such accusations, and in this instance, clearly derives from Acts' depiction of Jews: "It is clear that the Jews wielded considerable influence at court. There can be no doubt that the Roman Jews would have done all they could to fight Paul and his disciples here on their own ground in the empire's capital. The evidence, *scanty though it be*, clearly points to the leadership of the Roman synagogues, that is, to the very men who stormed out of Paul's lodgings rejecting his Gospel, as the ones who preferred the charge of *crimen laesae maiestatis* against him, the charge on which he was arrested for the final time, tried, condemned, and martyred. As the synagogal leaders had considerable influence in court circles, their depicting the Pauline Christians as subversives and their leader as an enemy of the state would not have been an arduous task. Once again, as throughout his career since the Christophany on the road to Damascus, Paul, the former Saul, born 'of the people of Israel, of the tribe of Benjamin, a Hebrew born of Hebrews; as to the law a Pharisee,' had to face as a consequence of preaching Jesus Christ the deadly hatred of the synagogue" (83–84, emphasis added).

29. Here, my work intersects with the arguments of Melanie Johnson-DeBaufre, *Jesus among Her Children: Q, Eschatology and the Construction of Christian Origins* (HTS 55; Cambridge: Harvard University Press, 2005). Johnson-DeBaufre challenges the notion that Q's primary interest is to explicate Jesus' identity and assert his superlative value, and suggests instead the profitability of reading Q as concerned primarily with the *basileia* (imperial reign) of God. Once concern for the *basileia* of God is recognized as central to Q, it is possible to imagine the Q community in alliance with other Jews, regardless of their assent or resistance to messianic claims about Jesus.

30. "Theology as a Vision for Colonialism: From Supersessionism to Dejudaization in German Protestantism," in *Germany's Colonial Pasts: An Anthology in Memory of Susanne Zantop* (ed. Marcia Klotz et al.; Lincoln: University of Nebraska Press, 2005), 148–64; "From Jesus to Shylock: Christian Supersessionism and 'The Merchant of Venice,'" HTR 99 (2006): 407–31; *The Aryan Jesus: Christian Theologians and the Bible in Nazi Germany* (Princeton: Princeton University Press, 2008).

31. The phrase "virgin womb of the God of Judaism" is cited from Gustav Volkmar's nineteenth-century work on the Religion of Jesus. See Heschel, "From Jesus to Shylock," 428.

32. Shawn Kelley, *Racializing Jesus: Race, Ideology and the Formation of Modern Biblical Scholarship* (Biblical Limits; London: Routledge 2002), 64–88; Craig C. Hill,

Hellenists and Hebrews: Reappraising Division within the Earliest Church (Minneapolis, Minn.: Fortress, 1992), 5–101; Todd Penner, *In Praise of Christian Origins: Stephen and the Hellenists in Lukan Apologetic Historiography* (London: T&T Clark, 2004), 8–59.

33. What Acts intends to signal with these terms at the time of its composition is currently controverted, in part, because each usage of Ἑλληνιστής in the text seems to have a distinct connotation (cf. Acts 6.1, 9.29, 11.20; and the discussion of H. Alan Brehm, "The Meaning of Ἑλληνιστής in Acts in Light of a Diachornic Analysis of ἑλληνίζεν," in *Discourse Analysis and Other Topics in Biblical Greek* [ed. Stanley E. Porter and D. A. Carson; JSNTSup 113; Sheffield: Sheffield Academic Press, 1995], 180–99). Current consensus is that while in 6.1 the Hellenists are Jesus-believing Jews who quarrel with other Jesus believers named "Hebrews," in 9.29 Hellenists are nonbelieving Jews who oppose Paul; and finally in 11.20, the contrast appears to be between "Hellenists/Gentiles" and non-Hellenists/Jews. All agree that, at minimum, the distinction between the two markers *Hellēnistēs* and *Hebraios* has a linguistic component—Greek speakers vs. Aramaic speakers.

34. F. C. Baur, *Paul, the Apostle of Jesus Christ, His Life and Works, His Epistles and Teachings: A Contribution to a Critical History of Primitive Christianity* (2 vols.; trans. A. P. Menzies and A. Menzies; London: Williams & Norgate, 1873–75), 1.59, emphasis added.

Differently from Baur, Rudolf Bultmann suggests that Paul's role in the stoning of Stephen might be legendary. Yet, he still reads the persecution of Stephen as ultimately responsible for the transfer of Christianity from Jesus to Paul. See his essay, "The Significance of the Historical Jesus for the Theology of Paul," in *Faith and Understanding* (2 vols.; trans. Louise Pettibone Smith; New York: Harper & Row, 1969), 1.220–246, esp. 1.221: "Paul must therefore have come to know Christianity in a form which was already critical of the law, which had in a measure transcended it. That is, he made the acquaintance of Christianity in the form of the Hellenistic Christianity which had arisen in Syria as a result of the propaganda of the Hellenistic Jewish Christians driven from Jerusalem by the death of Stephen."

35. Baur, *Paul the Apostle*, 49.

36. Ibid., 48. While Baur understands Paul's conversion to Christianity as rendering him able to adopt "the exact opposite" of what he had previously clung to (59), he also understands Jewish vices to be innate, or almost innate: "[these vices] must really have been their truest and most characteristic nature, because from the beginning—from the first moment in which they began to be a nation—they showed no other inclination. But what is so deeply rooted in the inmost being of an individual or of a nation as to be almost an innate and natural passion, must always exhibit itself outwardly in the occurrence of the same behavior"(49–50). The slipperiness of Baur's rhetoric concerning the innate quality of national characteristics, on the one hand, and the ease by which Paul sheds his Jewishness, on the other, provides one window onto the dynamic of fluidity and fixity that are both essential to racial discourse. See Ann Laura Stoler, "Racial Histories and Their Regimes of Truth," *Political Power and Social Theory* 11 (1997): 183–206; Buell, *Why This New Race*, 6–9.

37. Baur, *Paul the Apostle*, 58 (emphasis added).

38. On the possible narrative function of the Jerusalem apostles in rebutting marcionite arguments that Paul's apostleship signals radical discontinuity between Christians and Jews, see Tyson, *Marcion and Luke-Acts*. For further discussion of Acts as a response to marcionite contests, see my engagement with Tyson in chap. 1.

39. Baur, *Paul the Apostle*, 38–39. The repeated invocation of the "Hellenist-only" persecution in Acts scholarship is carefully documented in Hill, *Hellenists and Hebrews*, 19–40.

40. Castelli, *Martyrdom and Memory*, 20. On the paradox of cultural memory as both malleable and prone to fixedness over time, see 17–19.

41. Ibid., 4.

42. Ibid., 24.

43. Cf. Luke 1.1–4 for the orderly narrative: *diēgēsis akribōs kathexēs*; the elite patron: *kratiste Theophile*; certainty, assurance: *asphalia*; the divine plan: *tōn peplērophorēmenōn*.

44. Cf. John T. Squires, *The Plan of God in Luke-Acts* (SNTSMS 76; Cambridge: Cambridge University Press, 1993); Clare K. Rothschild, *Luke-Acts and the Rhetoric of History: An Investigation of Early Christian Historiography* (WUNT 2/175; Tübingen: Mohr, 2004), 99–212.

45. See, e.g., Charles Talbert's extensive study of patterns in Luke-Acts: *Literary Patterns, Theological Themes and the Genre of Luke-Acts* (Missoula, Mont.: SBL & Scholars Press, 1974); Robert C. Tannehill's *The Narrative Unity of Luke-Acts: A Literary Interpretation* (2 vols.; Philadelphia: Fortress, 1986–90); Mary Rose D'Angelo, "Women in Luke-Acts: A Redactional View," *JBL* 109 (1990): 441–61; David Moessner, "'The Christ Must Suffer': New Light on the Jesus—Peter, Stephen, Paul Parallels in Luke-Acts," *NovT* 28 (1986): 220–56. For one of numerous studies of how Luke patterns his characters after types from Hebrew Scripture, see François Bovon, "La figure de Moïse dans l'oeuvre de Luc," in *La Figure de Moïse: écriture et relectures* (ed. Robert Martin-Achard et al.; Geneva: Labor et Fides, 1978), 47–65.

46. Of course, even in a narrative as tightly woven as Luke-Acts, gaps, fissures, and ambiguities exist. It is in these narrative breaks that source and redaction critics have attempted to get a toe hold; it is because of these ambiguities that Acts has provoked a rich multiplicity of interpretations. These narrative breaks and ambiguities notwithstanding, agreement that Acts strives for continuity over disruption and unity over divisiveness is widespread. Less agreement exists on whether Acts defers to, rather than attempts to subvert, Roman authority, on which see discussion in chap. 1.

47. Keith Jenkins, *On "What Is History?": From Carr to Elton to Rorty and White* (London: Routledge, 1995), 138.

48. Note, for instance, the anxiety expressed by scholars of Christian origins that, in spite of their best efforts to resist Acts' narrative framing, they have succumbed to its hold. Consider the lament of Merrill P. Miller ("Antioch, Paul and Jerusalem: Diaspora Myths of Origins in the Homeland," in *Redescribing Christian Origins* [ed. Ron Cameron and Merrill P. Miller; Symposium 28; Atlanta: Society of Biblical Literature, 2004], 177–235, esp. 235) with regard to the constraining power of Acts and the Pauline Epistles: "we are trapped in the myth of origins we wish to explain." See

also Burton Mack, on imagining a Jerusalem group with some connection to the Jesus movements: "The challenge is great because such an imagination will have to be achieved without appeal to the Lukan or Christ-cult models and with very little hard evidence. The temptation will be to suggest that, since there is not enough evidence to construct scenarios other than the traditional Lukan portrayals, must we not allow this or that feature of the regnant model to remain in play, at least as a possibility?" ("A Jewish Jesus School in Jerusalem?" in *Redescribing Christian Origins*, 253–62, esp. 254).

Consider also Todd Penner's insightful arguments concerning the "power of ideology to shape both the text and the interpreter, often resulting in a causal connection between the discursive character of the text and its mimetic reinscription in contemporary scholarly analysis." *Praise*, 8.

49. Baur, *Paul the Apostle*, 1.38, 54. Gerd Lüdemann, *Early Christianity according to the Traditions in Acts: A Commentary* (trans. John Bowden; Minneapolis: Fortress, 1989).

In Todd Penner's survey of the history of scholarship on the Hellenist periscope of Acts 6.1–8.3, he repeatedly underscores that F. C. Baur reads differently than modern exegetes. Because Baur's reading of the Hellenistic pericope is grounded in a particular Hegelian philosophy of history that understands the emergence of Christianity as a coming into consciousness of the Spirit, for him ideas are more essential than specific persons. Therefore, while for modern exegetes such as Martin Hengel, it is crucial to contextualize the ideas of the early Christian period in real people and factual historical events, in Penner's reading of Baur, "the historical existence of Stephen is ultimately much less of an issue of focus . . . than is the presentation of the ideas existing in the speech and narrative of Stephen" (*Praise*, 53; see also 29, 54, 17, 18–19, 27). This may be so. But if so, Baur's repeated insistence nonetheless that the martyrdom of Stephen is "indubitably" historical becomes all the more noteworthy.

50. Baur, *Paul the Apostle*, 54–55.

51. A notable exception to the consensus concerning the certainty of Stephen's historical existence is offered by Hans Joachim Schoeps, who suggests that Stephen is a symbolic character invented by Luke to displace James as first martyr (*Theologie und Geschichte des Judenchristentums* [Tübingen: Mohr, 1949] 441–48). Schoeps' argument receives more consideration in my chap. 3.

52. Eduard Zeller, *The Contents and Origin of the Acts of the Apostles Critically Investigated* (2 vols.; trans. Joseph Dare; Edinburgh: Williams & Norgate, 1875–1976), 1.237, emphasis added.

53. Lüdemann, *Early Christianity*, 93.

54. N. H. Taylor, "Stephen, the Temple, and Early Christian Eschatology," *RB* 110 (2003): 62–85, esp. 62, 64–65.

55. While granting that Acts scholars cannot subject the text to the method of multiple attestation as it applies in Jesus research owing to the singularity of the narrative, there are yet outside sources against which Acts can be compared for purposes of historical analysis.

56. Note the observation of François Bovon, who does consider Luke to be preserving a historical event here, on the lack of corroboration between the Pauline Letters and the Stephen story: "The absence in the Pauline corpus is particularly

surprising. The theological affinity between the two men should have urged the apostle to the nations to find strength in his memory of Stephen." In "The Dossier on Stephen, the First Martyr," *HTR* 96 (2003): 279–315, esp. 287–88.

57. And even into the late second century and beyond, the Stephen tradition gets a mixed reception. While Irenaeus and Tertullian know the tradition of Stephen as first martyr, the Pseudo-Clementine *Recognitions* 1.27–71 does not. For more on the version of murder and parting preserved in *Rec.* 1.27–71, see chap. 3.

58. The significance of Hegesippus' story of the martyrdom of James is considered in greater detail in chap. 3.

59. Summaries of scholarship are included in Penner, *Praise*, 60–103; Hill, *Hellenists and Hebrews*, 41–101; Taylor, "Stephen," 64, n. 4.

60. See, e.g., Richard Pervo, "'Antioch, Farewell! For Wisdom Sees. . .': Traces of a Source Describing the Early Gentile Mission in Acts 1–15" (paper read at the fall meeting of the Westar Institute, Sonoma, Calif., 2006); Hans Conzelmann, *The Acts of the Apostles* (Hermeneia; trans. James Limburg et al.; ed. Eldon Jay Epp; Philadelphia: Fortress, 1987), 44.

61. *The Acts of the Apostles* (Crown Theological Library; NTS 3; trans. J. R. Wilkinson; New York: Putnam 1909), 169–78. Cf. Richard Pervo's proposal for a "modified" Antiochene source, which, at least in regards to Stephen, follows closely the contours of Harnack's proposal ("Antioch, Farewell"); Hill, *Hellenists and Hebrews*, 93–95; Penner, *Praise*, 60–78, esp. 76–77.

62. Nor is it to deny the possibility of writing history, or the fact that events happened. On which, see more below, pp. 20–24.

63. Given the centrality of temple and torah as twin pillars of Judaism, as argued by Seth Schwartz (*Imperialism and Jewish Society 200 B.C.E. to 600 C.E.* [Princeton: Princeton University Press, 2001], 59–69), and given Acts' interest in identity construction, it might be fruitful to understand the temple/torah accusation as a means of depicting Stephen as charged with the crime of standing "against Judaism."

64. "And Stephen was the first after his Lord with respect to his ordination, and in addition, as if he had been brought forward for this very purpose, because he was stoned to death by those who murdered the Lord. And so, he was the first to carry off the prize gained by the worthy martyrs of Christ, the crown [στέφανον], well suited to his name [τὸν αὐτῷ φερώνυμον]." (Eusebius, *Hist. eccl.* 2.1.1).

65. Zeph Stewart argues that the association of martyrdom with receiving the victorious crown in an athletic contest is a feature distinctive to Christian martyrdom, which does not surface before the mid-second century *Martyrdom of Polycarp* and which is without Jewish precedent ("Greek Crowns and Christian Martyrs," in *Mémorial André-Jean Festugière; Antiquité Païenne et Chrétienne* [ed. E. Lucchesi and H. D. Saffrey; Geneva: P. Cramer, 1984], 119–24). But this argument fails to account for the frequency of the association of the crown with the prize of immortality in Jewish (including New Testament) texts pre-dating *Polycarp* (e.g., 1 Cor. 9.25; Rev. 2.10, 3.11; James 1.12; 2 Tim. 4.8). Moreover, Stewart inexplicably disregards 4 Maccabees with its clear associations of martyrs and crowns (e.g., 4 Mac. 17.15). Even if Acts is written before the association of crowns with martyrs is firmly fixed, it is still written

in a milieu in which symbolic associations exist between concepts of struggle, persecution, crowns, and the reward of immortality. That is, Acts is written within a time frame in which an author with a penchant for symbolic characters could light upon *Stephanos* as the perfect name for his persecuted protagonist.

66. *Pace* Heikki Räisänen, who argues, "Luke must have had some traditional information at his disposal when composing the account of Stephen's martyrdom. He could not invent by himself the fact that Stephen was arrested and killed." Cf. "The 'Hellenists': A Bridge between Jesus and Paul?" in *Jesus, Paul and Torah: Collected Essays* (JSNTSup 43; Sheffield: Sheffield Academic Press, 1992), 166.

67. Thus, Hayden White contrasts the form of historical narrative, on the one hand, with that of a medieval annals, on the other: "What is lacking in the list of events [the annals] to give it a similar regularity and fullness [to the narrative] is a notion of a social center by which to locate them with respect to one another and to charge them with ethical or moral significance. Without such a center, Charles's campaigns against the Saxons remain simply fights, the invasion of the Saracens simply a coming, and the fact that the battle of Poitiers was fought on a Saturday as important as the fact that the battle was even fought at all." See "Narrativity in the Representation of Reality," in *The Content of the Form: Narrative Discourse and Historical Representation* (Baltimore: John Hopkins University Press, 1987), 1–25, esp. 11. For a critique of White's own unarticulated "social center," see Harry Harootunian, *History's Disquiet: Modernity, Cultural Practice, and the Question of Everyday Life* (New York: Columbia University Press, 2000), 10–15.

68. John B. Thompson, *Ideology and Modern Culture: Critical Social Theory in the Era of Mass Communication* (Stanford: Stanford University Press, 1990), 62. In his use of Acts to undergird developing orthodoxy, Irenaeus stands as Exhibit A of this principle as it relates to this canonical text. To cite but one example of how Acts functions to undergird existing ecclesiastical structures in the present: Jaroslav Pelikan references the specification in Acts 2 that the replacement of Judas among the twelve apostles be chosen from "the men" (*andres*) who accompanied them as justification for contemporary restrictions on women's ministry (*Acts* [Brazos Theological Commentary on the Bible; Grand Rapids: Brazos, 2005], 206).

69. In addition to the work of Hayden White, cf. also the work of Michel de Certeau, *The Writing of History* (trans. Tom Conley; New York: Columbia University Press, 1988); Roland Barthes, "The Reality Effect," in *The Rustle of Language* (New York: Hill & Wang, 1986), 141–48. A recent call for scholars of antiquity to attend to critical theory comes from Elizabeth A. Clark, *History, Theory, Text: Historians and the Linguistic Turn* (Cambridge: Harvard University Press, 2004). Elisabeth Schüssler Fiorenza has addressed the issue especially as it pertains to biblical criticism. Her work is treated in greater detail below.

For this discussion in the discipline of classics, see A. J. Woodman, "From Hannibal to Hitler, the Literature of War," *University of Leeds Review* 26 (1983): 107–24; idem, *Rhetoric in Classical Historiography: Four Studies* (London: Croon Helm, 1988); T. P. Wiseman, "Lying Historians: Seven Types of Mendacity," in *Lies and Fiction in the Ancient World* (ed. C. Gill and T. P. Wiseman; Austin: University of Texas Press, 1993),

122–46. For the most comprehensive argument to date on the implications of the linguistic turn for Acts studies, see Penner, *Praise*.

70. See especially the large and comprehensive third chapter, "Writing History in Antiquity: Identity, Rhetoric, and Compelling Narration," *Praise*, 104–222.

71. Penner's arguments intersect with those of classicists Woodman, *Rhetoric in Classical Historiography*, and Wiseman, "Lying Historians." Cf. Rothschild, *Luke-Acts and the Rhetoric of History*, who also concludes that history and theology are intertwined in Luke-Acts in ways that are impossible to untangle, but who is more cautious about the implications of these findings for historical reconstruction.

72. Penner, *Praise*, 144.

73. The caveat: noting that the *ideal* reader is an elite Romanized male is not to say that the *actual* readers of Luke-Acts held such high status. Luke's readers were not *of* such status but *aspired* to it. Concerning the sociocultural placement of this text, I am persuaded by Loveday Alexander's arguments that the literary abilities of the author of Luke-Acts seem to be in the range of those who wrote *Fachprosa*—a sort of prose aligned with the mundane or workaday world—and hence that his text falls short of the "prestige code" of atticized Greek. Cf. "Septuaginta, Fachprosa, Imitatio: Albert Wifstrand and the Language of Luke-Acts," in *Acts in Its Ancient Literary Context* (Library of New Testament Studies 298; London: T&T Clark, 2006), 231–52.

74. Cf. here Penner, *Praise*, 5, n. 17, on the methodological problem of assuming "veracity by association," in the attempt to link Acts with Polybius and Thucydides.

On the genre of Acts, see Loveday Alexander, *The Preface to Luke's Gospel: Literary Convention and Social Context in Luke 1.1–4 and Acts 1.1* (SNTSMS 78; Cambridge: Cambridge University Press, 1993). Compare also her updated assessment, "On a Roman Bookstall: Reading Acts in Its Ancient Literary Context," in *Acts in Its Ancient Literary Context*, 1–20.

75. Penner, *Praise*, 331.

76. See Elisabeth Schüssler Fiorenza, "Revisioning Christian Origins: *In Memory of Her* Revisited," in *Christian Beginnings: Worship, Belief and Society* (ed. Kieran O'Mahoney; London: Continuum, 2003), 225–50, esp. 233–35; cf. also Fred Burnett, "historiography," in *Handbook of Postmodern Biblical Interpretation* (ed. A. K. M. Adam; St. Louis, Mo.: Chalice, 2000), 106–112; Clark, *History, Theory, Text*, 156–58.

77. See, e.g., *Rhetoric and Ethic: The Politics of Biblical Studies* (Minneapolis: Fortress, 1999); *Jesus and the Politics of Interpretation* (New York: Continuum, 2000); "Revisioning Christian Origins."

78. Schüssler Fiorenza, *Rhetoric and Ethic*, 197.

79. Buell, *Why This New Race*, xii. Cf. also Johnson-DeBaufre, *Jesus among Her Children*, 11–17.

80. My attention to the ethical component of historical reconstruction of Christian origins has most immediate consequences in terms of Jewish–Christian relations. This alternate model for constructing Christian relations with Jews, in as much as it dismantles Acts' exclusivity and condemnation of nonbelievers and calls for a reassessment of Christian principles of enemy love and non-retaliation, could also

have implications for present and future Christian practice toward other social/ religious groups as well.

81. Because the volumes share the same final redactor, and related rhetorical concerns, I necessarily consider the Third Gospel, as well as Acts, in this book and signal the connection between the two volumes through employing the hyphenated construction. Yet, occasional resort to the conventional hyphenated construction for the two volumes does not preclude my understanding that the second volume is not always parroting the rhetoric of the first but in some instances assumes its own distinctive rhetorical slant. On the relation between, and also the distinct nature of, the two volumes, see Mikeal Parsons and Richard Pervo, *Rethinking the Unity of Luke and Acts* (Minneapolis: Fortress, 1993).

CHAPTER ONE

1. Throughout this chapter, I will consistently utilize a lower case "m" in referencing marcionite thinking, to signal a cluster of ideas eventually projected onto the historical figure Marcion but which did not necessarily originate with Marcion himself. See below, pp. 46–47, for further elaboration of this distinction.

2. On the ambivalence and ambiguity of the colonial situation, see especially Homi Bhabha, *The Location of Culture* (London: Routledge, 1994). For a postcolonial engagement with the passion narrative of Luke, drawing on Bhabha's categories ambivalence and ambiguity, see Yong-Sung Ahn, *The Reign of God and Rome in Luke's Passion Narrative: An East Asian Global Perspective* (Biblical Interpretation Series 80; Leiden: Brill, 2006), esp. 35, 190, 192, 203, 209–13. See also Virginia Burrus, "The Gospel of Luke and the Acts of the Apostles," in *A Postcolonial Commentary on the New Testament Writings* (ed. Fernando Segovia and R. S. Sugirtharahah; the Bible and Postcolonialism 13; London: T&T Clark, 2007), 133–55; Brigitte Kahl, "Acts of the Apostles: Pro(to)-Imperial Script and Hidden Transcript," in *In the Shadow of Empire: Reclaiming the Bible as a History of Faithful Resistance* (ed. Richard Horsley; Louisville, Ky.: Westminster John Knox, 2008), 137–56.

3. Schüssler Fiorenza, *Rhetoric and Ethic*, 196.

4. Regina Schwartz, *The Curse of Cain: The Violent Legacy of Monotheism* (Chicago: University of Chicago Press, 1997), 17.

5. For two contemporary examples of how one might produce a "resistant" reading, see the distinctions made by Adele Reinhartz concerning ideal, implied, and actual readers in "The New Testament and Anti-Judaism: A Literary Critical Approach," *JES* 25 (1988): 524–37; and Dale Martin's elaboration of multiple and subversive readings of Galatians 3.28, in *Sex and the Single Savior: Gender and Sexuality in Biblical Interpretation* (Louisville, Ky.: Westminster John Knox, 2006), 88–90. For an example of a resistant reader of Acts from the ancient world, see my discussion in chap. 3 of how the canonical Acts is recast by the redactor of the Pseudo-Clementine *Recognitions* 1.27–71.

Though we employ different categories of analysis, the distinction I make between reading with and against the rhetorical grain shares affinity with distinctions made by Burrus ("Gospel of Luke") and Kahl ("Acts of the Apostles") between the surface and submerged readings and/or the public vs. hidden transcript in Acts. Both make compelling arguments for subversive readings of Acts, but neither argues that such readings arise merely from a straightforward embrace of Acts' rhetoric.

6. Vincent L. Wimbush, "Reading Texts as Reading Ourselves: A Chapter in the History of African-American Biblical Interpretation," in *Social Location and Biblical Interpretation in the United States* (vol. 1 of *Reading From This Place*; ed. Fernando F. Segovia and Mary Ann Tolbert; Minneapolis: Fortress, 1995), 95–108; Demetrius K. Williams, *"The Acts of the Apostles,"* in *True to Our Native Land: An African American New Testament Commentary* (ed. Brian K. Blount et al.; Minneapolis: Fortress, 2007), 213–48.

7. Ivoni Richter Reimer, *Women in the Acts of the Apostles: A Feminist Liberation Perspective* (Minneapolis: Fortress, 1995).

8. Here, understanding egalitarian impulses on a continuum. It is more egalitarian to grant that women and slaves could have the power of prophecy than to imagine them silent. It would be more egalitarian still, of course, for a community to imagine a utopia free from the institution of slavery. On various typologies of egalitarianism and utopianism and their relevance for reconstructing early Christianity, see Mary Ann Beavis, "Christian Origins, Egalitarianism and Utopia," *JFSR* 23 (2007): 27–49.

9. On the view that the syntax of 1.14 suggests that these women are the disciples' wives, see Kirsopp Lake and Henry Cadbury, *English Translation and Commentary* (vol. 4 of *The Beginnings of Christianity Part I: The Acts of the Apostles*; ed. F. J. Foakes Jackson and Kirsopp Lake; 1920–1933; repr., Grand Rapids: Baker, 1979), 11.

10. On the frequency and significance of Luke's employment of ANHP language, see D'Angelo, "ANHP Question." D'Angelo argues that both the author's careful distinctions between roles for women and men, and the frequency of "men/man" as a form of address stem from "the desire to depict the Christian message and its messengers—the speeches and speakers—as ambassadors suitable for the public and civic forum" (52).

11. On the burlesque nature of the episode of the mantic slave girl, see Richard Pervo, *Profit with Delight: The Literary Genre of the Acts of the Apostles* (Philadelphia: Fortress, 1987), 63.

L. Michael White has suggested that Peter's ecstatic vision in Acts 10 harkens back to 2.17: "your young men will see visions" (οἱ νεανίσκοι ὑμῶν ὁράσεις ὄψονται; "The Pentecost Event: Lukan Redaction and Themes in Acts 2," *Forum* 3 [2000]: 75–103). It would be perfectly in keeping with Acts' rhetorical aims to allow only a man like Peter to fulfill an aspect of Joel's prophecy.

12. I am persuaded by Richard Pervo's argument (*Dating Acts*) that the author of Acts has familiarity with the Pauline correspondence.

13. On attention to gaps, ruptures, and absences in texts by scholars whom she classifies as the "new intellectual historians," see Clark, *History, Theory, Text*, 113–24.

14. D'Angelo, "ANHP Question"; Turid Karlsen Seim, *The Double Message: Patterns of Gender in Luke-Acts* (Studies of the New Testament and Its World;

Edinburgh: T&T Clark, 1994); Shelly Matthews, *First Converts: Rich Pagan Women and the Rhetoric of Mission in Early Judaism and Christianity* (Contraversions; Stanford: Stanford University Press, 2001), 51–100.

15. Laura Nasrallah, "The Acts of the Apostles, Greek Cities, and Hadrian's Panhellenion," *JBL* 127 (2008): 533–66.

16. I adopt the neologism, coined by Elisabeth Schüssler Fiorenza, *kyriarchal/kyriocentric* rather than the more customary *patriarchal/androcentric*, to speak of domination systems in the ancient world. Derived from the Greek term for lord, this term better underscores the interlocking and hierarchically structured systems of domination. See *Rhetoric and Ethic*, ix.

17. As Ernst Haenchen recognized long ago, the anti-Jewish and pro-Roman orientations of Acts are flip sides of the same coin. Distancing its own community from actual Jews, while simultaneously carting off any Jewish prestige markers as true signs of the worthiness of "the Way," is a means for rhetorically carving out safe space for Jesus believers within the empire. See Ernst Haenchen, *The Acts of the Apostles* (trans. Bernard Noble and Gerald Shinn; Philadelphia: Westminster, 1971), 99–103; idem, "Judentum und Christentum in der Apostelgeschichte," *ZNW* 54 (1963): 155–89.

For others who argue along similar lines with respect to the denigration of non-confessing Jews in Acts, see Jack T. Sanders, *The Jews in Luke-Acts* (Philadelphia: Fortress, 1987), 37–83; Wills, "Depiction of Jews"; idem, *Not God's People: Insiders and Outsiders in the Biblical World* (Lanham, Md.: Rowman & Littlefield: 2008), 195–209; Richard Pervo, *Dating Acts*, 324–27.

18. Attempts to summarize and synthesize this scholarship include Joseph B. Tyson, *Luke, Judaism, and the Scholars: Critical Approaches to Luke-Acts* (Columbia: University of South Carolina Press, 1999); Jon A. Weatherly, *Jewish Responsibility for the Death of Jesus in Luke-Acts* (JSNTSup 106; Sheffield: Sheffield Academic Press, 1994), 1–49; Daryl Schmidt, "Anti-Judaism and the Gospel of Luke," in *Anti-Judaism and the Gospels* (ed. William R. Farmer; Harrisburg, Pa.: Trinity, 1999), 63–96.

19. See, e.g., James D. G. Dunn's arguments that Luke cannot be motivated by anti-Jewish malice, in *The Parting of the Ways: Between Christianity and Judaism and Their Significance for the Character of Christianity* (London: SCM 1991), 140–51; Günter Wasserberg's conclusion that Luke is not anti-Jewish, in *Aus Israels Mitte—Heil für die Welt: Eine narrativ-exegetische Studie zur Theologie des Lukas* (BZNW 92; Berlin: de Gruyter, 1998), 361–66; and Daniel Marguerat's insistence that Acts is "open" to Jews and neither denigrates nor demonstrates the inferiority of Judaism, *The First Christian Historian: Writing the 'Acts of the Apostles'* (SNTSMS 121; Cambridge: Cambridge University Press, 2002), 129–54.

20. The strongest voice for the view that Luke presents a positive depiction of first-century Judaism in Acts has been Jacob Jervell's. See his representative works, *Luke and the People of God: A New Look at Luke-Acts* (Minneapolis: Augsburg, 1972); *The Unknown Paul: Essays in Luke-Acts and Early Christian History* (Minneapolis: Augsburg, 1984); and his commentary on Acts, *Die Apostelgeschichte* (KEK 3; Göttingen: Vandenhoeck & Ruprecht, 1998). Unlike those cited below (see n. 21),

Jervell acknowledges that from the vantage point of the author of Acts, the Jewish mission is long over. *Luke and the People*, 68–69.

Consider also the conclusions drawn by Robert Brawley concerning Luke-Acts' strong emphasis on things Jewish: "Rather than setting Gentile Christianity free, Luke ties it to Judaism. And rather than rejecting the Jews, Luke appeals to them . . ." (*Luke-Acts and the Jews: Conflict, Apology, and Conciliation* [SBLMS 33; Atlanta: Scholars Press, 1987], 159); see also idem, "The God of Promises and the Jews in Luke-Acts," in *Literary Studies in Luke-Acts: Essays in Honor of Joseph B. Tyson* (ed. Richard. P. Thompson and Thomas E. Phillips; Macon, Ga.: Mercer University Press, 1998), 279–96.

21. Robert C. Tannehill, "Israel in Luke-Acts: A Tragic Story," *JBL* 104 (1985): 69–85; Marilyn Salmon, "Insider or Outsider? Luke's Relationship with Judaism," in *Luke-Acts and the Jewish People: Eight Critical Perspectives* (ed. Joseph B. Tyson; Minneapolis: Augsburg, 1988), 76–82; David Tiede, *Prophecy and History in Luke-Acts* (Philadelphia: Fortress, 1980); idem, "'Fighting Against God': Luke's Interpretation of Jewish Rejection of the Messiah Jesus," in *Anti-Semitism and Early Christianity: Issues of Polemic and Faith* (ed. Craig Evans and Donald Hagner; Minneapolis: Fortress, 1993), 102–112; Craig Evans, "Faith and Polemic: The New Testament and First-Century Judaism," in *Anti-Semitism and Early Christianity*, 1–17.

Because they posit that Luke-Acts is part of an intramural debate, both Tiede and Tannehill argue that (1) the depiction of Jerusalem's destruction is a "tragic" element of the story, (2) that the condemnation of Jews for rejecting Jesus is part of a "vital intra-Jewish hermeneutical argumentation" concerning a "crises of national and theological identity," and that (3) Jesus' weeping over Jerusalem demonstrates sympathetic pathos, rather than animus, toward these rejected Jews. As someone who argues that Luke-Acts is not intramural, I suggest that the weeping of Jesus over Jerusalem might be better understood as akin to the "tears of Marcellus"—the tears of a victor over the vanquished, springing both from pity and from awareness that a historical era has come to completion. See Andreola Rossi, "The Tears of Marcellus: History of a Literary Motif in Livy," *GR* 47 (2000): 56–66.

22. For further elaboration of this argument, see chap. 2, pp. 59–60.

23. So, Daniel Marguerat, *First Christian Historian*, 150–51, concerning the openness of Paul's final speech in Acts 28.17–31: "just as the prophet does not curse the people of God, but calls them to change, so the apostle Paul presented by Luke is shown in these last verses as preaching the Kingdom of God to 'all who (πάντας) came to him' (28.30). With regard to the Jews, this πάντας does not close the door, but leaves it open." Compare also Daryl Schmidt on this final speech: ("Anti-Judaism," 91) "Any sense of complete separation between Jews and Christians is a projection beyond the end of the narrative. The language of rejection is limited to those Jews who refuse to be convinced by Paul's arguments. The statement is itself a direct echo of deuteronomistic language: The wise have rejected the word of the Lord . . . but Luke-Acts always stops short of the reverse deuteronomistic charge: and the Lord has rejected them."

24. The full citations emphasize both Paul's Jewishness and his humanity/ masculinity: ἐγὼ ἄνθρωπος μέν εἰμι Ἰουδαῖος (21.39); ἐγώ εἰμι ἀνὴρ Ἰουδαῖος (22.3).

25. Heschel, "From Jesus to Shylock"; Buell, *Why This New Race*, 161.

26. By pressing upon Luke the charge of anti-Semitism, Jack Sanders has unnecessarily opened himself up to criticism on the level of terminology, a criticism that has distracted from the main thrust of his argument concerning the nature of Acts' hostile depictions of non-confessing Jews. See, e.g., Jack T. Sanders, "The Parable of the Pounds and Lucan Anti-Semitism," *TS* 42 (1981): 667.

On fixity and fluidity as they pertain to racial discourse, see Stoler, "Racial Histories," 183–206; Buell, *Why This New Race*, 6–9.

27. Wills, "Depiction of Jews," 645–46.

28. Boyarin, *Dying for God*; idem, *Borderlines*; and discussion in my Introduction at pp. 6–8. In view of the place of Luke-Acts in constructing Christian identity, apart from Judaism, I disagree with the insistence of the contributors to *Anti-Semitism and Early Christianity* that *all* New Testament Polemic is intramural.

29. Though, as Tat-siong Benny Liew notes ("Acts," in *Global Bible Commentary* [ed. Daniel Patte et al.; Nashville: Abingdon, 2004], 420–23), faith in Christ is not the sole requisite for incorporation into the Christ community.

30. Acts 3.22–23 is a near quotation of Deut. 18.18–19 (LXX), though in Acts, ἐξολεθρεύω has been substituted for ἐκδικέω. Cf. also Lev. 23.29 (LXX).

31. This is not the case with the Pauline Epistles themselves, where the argument has been posited that Paul affirms two paths to salvation, one for Jews and one for Gentiles. For an overview of this position, see Wills, *Not God's People*, 167–78. For one discussion of Acts and the question of universal restoration (*apokatastasis*), see Pelikan, *Acts*, 66–68.

32. On the anti-Judaism implicit in the contrast between Jewish "exclusivity" and Christian "universalism," see Denise Buell, *Why This New Race*, 10–13. For one postcolonial critique of the hegemonic implications of Christian celebration of universalism, see Musa Dube, *Postcolonial Feminist Interpretation of the Bible* (St. Louis, Mo.: Chalice, 2000).

33. Amy-Jill Levine, "Anti-Judaism and the Gospel of Matthew," in *Anti-Judaism and the Gospels* (ed. William R. Farmer; Harrisburg, Pa.: Trinity), 9–36, esp. 17.

34. Brawley, "God of Promises," 206. See also idem, "Ethical Borderlines between Rejection and Hope: Interpreting the Jews in Luke-Acts," *CurTM* 27 (2000): 414–23.

35. Müller, "Reception of the Old Testament"; Geir Otto Holmås, "'My House Shall Be a House of Prayer,' Regarding the Temple as a Place of Prayer in Acts within the Context of Luke's Apologetical Objective," *JSNT* 27 (2005): 393–416.

36. As, e.g., when Matthew asserts that the prophecy of Hosea 11.1, "out of Egypt I have called my son," is fulfilled by the return of the Holy family from their flight into Egypt. For one treatment of Midrash prophecy in the Gospel of Matthew, see Jacob Neusner's *What Is Midrash?* (Philadelphia: Fortress, 1987).

37. "Go and say to this people: 'Keep listening but do not comprehend; keep looking, but do not understand.' Make the mind of this people dull, and stop their ears, and shut their eyes, so that they may not look with their eyes, and listen with their ears, and comprehend with their minds, and turn and be healed."

38. This comprehensive view of Scripture leads Jervell to conclude that Luke was "the fundamentalist" among New Testament authors. See "The Center of Scripture in Luke," in *The Unknown Paul*, 122–37, 179–83, esp. 122.

39. Note, for instance, Holmås' analysis of the paradoxical view of the temple in Paul's defense speech at Acts 22.17–21. On the one hand, Paul's reference here to his vision while at prayer in the temple serves to refute charges that he is an enemy of "the holy place." But at the same time that the vision affirms Paul's temple piety, it also strikes a blow to the temple's legitimacy. In this temple vision, as Holmås notes, "Jesus asks Paul to leave Jerusalem because of the city's rejection of the message of salvation and, instead, to go to the Gentiles. In a scene that recalls Isaiah's call in the temple . . . Paul receives the commission to preach the gospel to the Gentiles. But, with that, the command to leave Jerusalem is *de facto* to undermine the significance of the temple" (Holmås, "My House," 405).

40. Holmås, "My House," 416.

41. Exceptions exist. The Pharisee Gamaliel is coded positively, though he is not depicted as having converted (5.33–39). The Pharisees as a group defend Paul's innocence after his arrest (23.9). I read this as part of Acts' use of Jewish institutions to prove the legitimacy of the Way, while recognizing that others have argued that Luke-Acts is favorably disposed to and particularly respectful of this party in Judaism apart from any interest in the rhetoric of legitimation. See, e.g., David Balch, "Response to Daryl Schmidt: Luke-Acts Is Catechesis for Christians, Not Kerygma to Jews," in *Anti-Judaism and the Gospels* (ed. William R. Farmer; Harrisburg, Pa.: Trinity, 1999), 97–110, esp. 105. Whether the author of Luke-Acts could imagine these nonbelieving Pharisees as somehow standing outside of its condemnation of nonbelievers is not a question taken up in Acts.

42. Wills, "Depiction of Jews."

43. Ibid., 653–54. For further discussion of the negative depictions of Jews in Acts, see Dixon Slingerland, "'The Jews' in the Pauline Portion of Acts," *JAAR* 54 (1986): 305–21, esp. 314–19; Sanders, *Jews in Luke-Acts*; and the discussion in chap. 2, pp. 58–61.

44. *Marc.* 3.6–3.7.

45. Stephen G. Wilson, "Marcion and the Jews," in *Separation and Polemic* (vol. 2 of *Anti-Judaism in Early Christianity*; ed. Stephen G. Wilson; Studies in Christianity and Judaism 2; Waterloo, Ontario: Wilfrid Laurier University Press, 1986), 45–58, esp. 58. Cf. also John G. Gager, *The Origins of Anti-Semitism: Attitudes toward Judaism in Pagan and Christian Antiquity* (New York: Oxford University Press, 1983), 172.

46. Both Hans Conzelmann (*Theology of St. Luke* [trans. Geoffrey Buswell; New York: Harper & Row, 1961] trans. of *Die Mitte der Zeit: Studien zur Theologie des Lukas* [BHT 17; Tübingen: Mohr, 1964]), 137–49; and F. F. Bruce (*Commentary on the Book of Acts* [Grand Rapids: Eerdmans, 1956], 15–27) have argued that Acts is a political apology for the church to Rome. According to W. Gasque, *A History of the Criticism of the Acts of the Apostles* (BGBE 17; Tübingen: Mohr, 1975), 21–22, the first to identify the pro-Roman slant in Luke-Acts was the early eighteenth-century scholar, Christoph Heumann.

47. Conzelmann, *Theology of St. Luke*, 9–31.

48. For recent iterations of how best to understand the apologetic function of Acts, see Robert Maddox, *The Purpose of Luke-Acts* (Studies in the New Testament World; Edinburgh: T&T Clark, 1982); Paul W. Walaskay, *'And So We Came to Rome': The Political Perspective of St. Luke* (Cambridge: Cambridge University Press, 1987); Klaus Wengst, *Pax Romana and the Peace of Jesus Christ* (trans. John Bowden; Philadelphia: Fortress, 1987), 87–105; Robert Stoops, "Riot and Assembly: The Social Context of Acts 19:23–41," *JBL* 108 (1989): 73–91; Gregory E. Sterling, *Historiography and Self-definition: Josephus, Luke-Acts and Apologetic Historiography* (NTS 64; Leiden: Brill, 1992), 381–89; Fredrich W. Horn, "Die Haltung des Lukas zum Römischen Staat im Evangelium und in der Apostelgeschichte" in *The Unity of Luke-Acts* (ed. J. Verheyden; BETL 142; Leuven: Leuven University Press, 1999), 203–224; Penner, *Praise*; Loveday Alexander, "The Acts of the Apostles as an Apologetic Text," in *Acts in Its Ancient Literary Context*, 183–206.

49. Philip Esler, *Community and Gospel in Luke-Acts: The Social and Political Motivations of Lucan Theology* (SNTSMS 57; Cambridge: Cambridge University Press, 1987), 16–23, 205–19. See also Richard Pervo, *Acts* (Hermeneia; ed. Harold W. Attridge; Minneapolis: Fortress, 2009), 21–22.

50. Nasrallah, "Acts of the Apostles," 564. See also Denise Buell's brief but incisive comments on how Luke-Acts replicates the hegemonizing universalist discourse of empire through its logic of a third (and superior) people, *Why This New Race?* 86–87.

51. Richard J. Cassidy reads both volumes of Luke-Acts with this liberation lens. See his *Jesus, Politics and Society: A Study of Luke's Gospel* (Maryknoll, N.Y.: Orbis, 1978) and *Society and Politics in the Acts of the Apostles* (Maryknoll, N.Y.: Orbis, 1987). See also the contributors to *Political Issues in Luke-Acts* (ed. Richard J. Cassidy and Philip Scharper; Maryknoll, N.Y.: Orbis, 1983).

52. Gary Gilbert, "The List of Nations in Acts 2: Roman Propaganda and the Lukan Response," *JBL* 121 (2002): 497–529; idem, "Roman Propaganda and Christian Identity in the Worldview of Luke-Acts," in *Contextualizing Acts: Lukan Narrative and Greco-Roman Discourse* (ed. Todd Penner and Caroline Vander Stichele; SBLSymS 20; Atlanta: Society of Biblical Literature, 2003), 233–56.

Allen Brent, *The Imperial Cult and the Development of Church Order: Concepts and Images of Authority in Paganism and Early Christianity before the Age of Cyprian* (Supplements to Vigilae Christianae 45; Leiden: Brill 1999). Brent is in dialogue with important essays by François Bovon, in which Luke's employment of the language of imperial cult is recognized. See "Studies in Luke-Acts: Retrospect and Prospect," *HTR* 85 (1992): 175–96; and "Israel, the Church and the Gentiles in the Twofold Work of Luke," in *New Testament Traditions and Apocryphal Narratives* (Allison Park, Pa.: Pickwick, 1995), 81–95.

Because Gilbert and Brent, along with Kavin Rowe and David Balch (see below), focus on empire as a lens with which to clarify selected New Testament texts, their readings share some space with those informed by postcolonial methods of biblical interpretation. Yet, they do not engage explicitly with postcolonial studies, nor are they "intent on keeping the ancient imperial contexts in tensive dialogue with the contemporary contexts in which the biblical texts are appropriated," and hence, I refer to their work as "empire-critical" rather than postcolonial. For this distinction, see Stephen D. Moore and Fernando F. Segovia, "Postcolonial Biblical Criticism: Beginnings, Trajectories, Intersections," in *Postcolonial Biblical Criticism: Interdisciplinary Intersections* (ed. Stephen D. Moore and Fernando Segovia; London: T&T Clark, 2005), 1–22, esp. 7–8. On postcolonial engagement with Luke and Acts, see n. 3 above.

53. Gilbert, "List of Nations," 529.

54. Brent, *Imperial Cult*, 123, emphasis added.

55. C. Kavin Rowe, "Luke-Acts and the Imperial Cult: A Way Through the Conundrum?" *JSNT* 27 (2005): 279–300, esp. 292–94. Rowe is careful to note that one cannot discern Acts' intention and therefore shifts to a question of reading communities and what they might have heard. Rowe's recent monograph treating the question of Acts and the Roman Empire appeared too late for me to address. See *World Upside Down: Reading Acts in the Graeco-Roman Age* (Oxford: Oxford University Press, 2009).

For another argument that Luke's use of the imperial titles Lord, King, and Savior for Jesus constitutes an act of subversion, see Steve Walton, "The State They Were In: Luke's View of the Roman Empire," in *Rome and the Bible in the Early Church* (ed. Peter Oakes; Grand Rapids: Baker, 2002), 1–41, esp. 26–28.

56. "ΜΕΤΑΒΟΛΗ ΠΟΛΙΤΕΙΩΝ—Jesus as Founder of the Church in Luke-Acts: Form and Function," in *Contextualizing Acts: Lukan Narrative and Greco-Roman Discourse* (ed. Todd Penner and Caroline Vander Stichele; SBLSymS 20; Atlanta: Society of Biblical Literature: 2003), 139–88. Cf. also Balch's "Response to Daryl Schmidt." Here, Balch speaks of Luke-Acts as having an overarching concern to demonstrate that Jews and Christians are philanthropic in relation to foreigners.

57. Balch, "ΜΕΤΑΒΟΛΗ ΠΟΛΙΤΕΙΩΝ," 152, n. 54. For a comparable suggestion that Acts' story of the "Eastern" Paul invading Greek cultural territory is an act of "narrative aggression," see Loveday Alexander, "'In Journeyings Often': Voyaging in the Acts of the Apostles and in Greek Romance," in *Acts in Its Ancient Literary Context*, 69–95, esp. 84–86.

58. Balch, "ΜΕΤΑΒΟΛΗ ΠΟΛΙΤΕΙΩΝ," 186. The tensions Balch identifies here concerning East/West and Roman/Greek/barbarian are more helpfully analyzed under the rubric of the so-called Second Sophistic. See here Buell, *Why This New Race*, and Nasrallah, "Acts of the Apostles."

59. Gilbert, "List of Nations," 524, n. 101.

60. Brent, *Imperial Cult*, 101–6; also, 109: "The purpose of *Luke-Acts was to reassure this inner-Church group of their association with the humble and meek*" (emphasis added).

61. Rowe, "Luke-Acts and the Imperial Cult," 298–99. Rowe cites here the κύριος of Luke 12.37 as an instance of a generous lord who will "serve" his slaves at table, if they are prepared when he arrives.

62. Balch, "ΜΕΤΑΒΟΛΗ ΠΟΛΙΤΕΙΩΝ," 153.

63. On reading Acts against Acts, see especially the discussion of Kahl, "Acts of the Apostles," 149–51.

64. On this division between Luke-Acts, see Sanders, *Jews in Luke-Acts*, 132–53; and Parsons and Pervo, *Rethinking the Unity*, 38–40. Cf. also Demetrius Williams' concluding remarks in "Acts of the Apostles," 213–48, esp. 242–43.

65. Consider the insightful comments of D'Angelo on the ideal reader of Acts as an elite Christian male, in "ANHP Question," 47–48. See also Matthews, *First Converts*, 85–92.

66. See, e.g., Cassidy, *Society and Politics*, 57–59.

67. See, e.g., Kate Cooper, *The Virgin and the Bride: Idealized Womanhood in Late Antiquity* (Cambridge: Harvard University Press, 1996); Matthews, *First Converts*; D'Angelo, "ANHP Question."

68. If Acts were our only account of the earliest postcrucifixion Jesus movement, we would know nothing of the ministries of Phoebe, Junia, Euodia, and Syntyche. The slander of Mary Magdalene in the Third Gospel (Luke 8.2) and the silence concerning her apostolic witness in Acts belies the strong Magdalene traditions that can be reconstructed from first- and second-century sources. See here especially Jane Schaberg, *The Resurrection of Mary Magdalene: Legends, Apocrypha, and the Christian Testament* (New York: Continuum, 2004).

69. Buell, *Why This New Race*, esp. 1–13, 44–62, 78–93, 138–65. On the value of cultural "mixity" in modern urban centers, see Doreen Massey, *World City* (Malden, Mass.: Polity, 2007), 4.

70. Buell, *Why This New Race*, 86; here quoting François Hartog.

71. On Paul in Lystra, see Amy Wordleman, "Cultural Divides and Dual Realities: A Greco-Roman Context for Acts 14," in *Contextualizing Acts: Lukan Narrative and Greco-Roman Discourse* (ed. Todd Penner and Caroline Vander Stichele; SBLSymS 20; Atlanta: Society of Biblical Literature, 2003), 205–32; on Lystra and Athens, see Nasrallah, "Acts of the Apostles," 559–64. On the Malta episode of Acts 28 as containing the hint of a "slender" thread of religious tolerance, see Liew, "Acts," 424–25. On the depiction of nonbelieving *Ioudaioi* as prone to *stasis*, see also the discussion in chap. 2, pp. 75–77.

It is telling that those who argue Acts' overarching message is one that challenges and subverts Rome generally do not attempt to account for Acts' depiction of nonbelieving *Ioudaioi* according to Roman prejudice. In Gilbert's argument that Luke-Acts expresses opposition to empire, he opts to avoid altogether the question of how this text presents the relation between Christians and Jews ("List of Nations," 527, n. 117). In his analysis of Luke 1.5–2.52, Brent reads the depiction of Jewish cultic practice as having nothing to do with Judaism per se but rather as an allegory concerning the imperial cult. "[In Luke 1.5–2.52] the author of *Luke-Acts* . . . has selected from the Jewish cult a particular act that evokes particular comparison by gentile readers in Asia Minor and in Syria, and even by Jewish readers in Caesarea Philippi . . . with the Imperial Cult. *It is arguable that the Imperial Cult represents the real, pagan backcloth for his seemingly Jewish backcloth*" (Brent, *Imperial Cult*, 90, emphasis added; see also, 74–75).

72. As Todd Penner cautions, "We should be careful not to be lulled into a false sense of security that the language of Christian texts is somehow more humane and gentle; radical discourses that revalue power relationships are themselves not politically

and socially innocent, since the strategies that undermine a dominant structure in many respects use the same coercive and manipulative power to do so." See "Civilizing Discourse: Acts, Declamation, and the Rhetoric of the Polis," in *Contextualizing Acts: Lukan Narrative and Greco-Roman Discourse* (ed. Todd Penner and Caroline Vander Stichele; SBLSymS 20; Atlanta: Scholars Press, 2003), 65–104, esp. 70.

73. On the logics of the slave society operative in Gospel parables, see Jennifer Glancy, *Slavery in Early Christianity* (New York: Oxford University Press, 2002), 102–29.

74. Though Acts' use in late second-century battles against perceived heresy is widely acknowledged. See, e.g., Mount, *Pauline Christianity*.

75. Richard Pervo, *Dating Acts*, 204–8; idem, *Acts*, 525–29.

76. The most significant primary text for reconstructing Marcion's arguments is Tertullian's five-volume refutation of them, *Adversus Marcionem*. Because Marcion employs a version of the Third Gospel as his one Gospel, volume 4 of *Adversus Marcionem* is a commentary on large portions of canonical Luke, in which Tertullian refutes Marcion's reading of it. Irenaeus provides his version of Marcion's teaching at *Adversus haereses* 1.27. For an exhaustive list of primary sources related to Marcion, see Adolf Harnack's foundational study, *Marcion: Das Evangelium vom Fremden Gott* (Leipzig: Hinrichs, 1924; repr., Darmstadt: Wissenschaftliche Buchgesellschaft, 1985). Note especially Harnack's reconstruction of Marcion's Antithesis, 89–92; 256*–313*. A modern English translation of Harnack's *Marcion* is available but seriously limited in that it does not include Harnack's substantial and invaluable appendices. See *Marcion: The Gospel of the Alien God* (trans. John E. Steely and Lyle D. Bierma; Durham, N.C.: Labyrinth, 1990).

For more recent scholarship on Marcion, see Barbara Aland, "Marcion/Marcioniten," *TRE* 22 (1992): 89–101; Gerhard May and Katharina Greschat, eds., *Marcion und seine kirchengeschichtliche Wirkung: Vorträge der Internationalen Fachkonferenz zu Marcion* (ed. with the assistance of Martin Meiser; Berlin: de Gruyter, 2002); Heikki Räisänen, "Marcion," in *A Companion to Second-Century Christian 'Heretics'* (ed. Antti Marjanen and Petri Loumanen; Leiden: Brill, 2008), 100–124.

77. On the significance of Tertullian's rebuttal of Marcion's view that Jesus was not born and did not have a fleshy body, see especially Judith Perkins, "The Rhetoric of the Maternal Body in the *Passion of Perpetua*," in *Mapping Gender in Ancient Religious Discourses* (ed. Todd Penner and Caroline Vander Stichele; Leiden: Brill, 2007), 313–32.

78. Marcion's Gospel apparently begins with a combined form of Luke 3.1a, "In the fifteenth year of the reign of Emperor Tiberius, when Pontius Pilate was governor of Judea," and Luke 4.31, "[Jesus] came down to Capernaum, a city of Galilee, and was teaching them on the sabbath." See Tyson, *Marcion and Luke-Acts*, 32.

79. Gregory, *Reception of Luke and Acts*, 173–209.

80. Ulrich Schmid, *Marcion und sein Apostlos: Rekonstruction und historische Einordnung der marcionitischen Paulusbriefausgabe* (ANTF 25; Berlin: de Gruyter, 1995), 284–311.

81. And hence, the sustained interest in and debate concerning Marcion's role in New Testament canon formation. See Harnack, *Marcion: The Gospel of the Alien*

God, 123–32; John Knox, *Marcion and the New Testament: An Essay in the Early History of the Canon* (Chicago: University of Chicago Press, 1942), 19–38; Hans von Campenhausen, *The Formation of the Christian Bible* (trans. J. A. Baker; Philadelphia: Fortress, 1972), 147–209; John Barton, "Marcion Revisited," in *The Canon Debate* (ed. Lee Martin McDonald and James A. Sanders; Peabody, Mass.: Hendrickson, 2002), 341–54.

82. Irenaeus, *Haer.* 3.13–14; Tertullian, *Against Marcion*, vol. 4 (for his employment of the Gospel of Luke); on Tertullian's use of Acts as proof of Paul's "orthodoxy," see *Marc.* 5.2–3. Cf. also the discussion of Mount, *Pauline Christianity*, 12–29.

83. Edgar Goodspeed, *The Formation of the New* Testament (Chicago: University of Chicago Press, 1926), 74–75; C. K. Barrett, "The First New Testament?" *NovT* 38 (1996): 94–104.

84. Knox, *Marcion*; Tyson, *Marcion and Luke-Acts.* See also the essay of William O. Walker, "The Portrayal of Aquila and Priscilla in Acts: The Question of Sources," *NTS* 54 (2008): 479–95, esp. 492–95.

85. Richard Pervo, Review of Joseph B. Tyson, *Marcion and Luke-Acts: A Defining Struggle, JR* 87 (2007): 435–36.

86. Räisänen, "Marcion," 103; Aland, "Marcion," 90–91.

87. Knox, *Marcion*, 11–12; Tyson, *Marcion and Luke-Acts*, 31: "From Justin we learn that Marcion had had an extensive ministry in the East prior to 150 C.E., and from Polycarp we can conclude that his teachings were known in the East by 130 C.E. Indications from Ignatius and the Pastorals suggest even earlier dates. We probably will not be far off if we conclude that Marcion's views were known, at least in part and in some locations, as early as 115–120 C.E."

88. Tyson, *Marcion and Luke-Acts*, 26–49. Cf. Knox, *Marcion*, 10–12.

89. Though neither Knox nor Tyson is altogether unaware of the problems of ancient heresiological models. See Knox, *Marcion*, 4–8; Tyson, *Marcion and Luke-Acts*, 27–29.

90. *What Is Gnosticism?* (Cambridge: Harvard University Press, 2003), 24. King observes that Gnosticism as an intellectual category has both served to define the boundaries of normative Christianity in relation to Judaism and also aided colonialism, "by contrasting Gnosticism as an Oriental heresy with authentic Western religion" (*What Is Gnosticism*, 7). The oriental/barbaric nature of Marcion receives much play in Tertullian's derisive treatment of Pontus at *Marc.* 1.1.3–7.

91. Though our analytical categories are not identical, I am aware of the affinity between the argument here and the observations made by Walter Bauer long ago: "The reckless speed with which, from the very beginning, the doctrine and ideology of Marcion spread can only be explained if it had found the ground already prepared. Apparently a great number of the baptized, especially in the East, inclined toward this view of Christianity and joined Marcion without hesitation as soon as he appeared, finding in him the classic embodiment of their own belief. What had dwelt in their inner consciousness in a more or less undefined form until then, acquired through Marcion the definite form that satisfied head and heart. No one can call that a falling away from orthodoxy to heresy." See his, *Orthodoxy and Heresy in Earliest Christianity*

(ed. Robert A. Kraft and Gerhard Krodel; translated by a team from the Philadelphia Seminar on Christian Origins; Philadelphia: Fortress 1971), 194.

92. Knox, *Marcion*, 9–12; Tyson, *Marcion and Luke-Acts*, 30.

93. *Haer.* 3.3.4: "And Polycarp himself replied to Marcion, who met him on one occasion, and said, 'Do you know me?' 'I do know you, the first-born of Satan."

94. According to Tertullian, it is not the case that Marcion argued that there was no final judgment whatsoever but rather that the Father God himself did not judge, reserving that function for the lesser, Creator God (*Marc.* 1.26–28). Yet, opponents of marcionite thinking show concern that the certainty of divine judgment had been called into question. Polycarp's claim that some say "there is no judgment" and his derision of such a claim are understandable in a context in which marcionite assertions concerning the Father God's nature as solely merciful and compassionate are being tested.

95. The well-known marcionite dualism distinguishes the higher God, who is "mild and peaceable, solely kind and supremely good" (*mitem, placidum et tantummodo bonum atque optimum*), from the Old Testament God, who is the fierce and warlike judge (*iudicem, ferum, bellipotentem, laterum* [Tertullian, *Marc.* 1.6.1]). Some decades after Luke-Acts is redacted, Tertullian demonstrates his preoccupation with refuting the marcionite assertion that the supreme God does not judge: "a better god has been discovered, one who is neither offended nor angry nor inflicts punishment, who has no fire warming up in hell, and no outer darkness wherein there is shuddering and gnashing of teeth: he is merely kind" (*deus melior inventus est, qui nec offenditur nec irascitur nec ulciscitur, cui nullus ignis coquitur in gehenna, cui nullus dentium frendor horret in exterioribus tenebris: bonus tantum est; Marc.* 1.27.2 [Evans]).

96. Knox, *Marcion*, 87–88; Tyson, *Marcion and Luke-Acts*, 90–100. Even among those who do not link Luke 1 and 2 to an anti-marcionite agenda, the distinctive and possibly late nature of these chapters has been noted. Cf. Raymond Brown, *The Birth of the Messiah* (Garden City, N.Y.: Doubleday, 1977), 239–53; Joseph Fitzmyer, *Gospel According to Luke (I–IX)* (Anchor Bible; Garden City, N.Y.: Doubleday, 1979), 310–13; Conzelmann, *Theology of St. Luke*, 172; Gregory, *Reception of Luke*, 203.

97. Luke 1.31a: "you will conceive in your womb and bear a son" (συλλήμψη ἐν γαστρὶ καὶ τέξῃ υἱόν); Luke 1.41–42: "When Elizabeth heard Mary's greeting, the child leaped in her womb [ἐσκίρτησεν τὸ βρέφος ἐν τῇ κοιλίᾳ αὐτῆς]. And Elizabeth . . . exclaimed . . . 'Blessed are you among women and blessed is the fruit of your womb' [ὁ καρπὸς τῆς κοιλίας σου]."

98. Paul Winter, "Magnificat and Benedictus—Maccabean Psalms?" *BJRL* 37 (1954–55): 328–47, esp. 342–43.

99. Winter, "Magnificat and Benedictus."

100. Richard A. Horsley, *The Liberation of Christmas: The Infancy Narratives in Social Context* (New York: Crossroad, 1989), 107–23, 183–84. This affirmation is part of Horsley's effort to cast the nativity story as one of social and political liberation, rather than one focused on otherworldly and spiritual release.

101. Lloyd Gaston, *No Stone on Another: Studies in the Significance of the Fall of Jerusalem in the Synoptic Gospels* (SNT 23; Leiden: Brill, 1970), 256–57: "One main reason for assuming an earlier tradition contained in the [birth stories] is the fact that much of the proclamation seems to be addressed to Israel. An important aspect of this proclamation says that the coming of the Messiah to Israel means the offer of the peace of God to the people of the promise. After A.D. 70 such a proclamation would have seemed a bitter mockery, and the optimistic tone with which parts of the Lucan writings speak of peace as a real possibility is a sure sign of their early origin."

102. In addition to Luke 19.41–44, see also the distinctively Lukan components of the passage on the desolation of Jerusalem, at Luke 21.20–22: "When you see Jerusalem surrounded by armies, then know that its desolation has come near . . . for these are days of vengeance" (ἐκδικήσεως).

103. On the transfer in Acts of "*ho laos*" as a designation for Israel to a designation for those, including Gentiles, who accept Jesus as Messiah, see discussion in chap. 2, at pp. 67-68.

104. I disagree both with David Tiede (*Prophecy and History*, 65–96), who argues that Luke 19.41–44 is intramural polemic and thus not a vindictive assertion that the destruction of Jerusalem owes to rejection of Jesus, and with Joel Green (*The Gospel of Luke* [New International Commentary on the New Testament; Grand Rapids: Eerdmans, 1997], 690), who regards the peace spoken of in Luke 1.42 as having "no connection to harmony with the Roman Empire or with the temple leadership" while also insisting that this peace encompasses "social, material, and spiritual realities."

105. J. Massyngbaerde Ford, *My Enemy Is My Guest: Jesus and Violence in Luke* (Maryknoll, N.Y.: Orbis, 1984), 13–36.

106. Brittany E. Wilson, "Pugnacious Precursors and the Bearer of Peace: Jael, Judith, and Mary in Luke 1:42," *CBQ* 68 (2006): 436–56.

107. "Pugnacious Precursors," 448.

108. *My Enemy*, 36.

CHAPTER TWO

1. LSJ, s.v. φερωνυμία, the accordance of a name with an event; φερώνυμος, well named.

2. For Irenaeus' role in rescuing Acts from obscurity and granting it privileged place in his heresiology, see Mount, *Pauline Christianity*, 11–44.

3. While Eusebius repeats the detail of James' death by sword from Acts 12.2 several times in his church history (*Hist. eccl.* 2.1.5, 2.9.1, 2.9.4, 3.4.2), he preserves only one extrabiblical fragment, from Clement's *Hypotyposes*, that departs from Acts 12.2 by elaborating more specifically on the details of the apostle's martyrdom (*Hist. eccl.* 2.9.2–3).

4. I do not mean to suggest that the author of Acts must have had access to full-blown martyrologies for James the brother, Peter, and Paul, but I do presume that

his silence cannot be explained away as owing to complete ignorance about their fates. Traditions about their violent deaths were in circulation before the full-blown martyrologies developed.

5. For arguments on the integral role of suffering to Christian subjectivity see Perkins, *Suffering Self*; Castelli, *Martyrdom and Memory*; Berkowitz, *Execution and Invention*, 181–213.

6. To be sure, in two scenes from Paul's missionary journeys, opposition to followers of "the Way" comes from Gentiles rather than Jews (Acts 16.16–40, 19.23–41). On similarities between these stories and stories of Jewish opposition in Acts, see Wills, *Not God's People*, 200.

Among exceptions to the otherwise positive portrayals of Roman officials are the depictions of Felix and Festus, who both possess the unsavory characteristic of eagerness to accept bribes. As Wills notes (*Not God's People*, 202–4) rather than speaking of Acts' depiction of Roman characters as uniformly favorable, it is more precise to say that Acts depicts Roman characters *as a Roman historian would*, acknowledging the unfavorable reputation of these two Roman officials in Roman sources, while also inscribing favorable portraits of Roman characters that a Roman historian would regard favorably.

7. As Beth Berkowitz distills the difference between Jews and Christians in Acts with respect to Paul's conversion: "This paradigm shows conversion to Christ to be a conversion from persecutor to persecuted. Whereas the pre-conversion Saul *binds* 'all those who call upon your name' . . . (9.14), the post-conversion Paul *suffers* 'for my name'. . . (9.16); the Saul who was consenting to Stephen's execution (*anairesis*) becomes the one whom others want to execute (*anelein*, 9.23, 24, 29). What it means to join the Christian community is to shift from executioner to executed, from judge to judged, from jailer to imprisoned. This shift is not incidental to Saul's conversion but constitutive of it." Berkowitz, *Execution and Invention*, 191.

8. J. Roloff, "Die Paulus-Darstellung des Lukas. Ihre geschichtlichen Vorausetzungen und ihr theologisches Ziel," *EvT* 39 (1979): 510–31, esp. 522–24; Walaskay, '*And So We Came to Rome*,' 18–22.

9. For discussion concerning the relationship of the Acts of the Apostles to the Apocryphal Acts, see Richard Pervo, "A Hard Act to Follow: The Acts of Paul and the Canonical Acts," *JHC* 2, no. 2 (1995): 3–32; Dennis R. MacDonald, "Apocryphal and Canonical Narratives about Paul," in *Paul and the Legacies of Paul* (ed. William S. Babcock; Dallas: Southern Methodist University Press, 1990), 55–70; Stan Stowers, "Comment: What Does *Unpauline* Mean?" in *Paul and the Legacies of Paul* (ed. William S. Babcock; Dallas: Southern Methodist University Press, 1990), 70–77.

10. A summary of options for explaining the absence of a narrative of Paul's martyrdom in Acts is contained in Colin J. Hemer, *The Book of Acts in the Setting of Hellenistic History* (Winona Lake, Ind.: Eisenbrauns, 1990), 383–87.

11. Lukas Bormann's argument that after the Stephen narrative, there are no further deaths of Jesus followers reported in Acts is a technical error but not a substantive one. The martyrdom of the Apostle James is granted precisely one verse's worth of attention in the narrative of chap. 12, a narrative whose focus clearly lies

elsewhere. See "Die Verrechtlichung der früheste Christlichen Überlieferung im Lukanischen Schrifttum," in *Religious Propaganda and Missionary Competition in the New Testament World: Essays in Honoring Dieter Georgi* (ed. Lukas Bormann et al.; Leiden: Brill, 1994), 283–311, esp. 304.

12. See, e.g., Dixon Slingerland, "The Composition of Acts: Some Redaction-Critical Observations," *JAAR* 56 (1988): 99–113, esp. 103–4; Walton, "The State They Were In," 19.

13. Cf. Stephen G. Wilson, "The Jews and the Death of Jesus in Acts" in *Paul and the Gospels* (vol. 1 of *Anti-Judaism in Early Christianity*; ed. Peter Richardson with David Granskou; Studies in Christianity and Judaism 2; Waterloo, Ontario: Wilfrid Laurier University Press, 1986), 155–64; Weatherly, *Jewish Responsibility*, 50–98; Slingerland, "Composition of Acts." Slingerland also argues that the charge is mitigated by acknowledgment that the deed was done in ignorance. For more on this argument, see discussion of Stephen's martyrdom below.

14. See especially Wilson, "The Jews," and Weatherly, *Jewish Responsibility*.

15. The "Herod" in question is Agrippa I, who in Acts' broad-brush strokes is assimilated to the archetypal Herodian tyrant.

16. While my arguments concerning the depiction of *hoi Ioudaioi* in the Pauline portion of Acts converge with those of Slingerland ("The Jews"), we reach different conclusions in our readings of the first half of Acts. To support his thesis that the anti-Jewish slant of Acts owes to the secondary hand of a redactor, Slingerland argues that the passages mentioning Jewish culpability for Jesus' death in chap. 1–13 "are intended either to excuse all together or to mitigate Jewish responsibility for Jesus' crucifixion" ("Composition of Acts," 103). Rather than reading the first half of Acts as limiting Jewish murderousness, and the second half as underscoring it, I see numerous threads running throughout the book of Acts connecting the depictions of murderous Jews in chap. 1–13 and 14–28. Furthermore, Slingerland's argument that the anti-Jewish material in the Stephen episode owes to a heavy-handed redactor of Acts ("The Jews," 107–10) overlooks the many ways in which the Stephen narrative, in its entirety, is connected to broader themes both within Acts and within the larger design of Luke-Acts as a two-volume work.

I note further that the desire for the deaths of Jesus, the apostles, Stephen, James, Peter, *and* Paul leads me to disagree with Brawley's argument that the hostility toward Paul in 13–28 reflects Acts' concern to depict Jews as narrowly anti-Pauline rather than widely anti-Jesus believer. See Brawley, *Luke-Acts and the Jews*, 68–83.

17. See Martin Dibelius, "The Speeches in Acts and Ancient Historiography," in *Studies in the Acts of the Apostles* (London: SCM, 1956), 138–85, esp. 158; Haenchen, *Acts*, 597. Consider also the recent study of how Paul's Miletus speech aligns with the farewell discourse of Jesus preserved in Luke's version of the Last Supper: Steve Walton, *Leadership and Lifestyle: The Portrait of Paul in the Miletus Speech and I Thessalonians* (SNTSMS 108; Cambridge: Cambridge University Press, 2000), 99–117.

18. For example, Wilhelm Schneemelcher, ed. and trans., "The Acts of Peter," in *Writings Related to the Apostles: Apocalypses and Related Subjects* (vol. 2 of *New Testament Apocrypha*; ed. Edgar Hennecke et al.), 259–322, esp. 317–18; *Mart. Pol.* 5. On concurrent

debates within early Christian and Jewish martyrdom discourse concerning the propriety of fleeing from death, framed as the opposing perspectives of the martyr and the trickster, see Boyarin, *Dying for God*, 42–66.

19. Marguerat, *First Christian Historian*, 206–26. For further arguments that the ending of Acts is coherent with the narrative method of the two-volume work as a whole, see Loveday Alexander, "Reading Luke-Acts from Back to Front," in *Acts in Its Ancient Literary Context*, 207–29; David Moessner, "'Completed End[s]ings' of Historiographical Narrative: Diodorus Siculus and the End[ing] of Acts," in *Apostelges-chichte und die hellenistische Geschichtsschreibung: Festschrift für Eckhard Plümacher zu seinem 65. Geburtstag* (ed. Ciliers Breytenbach et al.; AGJU 57; Leiden: Brill, 2004), 193–221.

20. For a contemporary scholar's reconstruction of Paul's death, which argues that Jews bear primary responsibility for it and reaches this conclusion by extrapolat-ing from the previous narrative of Jewish murderous desire, see Tajra, *Martyrdom of St. Paul*, 83–84, cited in my Introduction, p. 143, n. 28.

21. Josephus, *Life* 141 is often cited as expressing a parallel sentiment concerning willingness to die, should death be deserved, but in this context as well, a martyrdom is not in question.

22. Consider the case of Cyprian, and the discussion of Boyarin, *Dying for God*, 59–60.

23. Dibelius, "Speeches," 158.

24. For treatment of *pronoia* in Acts, see Squires, *Plan of God*.

See also Peter J. Tomson, "Gamaliel's Counsel and the Apologetic Strategy of Luke-Acts" in *The Unity of Luke-Acts* (ed. J. Verheyden; BETL 142; Leuven: Leuven University Press, 1999), 585–604, esp. 600–603.

25. As with Gamaliel's speech in Acts 5, Josephus in his speech bolsters his argument concerning God-fighting by citing historical precedent. See *J.W.* 5.379–412.

26. Recent discussion of Gamaliel's speech has focused on the question of character development—do these words convey an ironic or irenic expression of Gamaliel's own view of the apostles. See, for example, Tomson, "Gamaliel's Counsel," 585–604.

The Pseudo-Clementine *Recognitions* 1.27–71, a document that depends on Acts and which will be treated at greater length in the next chapter, opts for a sympathetic Gamaliel, prefacing his speech on *pronoia* with the assertion that he is a crypto-Chris-tian—a secret "brother in the faith" (*Rec.* 1.65.2).

27. The two other references to Judas: *J.W.* 2.117–18; *Ant.* 18.4–10. For historical reconstruction of Judas, see James McLaren, "Constructing Judaean History in the Diaspora: Josephus's Accounts of Judas," in *Negotiating Diaspora* (ed. John Barclay; London: T&T Clark, 2004), 90–108.

28. This dependence has been recently argued by Mason, *Josephus and the New Testament*, 185–229; and Pervo, *Dating Acts*, 149–60. For earlier arguments, see Alfred Loisy, *Les Actes des apôtres* (Paris: E. Nourry, 1920), 286–91; and Haenchen, *Acts*, 254–58. Note also that Heinz Schreckenberg, whose overall view of Lukan dependency on Josephus is resoundingly negative, hedges his bets with respect to Theudas and

Judas, conceding that Acts' use of Josephus as a source here cannot be entirely ruled out. See his "Flavius Josephus und die Lukanischen Schriften," in *Wort in der Zeit: Neutestamentliche Studien. Festgabe für Karl Heinrich Rengstorf zum 75. Geburtstag* (ed. Wilfrid Haubeck and Michael Bachmann; Leiden: Brill, 1980), 179–209, esp. 198.

29. Attempts of Josephan scholars to identify instances in which this author gives backhanded or slanted criticism of Rome include Tessa Rajak's "Friends, Romans, Subjects: Agrippa II's Speech in Josephus's *Jewish War*" in *Images of Empire* (ed. Loveday Alexander; JSOTSup 122; Sheffield: Sheffield University Press, 1991), 122–34; John Barclay's "The Empire Writes Back: Josephan Rhetoric in Flavian Rome," in *Flavius Josephus and Flavian Rome* (ed. J. Edmondson et al.; Oxford: Oxford University Press, 2005), 315–32; James McClaren, "Josephus on Titus: The Vanquished Writing about the Victor," in *Josephus and Jewish History in Flavian Rome and Beyond* (ed. Joseph Sievers and Gaia Lembi; JSJSup 104; Leiden: Brill, 2005), 279–96.

30. This distinguishes Acts from even the Third Gospel, where Pilate's act of shedding the blood of Galileans is mentioned (Luke 13.1).

31. Acts' diminishment of the widows' agency here aligns with the treatment of widows in the Pastorals, see Pervo, *Dating Acts*, 219–20. It also conforms to the approbation of Martha for engaging in service or "ministry" in Luke 10.38–42. See Elisabeth Schüssler Fiorenza, "A Feminist Critical Interpretation for Liberation: Martha and Mary: Luke 10:38–42," in *Religion and Intellectual Life* 3, no. 2 (1986): 21–36; Barbara Reid, "The Power of the Widows and How to Suppress It (Acts 6.1–7)," in *A Feminist Companion to the Acts of the Apostles* (ed. Amy-Jill Levine; FCNTECW 9; London: T&T Clark, 2004), 71–88.

32. Luke Timothy Johnson notes that the apparent discrepancy between the assigned role of the Seven to table service, and their actual function as prophets, may be ameliorated by recognition of the Lukan tendency to associate authority over material possessions with spiritual authority proper. See *The Acts of the Apostles* (SP 5; Collegeville, Minn.: Liturgical Press, 1992), 106.

33. The designation "Hebrews" in Acts appears only in this pericope. For use of term "Hellenist" in Acts, see my Introduction, pp. 11–12.

34. Nikolaos Walter, "Proselyt aus Antiochen, und die Nikolaiten in Ephesos und Pergamon: Ein Beitrag auch zum Thema: Paulus und Ephesos," *ZNW* 93 (2002): 200–206.

35. Pervo, *Dating Acts*, 155.

36. The grammar and syntax of 6.9 are puzzles—There may be only one, or as many as five, synagogues being invoked here. Cf. Haenchen, *Acts*, 271, for the argument that there are two groups in view; Conzelmann, *Acts*, 47, for the argument that Acts is depicting one synagogue with a varying makeup. See most recently, Pervo, *Dating Acts*, 166–67.

37. For discussion of these variant readings, see Bruce Metzger, *A Textual Commentary on the Greek New Testament* (Stuttgart: Biblia-Druck GmbH, 1975), 339–40.

38. For the structural relationship of the Stephen episode to these four branches of mission, I follow Gregory E. Sterling, "'Opening the Scriptures': The Legitimation of the Jewish Diaspora and the Early Christian Mission," in *Jesus and the Heritage of Israel: Luke's Narrative Claim upon Israel's Legacy* (ed. David P. Moessner; Harrisburg, Pa.: Trinity, 1999), 199–217.

39. To be sure, individual Jews, or even—as at 21.20—a group of Jews, may be exempt from the vilifying connotation of the term *Ioudaios/oi*, provided that they are Jesus believers.

40. Augustin George, "Israël dans l'œuvre de Luc," *RB* 75 (1968): 481–525. Others who have noted this shift in the use of *hoi Ioudaioi* after Stephen's martyrdom include Sanders, *Jews in Luke-Acts*, 71–72; Joachim Gnilka, *Die Verstockung Israels: Isaias 6,9–10 in der Theologie der Synoptiker* (Munich: Kösel, 1961), 145–46; and Gerhard Lohfink, *Die Sammlung Israels: Eine Untersuchung zur lukanischen Ekklesiologie* (Munich: Kösel, 1975), 57–59. Note the use of *ho laos* for a Gentile people at 15.14 and the phrase "my people" related specifically to followers of Jesus, rather than Jews, at 18.10.

41. For the inaugurative function of hate speech, see Judith Butler, *Excitable Speech: A Politics of the Performative* (London: Routledge, 1997), 1–41. While they do not employ theories of subjectivity as Butler does, Acts scholars have also spoken of Jews "becoming" Jews in the Acts narrative. Consider Conzelmann's oft-quoted assessment on Acts 13.46: "We can say that the Jews are now called to make good their claim to be 'Israel.' If they fail to do this, then they become 'the Jews.'" (*Theology of St. Luke*, 145); and Sanders: "By the end of the Acts the Jews have *become* what they from the first *were*; for what Jesus, Stephen, Peter and Paul say about the Jews—about their intransigent opposition to the purposes of God, about their hostility toward Jesus and the gospel, about their murder of Jesus—is what Luke understands the Jewish people to be in their essence. The narrative shows how existence comes to conform with essence, the process by which the Jewish people become the Jews . . ." (*Jews in Luke-Acts*, 81).

42. LXX: "when you bring my people out of Egypt, you shall worship God on this mountain."

43. Penner, *Praise*, 309.

44. Pervo notes (*Dating Acts*, 182) that rather than using technically precise language that would mark Joseph as *one of the twelve patriarchs* persecuted by *the other eleven*, Acts uses the broad-brush stroke—*the patriarchs*, out of jealousy, sold Joseph into slavery (οἱ πατριάρχαι ζηλώσαντες τὸν Ἰωσὴφ ἀπέδοντο εἰς Αἴγυπτον; Acts 7.9), thus distinguishing the hero in the story from the official leadership.

45. The notion of Jesus as the predicted "prophet like Moses" is also key in the recitation of history preserved in the Pseudo-Clementine *Recognitions* 1.27–71.

46. Comparable critiques of the temple are found in *Barn.* 16.1–2 and in the Pseudo-Clementine *Recognitions* 1.27–71.

47. Baur, *Paul the Apostle* 47–48. Cf. also Lightfoot's hailing of Stephen as the first "to sound the death-knell of Mosaic ordinances and the temple worship, and to claim for the Gospel unfettered liberty and universal rights" ("St. Paul and the Three," 297–98).

48. Baur, *Paul the Apostle*, 57–58.

49. For scholarship situating Baur's exegesis of this pericope within the frame of German idealism, see Penner, *Praise*, 8–14; and, more broadly Kelley, *Racializing Jesus*, 66–80.

50. Those who argue for either the softening or the erasure of Stephen's temple critique include Dennis Sylva, "The Meaning and Function of Acts 7.46–50," *JBL* 106 (1987): 261–75; J. J. Kilgallen, "The Function of Stephen's Speech (Acts, 2–53)," *Bib* 70 (1989): 177–81; Hill, *Hellenists and Hebrews*, 69–90; Edvin Larsson, "Temple-Criticism and the Jewish Heritage: Some Reflections on Acts 6–7," *NTS* 39 (1993): 379–95.

Todd Penner (*Praise*, 308–18) distinguishes between Stephen's temple speech, which he views as radically temple-critical, and what he regards as Luke's more positive overarching view of the temple, by arguing that, according to the rules of rhetoric guiding speech-in-character, Stephen's speech need not align with Luke's own temple perspective. I agree with his reading of Stephen's speech but not with his view of Luke's perspective on the temple, on which, see below.

51. Compare also Paul's denigration of temples built with human hands from the Athenian Areopagus, at 17.24.

52. Pervo, *Dating Acts*, 189.

53. One might consider Stephen's temple critique, for instance, within debates of the Second Sophistic concerning superstition and true piety. See chap. 3 of Laura Nasrallah, *Christian Responses to Roman Art and Architecture: The Second-Century Church amid the Spaces of Empire* (New York: Cambridge University Press, 2010).

54. See the discussion of the temple in Acts, chap. 1, p. 35.

55. See Acts 18.24–28 and discussion in Introduction, p. 7.

56. Odil Hannes Steck, *Israel und das gewaltsame Geschick der Propheten: Untersuchungen zur Überlieferung des deuteronomistischen Geschichtsbildes im Alten Testament, Spätjudentum und urchristentum* (WMANT 23; Neukirchen-Vluyn: Neukirchener Verlag, 1967).

57. Melanie Johnson-DeBaufre, "The Blood Required of This Generation: Interpreting Communal Blame in a Colonial Context," in *Violence in the New Testament* (ed. E. Leigh Gibson and Shelly Matthews; London: T&T Clark, 2005), 22–34.

58. Cf. 2 Chron. 36.15–23.

59. See chap. 4 for further discussion of resonance between Zechariah and Stephen.

60. Johnson-DeBaufre, "Blood Required," 30.

61. Shelly Matthews, "Ethical Issues in Reconstructing Intrareligious Violence in Antiquity: The Gospel of Matthew as a Test Case," in *Walk in the Ways of Wisdom: Essays in Honor of Elisabeth Schüssler Fiorenza* (ed. Shelly Matthews et al.; Harrisburg, Pa.: Trinity, 2003), 334–50, esp. 345–48.

62. For more on the significance of requiting Zechariah's death, in view of Stephen's dying forgiveness prayer, see chap. 4, pp. 108–09.

63. Dale Allison, *The Intertextual Jesus: Scriptures in Q* (Harrisburg, Pa.: Trinity, 2000), 84–87, 149–52. See Sheldon H. Blank, "The Death of Zechariah in Rabbinic

Literature," *HUCA* 13 (1938): 327–46, esp. 331, for the argument that the Zechariah in question is this son of Jehoiada. Both Allison and Blank suggest that the highlighting of Abel and Zechariah may reflect a scriptural corpus that ends with Chronicles, such that Abel and Zechariah are the first and last martyrs of this corpus.

64. Alison, *Intertextual Jesus*, 145.

65. Stoning is commonly associated with narratives of prophet prosecution. Twice in the Torah, Moses is threatened with stoning (Exod. 17.4; Num. 14.9–10). Josephus includes both of these references and adds another in his account of Moses' trials (*Ant.* 2.327, 3.12, 3.307; cf. also *Ant.* 4.12). For extrabiblical traditions that Abel was also stoned, see Allison, *Intertextual Jesus*, 85–86.

66. For general discussion of the links between Jesus, Stephen, and Paul, with bibliography, see Hill, *Hellenists and Hebrews*, 59; Earl Richard, *Acts 6:1–8:4: The Author's Method of Composition* (SBLDS 41; Missoula, Mont.: Scholars Press, 1978), 281; Moessner, "Christ Must Suffer"; Pervo, *Dating Acts*, 168.

67. I argue in chap. 4 that Jesus' dying prayer for forgiveness of tormentors (Luke 23.34a) is originally Lukan and serves as the type for Stephen's forgiveness prayer at Acts 7.60.

68. On the significance of this speech for illuminating Acts' temple ideology, see Holmås, "My House," 404–5.

69. Squires, *Plan of God*.

70. On the conflicting import of passages related to ignorance in Luke-Acts, see Conzelmann, *Theology of St. Luke*, 89–93. For further discussion of the forgiveness prayer, its function in Luke Acts, and the significance of the ignorance excuse, see my chap. 4, p. 102.

71. Charles H. Talbert, "Martyrdom in Luke-Acts and the Lukan Social Ethic," in *Political Issues in Luke-Acts* (ed. Richard J. Cassidy and P. J. Scharper; Maryknoll, N.Y.: Orbis, 1983), 99–110, esp. 102.

72. On the link between killing "without ignorance" and the unforgivable sin against the Holy Spirit (Luke 12.10–12), see chap. 4, p. 103.

73. Acts minimizes Roman involvement in Jesus' death narrative even more than the Third Gospel, see above, pp. 58–60.

74. Erika Heusler, *Kapitalprozesse im lukanischen Doppelwerk: Die Verfahren gegen Jesus und Paulus in exegetischer und rechtshistorischer Analyse* (NTAbh 2/38; Münster: Aschendorff, 2000), 2–5.

75. On the perspective of "imperial sociology," cf. Acts 13.44–50, 14.1–6, 14.19, 17.5–6, 18.12–17, 21.17–31, 23.2–21, 23.10; and Wills, "Depiction of Jews," who coins the phrase. Wills notes that this perspective on mob violence coalesces in the works of elite authors of the imperial period—e.g., Tacitus, Sallust, and Josephus—but is not pronounced in earlier Greek and Latin literature. Compare also the arguments concerning Jewish propensity for rioting in Ephesos, in Stoops, "Riot and Assembly."

For a contemporary sociologist's reflection on how the dominant class perceives gatherings of the lower classes that converges with Will's assessment, see James C. Scott, *Domination and the Arts of Resistance: Hidden Transcripts* (New Haven, Conn.: Yale University Press, 1990), 58–66. Contrast the argument by Moyer V. Hubbard,

"Urban Uprisings in the Roman World: The Social Setting of the Mobbing of Sosthenes," *NTS* 51 (2005): 416–28, which uncritically accepts the perspective of elite
authors as accurately reflecting social reality when they depict the masses as prone to
riot.

76. Haenchen, *Acts*, 295–96, emphasis added.

77. Contrast Jewish sources, in which stoning is understood as an ideal way
to signal corporate retribution and is prescribed for crimes perceived as offenses
against the entire community. Consider also Plato's *Laws* 9.873b, where he
suggests that the (already dead) criminal should be stoned by representatives
on behalf of the city so that atonement be made for the whole city. For further
sources, see Shelly Matthews, "The Need for the Stoning of Stephen," in
Violence in the New Testament (ed. Shelly Matthews and E. Leigh Gibson;
London: T&T Clark, 2004), 132–33.

78. Theodor Mommsen, *Römisches Strafrecht* (Leipzig: Duncker & Humblot,
1899).

79. Cf. Livy, 4.50.4–9; Horace, *Epod.* 5.99; Suetonius, *Cal.* 5.

80. See Nestle-Aland, *Novum Testamentum Graece*, 27th ed., for manuscripts
preserving the reading "πρωτομάρτυρος." On symbolic import of Stephen as
proto-martyr, see also Klaus Haacker, "Die Stellung des Stephanus in der Geschichte
des Urchristentums," *ANRW* 26.2:1515–53, esp. 1516.

G. W. Bowersock downplays the significance of early traditions granting Stephen
the role of proto-martyr, by noting that the tradition of "first martyr" was a fluid one in
earliest centuries and suggesting that the need for a first martyr is part of post-Con-
stantinian theology. See his *Martyrdom and Rome* (Cambridge: Cambridge University
Press, 1995), 75–76. This may be so *across early Christian literature*, but this should not
detract from the observation that constructing a "first martyr" is crucial to the narrative
method of Acts.

CHAPTER THREE

1. See Introduction, pp. 16–20. To argue that the two-volume work possesses
a relatively strong coherence is not to say that it is devoid of ambiguity (see chap. 1,
pp. 27–28) or that there are no argumentative shifts from vol. 1 to vol. 2 (see chap. 1,
pp. 40–41).

2. This, in spite of an increasingly widespread acknowledgment that it is
wrong to frame the Stephen event as indicative of a rift between Hellenists and
Hebrews over matters of temple and torah. In addition to sources cited in Introduction (p. 143, n. 32), consider the most recent argument of Richard Bauckham, "James
and the Jerusalem Community," in *Jewish Believers in Jesus: The Early Centuries* (ed.
Oskar Skarsaune and Reidar Hvalvik; Peabody, Mass.: Hendrickson, 2007), 55–95.
While Bauckham challenges traditional readings of the pericope that stress
Stephen's place within a "Hellenist–Hebrew" divide (63–65), in the end, he holds to
a remarkably positivistic view of what can be known of the historical Stephen from
the Acts narrative (92).

3. Because Peter, Paul, and Mary Magdalene are present within a number of early sources, their historical existence is generally assumed. Whether Thecla narratives, which appear first in second-century literature, arise from memories of a historical Thecla within the Pauline orbit is less certain.

4. On the importance of a social center for organizing historical narrative, see my Introduction, p. 21.

5. Though the precise contours of my argument differ from his, I acknowledge that it is in line with that of Hans Joachim Schoeps, a remarkable figure in Biblical scholarship from the early twentieth century, who proposed that Stephen was a fictional character created by Luke and who argued for close textual relationship between the speech of Stephen in Acts and of Peter in the Pseudo-Clementine *Recognitions* 1.45.1–1.65. See Schoeps, *Theologie und Geschichte*, esp. 441–44. Schoeps, a Jewish native of Germany, published a work on Jewish Christianity in 1937, soon banned in Germany as a dangerous book. Its second edition, published in 1949, includes dedications to his father, murdered in Theresienstadt (1942), and mother, murdered in Auschwitz (1944).

6. It is difficult to ascertain whether the final sentence belongs to Hegesippus or Eusebius. For more on the tradition linking the Jerusalem siege to the martyrdom of James, see John Painter, *Just James: The Brother of Jesus in History and Tradition* (Columbia: University of South Carolina Press, 1997; repr., Minneapolis: Fortress, 1999), 143–47.

7. For Eusebius as faithful preserver of Hegesippus, with extensive bibliography on the history of interpretation, see F. Stanley Jones, "The Martyrdom of James in Hegesippus, Clement of Alexandria, and Christian Apocrypha, Including nag Hammadi: A Study of the Textual Relations," *SBL Seminar Papers, 1990* (SBLSP 29; Atlanta: Scholars Press, 1990), 322–35, esp. 323–27. Wilhelm Pratscher argues only for minor interpolations of Eusebius into Hegesippus' text. See *Der Herrenbruder Jakobus und die Jakobustradition* (FRLANT 139; Göttingen: Vandenhoeck & Ruprecht, 1987), 104–6.

For further arguments on questions of dating, Hegesippus' ethnicity, and the heresiological slant of the *Hypomnemata*, see F. Stanley Jones, "Hegesippus as a Source for the History of Jewish Christianity," in *Le judéo-christianisme dans tous ses états: Actes du collogque de Jérusalem 6–10 Juillet 1998* (ed. Simon C. Mimouni and F. Stanley Jones; Paris: Cerf, 2001), 201–12; Pratscher, *Der Herrenbruder Jakobus*, 103–9.

8. Verbal allusions to the Gospels include James' cry concerning the Son of Man (cf. *Hist. eccl.* 2.23.13 with Mark 14.62; Matt. 26.64) and the dying forgiveness prayer. For more on James and *imitatio Christi*, cf. Pratscher, *Der Herrenbruder Jakobus*, 118–19. Some insist that the parallels between James and Stephen's martyrdom demonstrate that Hegesippus knows Acts 7, but there is no direct and obvious textual overlap.

9. For competing views on the source-critical questions related to the multiple early Christian versions of James' death, see Jones, "Hegesippus as a Source"; Pratscher, *Der Herrenbruder Jakobus*, 231–59; Richard Bauckham, "For What Offence Was James Put to Death?" in *James the Just and Christian Origins* (ed. B. Chilton and C. A. Evans; NovTSup 98; Leiden: Brill, 1999), 199–232, esp. 201–6; Painter, *Just James*, 121–22, 130–31, 179–81; Karlman Beyschlag, "Das Jakobusmartyrium und seine

Verwandten in der frühchristlichen Literatur," *ZNW* 56 (1965): 149–78; Gerd
Lüdemann, *Opposition to Paul in Jewish Christianity* (trans. M. Eugene Boring;
Minneapolis: Fortress, 1989), 155–85.

10. F. Stanley Jones, "Hegesippus as a Source," 208–11. Jones' argument that
Hegesippus works from oral report here is consistent with his earlier argument that
Hegesippus' account of the death of James is the written source from which all other
accounts draw. See Jones, "Martyrdom of James."

11. Pratscher, *Der Herrenbruder Jakobus*, 106.

12. Bauckham, "For What Offence," 206–18. Compare the similarly careful
analysis of exegetical methods undergirding the Epistle of Jude, in Richard
Bauckham, *Jude and the Relatives of Jesus in the Early Church* (London: T&T Clark,
2004), 179–234.

13. This storytelling method is also present in Greek sources, e.g., in the move
from metaphorical association between Pindar's song and bees to the legend that a bee
once built a honeycomb in Pindar's mouth. See M. R. Lefkowitz, *The Lives of the Greek
Poets* (London: Duckworth, 1981), 59, 155–56.

14. Bauckham, "For What Offense," 211–12.

15. Where the Greek text grants James special entrance into the *sanctuary* (τὰ ἅγια;
Hist. eccl. 2.23.6), both the Latin and the Syriac versions read "Holy of Holies." For
discussion, see Bauckham, "For What Offence," 215; Jones, "Martyrdom of James," 327.

16. On the common function of τὸ πτερύγιον in the temptation of Jesus stories
and the martyrdom of James, see Yaron Z. Eliav, "The Tomb of James, Brother of
Jesus, as *Locus Memoriae*," *HTR* 97 (2004): 33–59, esp. 50–51.

17. Bauckham, "For What Offense," 214–16.

18. On the passion narratives as prophecy historicized, see John Dominic
Crossan, *The Historical Jesus: The Life of a Mediterranean Jewish Peasant* (San Francisco:
HarperSanFrancisco, 1991), 367–91.

19. Beyschlag, "Das Jakobusmartyrium," 154–75, esp. 161. Beyschlag suggests
that both the Stephen pericope and the accounts of Paul's near martyrdoms in Acts
owe to Acts' dependence upon an *Ur*-martyrdom of James. The argument for such a
direction of dependency is compelling, as it is easier to imagine the Greek-speaking,
Hellenist-associated *Stephanos* as derivative of an earlier story in which the first martyr
is the Jerusalem-centered brother of Jesus than to posit dependency in the opposite
direction. Imagining such a direction of dependency is more plausible for those who
date Acts' composition to the second century.

20. See Introduction, p. 140, n. 8, for the typologies of martyrdom suggested by
van Henten and Boyarin.

21. For verbal and thematic links between the Stephen story and Zechariah
traditions, see chap. 2. Hegesippus' James is also like the legendary Zechariah, in that
he is linked to the temple and priesthood and dies on the temple grounds by stoning.
In the broader James tradition, James and Zechariah are also linked. Cf. *Protoevan-
gelium of James*, 23–24, which narrates the death of Zechariah and the congealing of
his blood into stone. In later pilgrimage traditions, the Temple Mount is a site
associated with both James and Zechariah. See Eliav, "Tomb of James," 54–55.

22. The employment of the terms *martyreo/martyria/martyrion* also suggests the interstitial location of these two texts. The terms are not employed exclusively for the evangelical confession that is sealed by death, as they will be in later Christian literature. The use of these terms still has some fluidity for Hegesippus and Acts, serving also to designate witnesses who proffer false testimony against Stephen (Acts 6.13) and the good reports others might offer on behalf of Paul and James (Acts 22.5; *Hist. eccl.* 2.23.10). Nevertheless, the notion that evangelical witness concerning Jesus leads to death is clearly expressed in both texts. Cf. the reference to the shedding of the blood of the martyr Stephen in Acts 22.20 and the links between James' testimony and his death in *Hist. eccl.* 2.23.14, 2.23.18.

23. As Beyschlag observes, the testimony on the temple steps is a common feature in Acts, Hegesippus, and the Pseudo-Clementines, though in Acts, this particular feature is associated with Paul, rather than Stephen. Cf. "Das Jakobusmartyrium," 158–60.

24. Mutual dependence upon the synoptic accounts of the trial of Jesus seems the best explanation for this common structure. Hegesippus follows more closely synoptic structure and terminology. Cf. *Hist. eccl.* 2.23.13–14 with the Gospel of Mark 14.62–64.

25. That in both instances the stoning is undertaken by riotous mobs calls into question Richard Bauckham's historicist arguments that because the deaths come by stoning and stoning is the Levitical punishment for blasphemy (Lev. 24.16), both Stephen and James must have been formally charged with committing blasphemy. See "For What Offence," 218–32; and "James and the Jerusalem Community," 64, 76. On the difficulties in accounting for first-century incidents of stoning with references to prescriptions in the Torah, see James McLaren, "Ananus, James, and Earliest Christianity: Josephus' Account of the Death of James," *JTS* 52 (2001): 1–25, esp. 16–17.

Pace Bauckham, who reads narratives of stoning in the Second Temple period as indications that the victims of such attacks are perceived to have violated specific provisions in the Torah punishable by stones; I read them as a means by which the authors of these accounts attempt to demonize the perpetrators as savage/lawless. See chap. 2 and also Matthews, "Need for the Stoning of Stephen," 130–33.

26. The question, τί ποιεῖτε, also draws attention to (and perhaps calls into question?) the explanatory clause in James' prayer, "forgive them, *for they know not what they do.*" Cf. Beyschlag, "Das Jakobusmartyrium," 152–53.

27. See Introduction, p. 7.

28. Hegesippus' rhetorical strategy perfectly illustrates Daniel Boyarin's observation that early Christianity's self-definition over and against Judaism is closely linked to its self-definition over and against heresy. See *Borderlines*, 1–17, and also the Pseudo-Clementine *Recognitions* 1.54–65.

29. See Alain Le Boulluec, *La notion d'hérésie dans la littérature grecque IIe-IIIe siècles* (2 vols.; Paris: Études Augustiniennes, 1985), 1: 95–100, esp. 96; for consideration of others employing the category of the Ten Tribes, see Burton L. Visotzky (*Fathers of the World: Essays in Rabbinic and Patristic Literatures* [Tübingen: Mohr, 1995],

146–49), who argues that references in rabbinic literature to the Ten Tribes might refer to "law-observant Jewish-Christian converts from Judaism."

30. *Hist. eccl.* 3.32.3–6, 3.20.1; see also 3.19, for the sects as persecutors of Simon and Jude.

31. Hegesippus himself appears responsible for introducing the "sects" into the narrative of the martyrdom of James (cf. *Hist. eccl.* 2.23.8: τινὲς οὖν τῶν ἑπτὰ αἱρέσεων τῶν ἐν τῷ λαῷ, τῶν προγεγραμμένων μοι [ἐν τοῖς Ὑπομνήμασιν], ἐπυνθάνοντο αὐτοῦ).

32. See chap. 2, pp. 67–68.

33. F. Stanley Jones, in keeping with his understanding that Hegesippus is the source of all other Christian traditions of the martyrdom of James, dates *Rec.* 1.27–71 to around 200 CE. See *An Ancient Jewish Christian Source on the History of Christianity: Pseudo-Clementine Recognitions 1.27–71* (SBLTT 37; Christian Apocrypha Series 2; Atlanta: Scholars Press, 1995), 157–68. Graham Stanton, pointing to similarities between *Rec.* 1.27–71 and Justin's *Trypho*, suggests a mid-second-century date. Cf. "Jewish Christian Elements in the Pseudo-Clementine Writings," in *Jewish Believers in Jesus: The Early Centuries* (ed. Oskar Skarsaune and Reidar Hvalvik; Peabody, Mass.: Hendrickson, 2007), 305–24. Further agreement holds that *Rec.* 1.44–52 is an interpolation of a later redactor (Jones, *Ancient Jewish Christian Source*, 135–36). On the Pseudo-Clementine literature, see Nicole Kelley, *Knowledge and Religious Authority in the Pseudo-Clementines: Situating the Recognitions in Fourth Century Syria* (WUNT 2/213; Tübingen: Mohr, 2006); Reed, "Jewish Christianity."

While my focus here is on affinities between this document and Acts, it is also the case that *Rec.* 1.27–71 has a close relationship to the Hegesippus' James narrative. For various views on the relationship of these two texts, see p. 172, n. 9.

34. Jones suggests that the original version of the story contains a murder of James by Paul that is emended by a redactor, in order to keep James alive so that he may continue to serve as the protagonist in the larger narrative of the basic source. *Ancient Jewish Christian Source*, 152.

35. As F. Stanley Jones has argued, the narrative demonstrates dependence upon the Book of Jubilees, for instance, in asserting that the sons of Noah receive their divisions of the world by lot or that Hebrew was the universal language before the confusion of tongues at Babel. *Ancient Jewish Christian Source*, 138–40. This is part of Jones' larger argument that *Rec.* 1.27–71 knows of and depends upon Stephen's recitation of history, but also in the spirit of competitive historiography, adapts and improves upon it.

36. All these features lead F. Stanley Jones to argue that *Rec.* 1.65.2–7 uses Acts as a source. See *Ancient Jewish Christian Source*.

37. Here, e.g., is F. Stanley Jones' translation of the Syriac version of Moses' reaction to the sin of the golden calf: "Evils had been added to them from the strong habits from the extended period in Egypt. . . . Because of this, even Moses, as he came down from Mount Sinai and saw the crime, understood, as a good and faithful steward, that it was not possible for the people easily to cease and stop all of the desire of the love of idolatry, in which thing, which had been added to it [*sic* the people] from

the evil upbringing, with the Egyptians, there had been the great length of time" (1.35.6–1.36.1).

38. "Lebbaeus began strongly to convict the people for why they would not believe Jesus, who had been so helpful to them by teaching the matters of God, by comforting the afflicted, by healing the sick, and by consoling the poor, but rather, for all these good things, they had paid him back with hate and death" (1.59.7; Latin version [Jones]).

39. Cf. Acts 3.22–23; *Rec.* 1.36.2; and the discussion of F. Stanley Jones, "An Ancient Jewish Christian Rejoinder to Luke's Acts of the Apostles: Pseudo-Clementine *Recognitions* 1.27–71," *Semeia* 80 (1997): 223–45, esp. 226–27.

40. *Post quem Barnabas . . . qui in locum Iudae subrogatus est apostolus, monere populum coepit, ne odio haberent Iesum neque blasphemarent eum. multo enim esse rectius, etiam ignoranti vel dubitanti de Iesu, amare eum quam odisse. caritati enim deus praemium posuit, odiis poenam.*

41. Acts 7.58–8.1: "Then they dragged [Stephen] out of the city and began to stone him; and the witnesses laid their coats at the feet of a young man named Saul. . . . And Saul approved of their killing him."

42. Because of the difficulty in establishing the original wording of Josephus' remarks concerning Jesus, I withhold the so-called *Testimonium Flavianum* from this discussion. I note here briefly, however, that if J. P. Meier is correct in the reconstruction he proposes, then Josephus' neutral-to-favorable assessment of Jesus is in line with his assessment of John the Baptist and James. Meier's reconstruction of *Ant.* 18.63–64 in "Jesus in Josephus: A Modest Proposal," *CBQ* 52 (1990): 76–103: "At this time there appeared Jesus, a wise man. For he was a doer of amazing deeds, a teacher of persons who receive truth with pleasure. He won over many Jews and many of the Greeks. And when Pilate condemned him to the cross—the leading men among us having accused him—those who loved him from the first did not cease to do so. And to the present the tribe of Christians, named after this person, has not disappeared."

43. This ascription of Herod's defeat as owing to divine vengeance may have influenced the (confused) reports in Origen (*Cels.* 1.47) and Eusebius (*Hist. eccl.* 2.23) that Josephus *himself* attributes the suffering that Jews endured during the war against the Romans to God's vengeance for the death of James.

44. I find the arguments that the James passage is authentically Josephan and not the work of Christian interpolators persuasive primarily because of the relatively casual way the connection between Jesus and James is made. For discussion and bibliography on the question of the authenticity of the James passage, see Painter, *Just James*, 133–35; Martin Dibelius, *James: A Commentary on the Epistle of James* (rev. Heinrich Greeven; Hermeneia; Philadelphia: Fortress, 1976), 14–15, n. 34.

45. For a recent discussion of the James reference in Josephus, see McLaren, "Ananus, James, and Earliest Christianity." McLaren argues, as I do here, for a new framework for analyzing the story so that it is not read as a high-profile conflict between Jews and Christians over dogmatic principles. See also my own argument about interpretive frameworks for assessing the violence of this story in, Matthews, "Ethical Issues," 348–50.

46. Many have argued that through opposing this group to the Sadducees and designating them as "strict observers of the law," Josephus hints that they are Pharisees. See, e.g., Mason, *Josephus and the New Testament*, 176–77. For an argument that disputes this designation, see McLaren, "Ananus, James, and Earliest Christianity," 5–12.

47. Mason, *Josephus and the New Testament*, 175–81.

48. Richard Horsley, "'Like One of the Prophets of Old': Two Types of Popular Prophets at the Time of Jesus," *CBQ* 47 (1985): 435–63.

49. For Acts' depiction of Theudas, see also chap. 2, pp. 64–65.

50. Reed, "Jewish Christianity," 204–13. In this argument against a linear historical progression of Christianity from the Jews to the Gentiles, and for a reading of *Rec.* 1.27–71 as a Jewish text expressing views that may have subsequently influenced Christian documents, Reed provides an apt illustration of the value of thinking about Judeo-Christian relations using models of hybridity, waves, continuums, and bidirectional conversation, rather than models that suggest only linear progression of Christians away from Judaism. See Boyarin, *Borderlines*, 13–27.

Reed's arguments concerning *Rec.* 1.27–71 are embedded in a larger argument concerning the Pseudo-Clementine literature that points to passages in the *Homilies* and the *Recognitions* which are even more sympathetic to Judaism than *Rec.* 1.27–71. Passages in these documents go so far as to authorize Moses and Jesus on an equal footing, offering two paths to salvation, whereby Jews are urged to follow the teachings of Moses, and Gentiles, the teachings of Christ (cf. *Rec.* 4.5.1–6 and Reed, "Jewish Christianity," 213–17). Those who hold to the view propounded in recent Pauline scholarship that Paul himself adhered to a "two-ways" model, by which Jews are saved under the Torah and Gentiles through Christ belief (see Wills, *Not God's People*, 167–78), may note irony in the fact that the Pseudo-Clementines, which depict Paul as the "enemy," adhere to a soteriology matching up rather closely with his.

51. Note that the violence and division so central to Acts distinguishes Acts from ancient institutional histories with which it otherwise shares considerable common ground. While Hubert Cancik has convincingly demonstrated that Acts conforms considerably to other ancient narrations of the origin and spread of an institution, he concludes that "nowhere else in ancient Western institutional history are the phenomena of 'division' and 'conflict' between 'new' and 'old schools' . . . depicted in so detailed and focused a manner as in the second *logos* of Luke's history." "The History of Culture, Religion and Institutions in Ancient Historiography: Philological Observations Concerning Luke's History," *JBL* 116 (1997): 673–95, esp. 693.

52. On the othering of the Egyptian in early Christian literature, see Gay L. Byron, *Symbolic Blackness and Ethnic Difference in Early Christian Literature* (London: Routledge, 2002). On the problem of "the pagan" as other in Pauline discourse, see Wills, *Not God's People*, 179–82.

53. See p. 174, n. 34, in this chapter for the view that the original narrative culminated in James' death.

54. See, e.g., Ulrich Luz, *Das Evangelium nach Matthäus* (EKKNT 1; Neukirchen-Vluyn: Neukirchener Verlag, 1997), 3.371; B. Reicke, "Judaeo-Christianity

and the Jewish Establishment, A.D. 33–66," in *Jesus and the Politics of His Day* (ed. Ernst Bammel and C. F. D. Moule; Cambridge: Cambridge University Press, 1984), 145–52.

55. Painter, *Just James*, 138, suggests that the crime was violation of a ritual law; Bauckham, "For What Offence," argues for blasphemy. For an important argument against reading the execution of James in terms of Jewish persecution of the nascent church, see McLaren, "Ananus, James, and Earliest Christianity."

56. John Painter is among those scholars who read the James narrative as closely linked to the story immediately following in which the new high priest, Ananias, violently exploits ordinary priests by robbing them of their support from tithes and effectively starving them to death. This reading, which places James on the side of the downtrodden priests, introduces issues of class struggle into the conflict of *Ant.* 20.199–203. Painter, *Just James*, 140.

57. One of Judith M. Lieu's important, as well as poignant, insights into Justin Martyrs' construction of Christians as sufferers is that he not only repeatedly depicts Jews as persecutors but also delegitimizes Jewish suffering itself (pp. 283–84). See "Accusations of Jewish Persecution in Early Christian Sources, with Particular Reference to Justin Martyr and the *Martyrdom of Polycarp*," in *Tolerance and Intolerance in Early Judaism and Christianity* (ed. Graham N. Stanton and Guy G. Stroumsa; Cambridge: Cambridge University Press, 1998), 279–95, esp. 283–84. Acts also constructs a world where only Jesus believers, and not other Jews, suffer.

CHAPTER FOUR

1. As J. S. Banks muses in his consideration of the merciful import of the dying forgiveness prayer in "Professor Deissmann on Jesus at Prayer," *ExpTim* 11 (1899/1900): 270–273, esp. 272: "Where is the God of the Psalms of revenge? Where is the God of the Maccabean martyrs, whose strength was two things at once—faith and hate?"

2. G. P. Carras, "A Pentateuchal Echo in Jesus' Prayer on the Cross: Intertextuality between Numbers 15,22–31 and Luke 23,34a," in *The Scriptures in the Gospels* (ed. C. M. Tuckett; BETL 131; Leuven: Leuven University Press, 1997), 605–616.

3. C. A. Evans, "Is Luke's View of the Jewish Rejection of Jesus Anti-Semitic?" in *Reimaging the Death of the Lukan Jesus* (ed. D. D. Sylva; Frankfurt am Main: Hain, 1990), 29–56, esp. 52–53.

4. Those arguing this position include the editors of the Nestle-Aland 27th edition of the Greek New Testament, who continue to place the phrase in double square brackets marking them as theologically significant in Christian tradition, but not original. See also Jacobus H. Petzer's argument that the words are a secondary insertion, intended to exculpate Romans for "not knowing what they do," as well as to intensify Jewish guilt for the crucifixion, "Anti-Judaism and the Textual Problem of Luke 23:34," *Filología Neotestamentaria* 5 (1992): 199–204.

For a most recent proposal that the prayer is a late scribal insertion, see the imaginative, if ultimately unconvincing, suggestion that the addition of the prayer was motivated by numerical concerns, so that Jesus would be made to speak precisely "seven" words from the cross within the canonical Gospels, in Jason A. Whitlark and Mikeal C. Parsons, "The 'Seven' Last Words: A Numerical Motivation for the Insertion of Luke 23.34a," *NTS* 52 (2006): 188–204.

5. Thus, Bruce Metzger, echoing the sentiment expressed already in Westcott and Hort, notes that the absence of the prayer in significant manuscripts "can scarcely be explained as a deliberate excision by copyists who, considering the fall of Jerusalem to be proof that God had not forgiven the Jews, could not allow it to appear that the prayer of Jesus had remained unanswered." *A Textual Commentary*, 180.

6. My arguments regarding external and internal considerations fall basically in line with those of Bart Ehrman, "The Text of the Gospels at the End of the Second Century," in *Codex Bezae: Studies from the Lunel Colloquium June 1994* (ed. D. C. Parker and C.-B. Amphoux; NTTS 22; Leiden: Brill, 1996), 95–122, esp. 109–113; Kim Haines-Eitzen, *Guardians of Letters: Literacy, Power, and the Transmitters of Early Christian Literature* (New York: Oxford University Press, 2000), 119–24; and Joël Delobel, "Luke 23:34a: A Perpetual Text-Critical Crux?" in *Sayings of Jesus: Canonical and Non-Canonical: Essays in Honour of Tjitze Baarda* (ed. William L. Petersen et al.; NovTSup 89; Leiden: Brill, 1997), 25–36.

7. *On Tatian*: If one grants, as most scholars do, that Ephrem is a reliable transmitter of Tatian's *Diatessaron* and further that Tatian is not inventing sayings, but working from Gospel sources, then the threefold citation of the forgiveness prayer in Ephrem's *Commentary on the Diatessaron* suggests that he is quoting from Tatian's original Gospel source (Ephrem, *Commentary* 10.15, 21.3, 21.18). Tatian, then, becomes a second-century witness to Jesus' forgiveness prayer as part of Gospel tradition. For this argument, see Delobel, "Luke 23:34a," 28–30.

On Hegesippus: Because I regard the Third Gospel as a source for both Hegesippus and Acts, as noted in chap. 3, and hold to the internal arguments for Lukan originality elaborated below, I am not convinced by arguments that dependency goes in the reserve direction. I disagree, therefore, with the proposal of David Flusser ("'Sie wissen nicht, was sie tun': Geschichte eines Herrnwortes," in *Kontinuität und Einheit* [ed. Paul-Gerhard Müller and Werner Stenger; Freiburg: Herder, 1981], 393–410) that the prayer originates in the James tradition and is secondarily absorbed into Jesus tradition.

8. On this close interlocking structure, see, e.g., Delobel, "Luke 23:34a," 34–35.

9. As B. Ehrman notes ("Text of the Gospels," 112), one reason for the difficulty in positing that a scribe inspired by Stephen's dying prayer then composed a similar, but not identical, prayer to retroject into the Lukan story of Jesus on the cross is that scribal harmonizations tend to be verbatim, rather than free form.

10. See especially Haines-Eitzen, *Guardians of Letters*; Bart Ehrman, *The Orthodox Corruption of Scripture: The Effect of Early Christological Controversies on the Text of the New Testament* (New York: Oxford University Press, 1996).

11. Eldon Jay Epp, "The 'Ignorance Motif' in Acts and Anti-Judaic Tendencies in Codex Bezae," *HTR* 55 (1962): 51–62; Ehrman, "Text of the Gospels," 109–13; Haines-Eitzen, *Guardians of Letters*, 123.

12. For arguments linking Luke 12.10–12 to both the ignorance motif and to the stoning of Stephen, see H.-T. Wrege, "Zur Rolle des Geisteswortes in frühchristlichen Traditionen (LC 12,10 parr.)," in *Logia: les paroles de Jésus* (ed. J. Coppens et al.; Louvain: Peeters, 1982), 373–77, esp. 377; and P. Hoffmann, "Jesus versus Menschensohn: Mt 10,32f und die synoptische Menschensohnüberlieferung," in *Salz der Erde, Licht der Welt: exegetische Studien zum Matthäusevangelium* (ed. L. Oberlinner and P. Fiedler; Stuttgart: Verlag katholisches Bibelwerk, 1991), 165–202.

13. This is the position of Matthais Blum, *". . . denn sie wissen nicht, was sie tun." Zur Rezeption der Fürbitte Jesu am Kreuz (Lk 23,34a) in der antiken jüdisch-christlichen Kontroverse* (NTABh 2/46; Münster: Aschendorff, 2001), 53, 205–208. I will suggest below that a further explanation for the ambiguity of the object of the prayer lies in the intransitive nature of clemency, which focuses primarily on the subject who grants it, rather than the object who receives it. Here, my argument is loosely aligned with that of Blum, who also notes that primary focus of the prayer is not its object (pp. 44–46). But while he suggests that the purpose of the prayer is to underscore the generosity of God's unconditional forgiveness, I note the power implicit in the assertion of pardon, and the futility of the prayer in effecting forgiveness for the Jews.

14. As, e.g., argued by Sanders, *Jews in Luke-Acts*, 11–13, 226–28.

15. This supersessionist reading is found, e.g., in Hippolytus' third-century treatise against the Jews, in which he has Jesus speak: "But as for me, in my prayer unto Thee, O Lord, I said, 'Father, forgive them,' namely the Gentiles, because it is the time for favor with Gentiles [διότι καιρὸς εὐδοκίας τῶν ἐθνῶν]" (*Demonstratio adversus Judaeos* 3.20.4).

16. For this reading in the third century, see Origen, *Peri Pascha* 43.33–36; *Didascalia* 25.

17. David Daube argues for the Jewish background of the forgiveness prayer through noting links between the forgiveness prayer and the atonement provisions in Leviticus (more on these atonement provisions below). See his "'For They Know Not What They Do': Luke 23,24," *StPatr* 4, no. 2 (1961): 58–70. Carras ("Pentateuchal Echo," 615) takes the argument one step further: "The fact that Jesus prayed for the Jewish religious establishment in spite of their inability to understand the events surrounding him as Messiah is a telling corrective to the view espoused by Sanders [of Luke's anti-Judaism]. Luke's passion account indicates that he has not given up on the Jewish leaders but prays for them. *Since the prayer is unique to Luke and its background accords with OT law, the view is strengthened that Luke has not given up on the Jews*" (emphasis added).

18. Blum, *denn sie wissen nicht*, 37.

19. Carras, "Pentateuchal Echo"; Daube, "'For They Know Not What They Do.'"

20. See Moessner, "Christ Must Suffer"; Bovon, "La figure de Moïse."

21. For classic statement of the absence of atonement theology in Luke's passion, see Conzelmann, *Theology of St. Luke*, 200–202; cf. the recent attempt to argue for some form of atonement theology in Luke-Acts in David Moessner, "The 'Script' of the Scriptures in Acts: Suffering as God's 'Plan' (βουλή) for the World for the 'Release of Sins,'" in *History, Literature, and Society in the Book of Acts* (ed. Ben Witherington; Cambridge: Cambridge University Press, 1996), 218–50.

22. On the use of Isaiah in Luke, see, e.g., Joel Marcus, "The Old Testament and the Death of Jesus: The Role of Scripture in the Gospel Passion Narratives," in *The Death of Jesus in Early Christianity* (ed. John T. Carroll and Joel B. Green; Peabody, Mass.: Hendrickson, 1995), 205–33, esp. 213–18.

23. For discussion and bibliography, see Blum, *denn sie wissen nicht*, 38. Note also that from the notion of intercessory prayer at Isa. 53.12 in Hebrew but not LXX, Flusser ("Sie wissen nicht") builds his argument that the forgiveness prayer makes its way first into the narrative of James' death in Palestinian, Jewish–Christian sources, and only secondarily into Luke's Jesus tradition.

24. Brian E. Beck, "'Imitatio Christi' and the Lucan Passion Narrative," in *Suffering and Martyrdom in the New Testament* (ed. William Horbury and Brian McNeil; Cambridge: Cambridge University Press, 1981), 28–47, esp. 44–45. Beck contrasts the suffering righteous who exhibits gentleness through persecution, with the martyr who aggressively condemns his persecutor (p. 35).

25. Origen, *Hom. Lev.* 2.5.

26. Heinrich Plett, "Intertextualities," in *Intertexuality* (ed. Heinrich Plett; Research in Text Theory 15; Berlin: de Gruyter, 1991), 1–20, esp. 11.

27. Richard B. Hayes, *Echoes of Scripture in the Letters of Paul* (New Haven, Conn.: Yale University Press, 1989), 19.

28. Focus on the mouth is frequent in noble death narratives of all sorts. In addition to the instances discussed here, consider Diogenes' legends of Zeno biting the tyrant's ear while he is stabbed to death in one version, or biting and spitting out his own tongue at the tyrant in another (*Diogenes Laertius* 9.26–27). See the comparable tongue-biting defiance of Anaxarchus, in *Diogenes Laertius* 9.58–59.

29. See 2 Macc. 7.14, 7.16, 7.19, 7.31–36.

30. On the importance of vengeance to martyrdom literature specifically, see Ulrich Kellermann, "Das Danielbuch und die Märtyrertheologie der Auferstehung," in *Die Entstehung der jüdischen Martyrologie* (ed. J. W. van Henten; StPB 38; Leiden: Brill, 1989), 51–75, esp. 72–75; Jan Willem van Henten, "Zum Einfluss jüdischer Martyrien auf die Literatur des frühen Christentums, II. Die Apostolischen Väter," *ANRW* 27.1:700–23; and Ernst Dassmann, *Sündenvergebung durch Taufe, Busse und Martyrerfürbitte in den Zeugnissen frühchristlicher Frömmigkeit und Kunst* (Münsterische Beiträge zur Theologie 36; Münster: Aschendorff, 1973), 153–82.

Note that in the rabbinic legends of the mother and her seven sons, the affirmation of the name of God is substituted for the Maccabean cry of vengeance. See *Lam. Rab.* 1.16; *b. Git.* 57b.

31. See David M. Moffitt, "Righteous Bloodshed, Matthew's Passion Narrative, and the Temple's Destruction: Lamentations as a Matthean Intertext," *JBL* 125 (2006):

299–320, esp. 301–04; Johnson-DeBaufre, "Blood Required," 27–28; Allison, *Intertextual Jesus*, 149–51; Blank, "Death of Zechariah."

32. Cf. also *b. Sanh.* 96b; *Eccl. Rab.* 3.16, 10.4; *Lam. Rab.* proem 23; *Liv. Pro. Zech.* 23.1.

33. And thus, the tradition of the urgent nature of Zechariah's blood requital is tied to both the James and the Stephen traditions.

34. See chap. 3, pp. 86–87.

35. Bauckham, "For What Offence," 212–18, and chap. 3, pp. 83–84.

36. The verb in the Hebrew text, *mvl*, is a hapax, whose meaning is not certain. *HALOT* s.v. *mvl* suggests relation to an Arabic stem meaning "to be hostile towards," and translates at Ps. 118.10–12, "to fend off."

37. Hereafter referenced as SM/SP. As a means to evoke the scholarly energy that has been poured into the interpretation of this body of teaching, even the standard phrase "the literature is large" seems a vast understatement. Entry points can be found in the recently translated and revised commentary of Ulrich Luz, *Matthew 1–7: A Commentary* (vol. 1 of *Matthew, A Commentary*; trans. James E. Crouch; ed. Helmut Koester; Hermeneia; Minneapolis: Fortress, 2007), 170–72, 226, 283; Willard M. Swartley, "War and Peace in the New Testament," in *ANRW* 26.3: 2298–408; and Hans Dieter Betz, *The Sermon on the Mount: A Commentary on the Sermon on the Mount Including the Sermon on the Plain (Matthew 5:3–7:27 and Luke 6:20–49)* (ed. Adela Yarbro Collins; Hermeneia; Minneapolis: Fortress, 1995).

38. In Matt. 5.44, enemies are linked with "those who persecute you" (τῶν διωκόντων ὑμᾶς). In Luke 6.27–28, enemies are marked as those who "hate you" (μισοῦσιν ὑμᾶς), "curse you" (καταρωμένους ὑμᾶς), and "abuse you" (ἐπηρεαζόντων ὑμᾶς).

39. On the rhetorical figure joining the commands "to love" and "to pray for" in Matt. 5.44, see Betz, *Sermon on the Mount*, 312, n. 885.

40. *Synoptische Überlieferung bei den apostolischen Vätern* (Berlin: Akademie, 1957), 44. See also Karlmann Beyschlag ("Zur Geschichte der Bergpredigt in der Alten Kirche," *ZTK* 74 [1977]: 291–322, esp. 314), who notes that the saying is known among all "parties" of Christians, save the Gnostics. See, e.g., *Did.* 1.3; *Diogn.* 5.11, 6.6; Pol. *Phil.* 12.3; Justin, *Apol.* 1.14, 1.15.9; Athenagoras, *Leg.* 11.1; Theophilus, *Autol.* 3.14; Aristides, *Apol.* 15.5, 17.3; Irenaeus *Haer.* 4.13.3; Tertullian *Scap.* 1., *Pat.* 6, *Spect.* 16, *Apol.* 31, 37.

41. W. C. van Unnik, "Die Motivierung der Feindesliebe in Lukas 6:32–35," *NovT* 8 (1966): 284–300, esp. 286.

42. John Whittaker, "Christianity and Morality in the Roman Empire," *VC* 33 (1979): 209–25.

The debate over whether the SM/SP is best understood as a Christian *proprium* or as standing within Jewish and/or Greco-Roman ethical traditions continues. How one answers the question depends in part on judgments made about what constitutes a parallel, what can be dismissed as an "exception" rather than a precedent, and the point at which one distinguishes between the "background" of an idea and the idea itself. A sampling of the scholarly spectrum:

Arguments for continuity between SM/SP and Hebrew Scripture: Citing passages from Hebrew Scripture in which enemies are treated humanely (e.g., 1 Sam. 26.17–25; 2 Kings 6.22–23), William Klassen has argued that a number of passages in Hebrew Scripture already embody the principle of enemy love that Jesus then accentuates in the Gospel (*Love of Enemies: The Way to Peace* [OBT 15; Philadelphia: Fortress, 1984]). Noting the connection between the command to love neighbor in Lev. 19.18 with preceding exhortations against taking vengeance or bearing grudges, Hans-Peter Mathys has suggested that the command to love neighbor in Lev. 19.18 already includes a command to love one's enemy (*Liebe deinen Nächsten wie dich selbst. Untersuchungen zum alttestamentlichen Gebot der Nächstenliebe (Lev 19.18)* [OBO 71: Göttingen: Vandenhoeck & Ruprecht, 1986], 68–81). These modern arguments are restatements of those made by early Christians engaged in battles with Marcion, as the *Dialogue of Admantius* demonstrates (see below).

Arguments for radical distinction between Christian enemy love and Jewish ethical teaching: For a vigorous defense of this view, consider P. E. Lapide: "Rejoicing in the misfortunes of others, hating enemies, and repaying evil with evil are certainly forbidden, while generosity and kindness toward ones enemy are commanded—but Judaism does not recognize enemy-love as a moral principle. This particular imperative is possibly the only one in all three chapters of the Sermon on the Mount that lacks a clear parallel or analogy in rabbinic literature," in "Die Bergpredigt—Theorie und Praxis," *ZEE* 17 (1973): 369–72. See also John Piper, *'Love Your Enemies': Jesus' Love Command in the Synoptic Gospels and in the Early Christian Paraenesis* (SNTSMS 38; Cambridge: Cambridge University Press, 1979); Gordon M. Zerbe, *Non-retaliation in Early Jewish and New Testament Texts: Ethical Themes in Social Contexts* (JSPSup 13; Sheffield: Sheffield Academic Press, 1993), 294.

Enemy love and Greco-Roman ethical norms: In spite of Whittaker's argument, most scholars still frame the significance of the SM/SP in terms of difference from Greco-Roman norms (even if they concede that the difference is slight). Betz privileges the Socratic and Stoic materials to argue that when the Sermon on the Mount was formulated, "retaliation was thoroughly discredited as far as ethical thought was concerned." Yet, he argues that Jesus' teaching on enemy love is still an advance beyond what came previously: "one can conclude, therefore, that Jesus' demand in the SM has precedent or preparation in the history of ideas, although it did represent a new step at the time" (*Sermon on the Mount*, 288, 311, n. 882). Cf. Luz, *Matthew 1–7*, 286; Marius Reiser, "Love of Enemies in the Context of Antiquity," *NTS* 47 (2001): 411–27; Beyschlag, "Zur Geschichte der Bergpredigt."

Those who acknowledge that treating enemies fairly or kindly is a broad principle but wish to preserve enemy *love* as the Christian *novum* must skirt around the exhortation to love persecutors in Epictetus' *Discourses* 3.22.54: "For this too is a very pleasant strand woven into the Cynic's pattern of life; he must needs be flogged like an ass, and while he is being flogged *he must love the men who flog him*, as though he were the father or brother of them all" (emphasis added).

43. Tertullian refers to this marcionite antithesis explicitly at *Marc.* 4.16.1–8 and 2.28.2. See also the discussion of Tertullian on the continuity between the talion and enemy love below.

Similar to Marcion, the second-century Letter of Ptolemy to Flora also expresses concern over the violence of the talion, relegating it to the portion of the law that is "interwoven with injustice." See Ptolemy, *Flor.* 5.4–5.

44. *Marc.* 1.27.2: *deus melior inventus est, qui nec offenditur nec irascitur nec ulciscitur, cui nullus ignis coquitur in gehenna, cui nullus dentium frendor horret in exterioribus tenebris: bonus tantum est.* Harnack casts this distinction as one between the just God and the good God. See *Marcion,* *262–65. For the argument that Marcion is more concerned with the capriciousness of the God who judges in the Old Testament than with the abstract concept of justice, see Winrich Löhr, "Did Marcion Distinguish between a Just God and a Good God?" in *Marcion und seine kirchengeschictliche Wirkung: Vorträge der Internationalen Fachkonferenz zu Marcion, gehalten vom 15–18. August 2001 in Mainz* (ed. Gerhard May and Katharina Greschat; TUGAL 150; Berlin: de Gruyter, 2002), 131–146.

45. Daniel Boyarin has also noted Justin's concern to make the distinction between Christianity and Judaism on the theological plane, over the question of belief in the Logos. See *Borderlines,* 39.

46. Since the influential argument of Louis Martyn (*History and Theology in the Fourth Gospel* [2d ed.; Nashville: Abingdon, 1979]), the threefold charge of cursing Christ in the synagogue (*Trypho* 16.4, 47.4, 96.2) has been linked both to the *Birkat Ha-Minim* and to the references to synagogue expulsion in the Fourth Gospel, as signs of Jewish violence against Christians (and as explanation for the anti-Judaism of the Fourth Gospel). For critique of this hypothesis, see Reuven Kimelman, "*Birkat Ha-Minim* and the Lack of Evidence for an Anti-Christian Jewish Prayer in Late Antiquity," in *Jewish and Christian Self-definition* (2 vols.; ed. E. P. Sanders; Philadelphia: Fortress, 1981), 2.226–44, 2.391–403. Cf. Boyarin, *Borderlines,* 67–73.

For an analysis of Justin's accusations, which includes discussion of, but is not focused on, the *Birkat Ha-Minim,* see Lieu, "Accusations of Jewish Persecution," 290–91.

47. Compare also the assertions of Jewish hatred, paired with Christian prayer in *Trypho,* 35 and 85.

48. I contrast here only the *inscribed* audience of Justin's two works, one Jewish and one Gentile, while recognizing the difficulty of moving from inscribed to actual audience for this author.

49. Walter Bauer, "Das Gebot der Feindesliebe und die alten Christen," *ZTK* 27 (1917): 37–54; repr. in *Aufsätze und Kleine Schriften* (ed. Georg Strecker; Tübingen: Mohr, 1967), 243–44. There are precisely two instances in the Apocryphal Acts in which invoking Christian teaching of enemy love leads to charitable treatment of enemies. When in the *Acts of Peter* an angry crowd proposes to subject Simon Magus to execution by fire, Peter quiets them by the reminder that "we have learned to love our enemies and pray for our persecutors," thus saving Simon from the pyre (*Acts Pet.*

28). In the *Acts of John*, the principle of enemy love is invoked as a rationale for raising an unbeliever from the dead (*Acts John* 81).

50. Bauer, "Das Gebot der Feindesliebe," 247.

51. For further condemnations of the Jews as Christ killers in Irenaeus, see *Haer.* 4.36.2; *Epid.* 69.

Acknowledging the propensity to read the prayers intransitively might also serve to explain the puzzle of the ambiguous antecedent in the original dominical prayer. As noted earlier in this chapter, owing to the vagueness of any textual clues concerning the identity of the antecedent, there is debate over whether Jesus' prayer to forgive "them" is aimed at Jews or Romans. But such debate is premised on the assumption that the object, the "them," is crucial to the meaning of the utterance. If it is recognized instead that the prayer functions much more to idealize Jesus, than to effect forgiveness of any group, the importance of attaching a group identity to the pronoun "them" recedes.

52. On issues of gender and contest in this text, see Stephen D. Moore and Janice C. Anderson, "Taking It Like a Man: Masculinity in 4 Maccabees," *JBL* 117 (1998): 249–73.

53. On the verticality of the power dynamic of clemency, consider also Plautus' *Epidicus*, in which the humorous inversion of the power dynamics, so that the slave Epidicus grants clemency to his master, relies on the understanding that such power dynamics have been turned upside down in the play, as argued in Melissa Dowling, *Clemency and Cruelty in the Roman World* (Ann Arbor: University of Michigan Press, 2006), 12–13.

54. Cf. Sheila Dillon's discussion of images of clemency on Trajan's column, "Women on the Columns of Trajan and Marcus Aurelius and the Visual Language of Roman Victory," in *Representations of War in Ancient Rome* (ed. Sheila Dillon and Katherine E. Welch; Cambridge: Cambridge University Press, 2006), 244–71.

55. Dowling, *Clemency and Cruelty*, 139.

56. Joel Marcus, "Crucifixion as Parodic Exaltation," *JBL* 125 (2006): 73–87, esp. 78.

57. Ibid., 87.

58. Cf. John S. Kloppenborg, "The Death of Jesus in Luke," *TJT* 8 (1992): 121–33, esp. 112–13. Kloppenborg himself suggests that the dying forgiveness prayer is a gesture toward the Roman virtue of clemency, but he does not elaborate on the power dynamics of such a gesture.

59. This merging of discourse concerning the emperor and Jesus is continued in Luke-Acts through the depiction of Jesus' ascension. Compare here the arguments of Gilbert that the language of Jesus' ascent mirrors accounts of imperial ascent and deification in "Roman Propaganda and Christian Identity," 242–47.

60. *Magni autem animi proprium est placidum esse tranquillumque et iniurias atque offensiones superne despicere. Muliebre est furere in ira, ferarum . . . praemordere et urguere proiectos.*

61. *Clem.* 2.6.4 characterizes *misericordia* as "a weakness of the mind that is over-much perturbed by suffering, and if any one requires it from a wise man, that is very much like requiring him to wail and moan at the funerals of strangers" [Basore, LCL]

(*misericordia vitium est animorum nimis miseria paventium, quam si quis a sapiente exigit, prope est, ut lamentationem exigat et in alienis funeribus gemitus*).

62. *patrem clementia, dominum disciplina, patrem potestate blanda, dominum severa*. . . . For further employment of metaphors for God as supreme Father and Lord of household, see also Tertullian's reference to God as stern disciplinarian in *Marc.* 1.27.3–4; and his enthusiasm for the right of the lord of the household to inflict corporal punishment on his slaves, *Marc.* 4.29.12.

63. Tertullian explicitly refers to Marcion's God as a castrated God, with respect to his inability to create, *Marc.* 4.17.5.

64. For introduction to Asterius, see Boudewijn Dehandschutter, "Asterius of Amasea," in *"Let Us Die That We May Live": Greek Homilies on Christian Martyrs from Asia Minor, Palestine and Syria c. AD 350–AD 450* (ed. Johan Leemans et al.; London: Routledge, 2003), 162–93; Cornelis Datema, *Asterius of Amasea. Homilies I–XIV: Text, Introduction and Notes* (Leiden: Brill, 1970).

65. Jerome, *Epistle* 120.8.2 (PL 22.993): *In tantum autem amavit Hierusalem dominus, ut fleret eam et plangeret et pendens in cruce loqueretur: "pater, ignosce eis, quod enim faciunt, nesciunt." Itaque impetravit, quod petierat, multaque statim de Iudaeis milia crediderunt et usque ad quadragesimum secundum annum datum est tempus paenitentiae*. Similar legends of mass conversion around the cross, attributed to the "Gospel of the Nazoreans," and hence of possible early date, are preserved in Haimo of Auxerre's medieval commentary on Isaiah at 53.12, and in a medieval manuscript known as the *Historia passionis Domini* f.55^r. For the latter two in English translation, see Philipp Vielhauer and Georg Strecker, eds. and trans., "Jewish-Christian Gospels," in *Gospels and Related Writings* (vol. 1 of *New Testament Apocrypha*; ed. Wilhelm Schneemelcher and R. McL. Wilson; Louisville, Ky.: Westminster John Knox, 1991), 134–78, esp. 162, n. 24; 164, n. 35. For Latin text of each of these three conversion legends, see also Kurt Aland, *Synopsis Quattuor Evangeliorum* (15th ed.; Stuttgart: Deutsche Bibelgesellschaft, 1996), 484. For discussion, see Flusser, "Sie wissen nicht," 404–07.

66. For another variation, consider the martyrdom of James in the fragment from Clement's *Hypotyposes* preserved in Eusebius' *Ecclesiastical History*. Here, prayer for forgiveness is granted from the martyr for his jailor, but only after the official in question is poised for conversion: "Clement adds in the seventh book. . . a story. . . to the effect that he who brought James to the court was so moved at seeing him testify as to confess that he also was himself a Christian. 'So they were both led away together' he says, 'and on the way he asked for forgiveness for himself from James. And James looked at him for a moment and said, 'Peace be to you,' and kissed him. So both were beheaded at the same time'" (*Hist. eccl.* 2.7.2–3 [Lake, LCL]).

67. Zerbe, *Non-retaliation*, 37–39, 75–77, 92–93, 98–99, 119–26, 158–60, passim. See also J. Licht, "Taxo, Or the Apocalyptic Doctrine of Vengeance," *JJS* 12 (1961): 95–103.

68. Cf. also, Prov. 24.17–18, 25.21–22; *T. Gad* 6.7, 7.4–5; *Jos. Asen.* 28.10, 28.14; *2 En.* 50.2–4; *T. Mos.* 9–10; CD 9.2–5.

69. While many New Testament scholars have wished to soften Paul's apparent vindictiveness here, Krister Stendahl argued more than forty years ago (in his typically perspicacious and provocative manner) that Paul's argument in Romans should be read as exhibiting the same vindictiveness as found in the Dead Sea Scrolls. See his "Hate, Non-retaliation, and Love: 1QS x,17–20 and Rom. 12:19–21," *HTR* 55 (1962): 337–55. For a recent review of literature on Romans 12.17–21, see Zerbe, *Non-retaliation*, 211–69.

70. "Hate, Non-retaliation, and Love," 355. Note that Betz argues to the contrary that the Sermon on the Mount itself does not exhort non-retaliation on the basis of referring such vengeance to God (*Sermon on the Mount*, 285, n. 687).

71. Zerbe, *Non-retaliation*, 176–210, esp. 210.

72. The anti-marcionite *Dialogue of Admantius* also asserts continuity between New and Old Testaments, through citation of passages from the Torah on returning an enemy's livestock as precedent for Jesus' enemy love teaching and the exempla of Moses, David, and Saul enacting practices of prayer and love for enemies. See *Dialogue of Admantius*, 812D, 812E–F, and 830D.

73. The deficient understanding of the Jews is identified by Tertullian as the reason for the incorporation of the *lex talionis* into the law in the first place: "To that stiff-necked people, devoid of faith in God, it seemed a tiresome thing, or even beyond credence, to expect from God that vengeance which was afterwards to be promised by the prophet" (*Marc.* 2.18.1 [Evans]).

74. Tertullian does make reference to Luke 23.34b, the casting of lots for Jesus' clothing, and accuses Marcion of having excised that very passage from the text (*Marc.* 4.42.4).

75. While many have suggested that the forgiveness prayer at Luke 23.34a is one of the *ipsissima verba* of Jesus, its late appearance and the lack of multiple attestation make this a difficult argument to sustain.

76. Lieu, "Accusations of Jewish Persecution," 283–84.

77. Heschel, "From Jesus to Shylock," 422.

EPILOGUE

1. For one brief overview of the impact of the conquest of Judea, along with Roman imperial propaganda regarding that conquest, on the composition of Acts, see Kahl, "Acts of the Apostles," 139–41. The Diaspora revolts of 115–17 and the Bar Kokhba rebellion of 132–35 are also flash points in violent interactions among Jews and their overlords in the Roman Empire. Any of these situations, serving as a backdrop for a reading of Acts, sets in bold relief Acts' claim that "Romans do no harm."

2. I am convinced by the arguments of Daniel Boyarin and Judith Lieu on the significance of the dying words that come to be associated in the second century with Christian martyrs—"I am a Christian"—and with Jewish martyrs—"the Lord is One." As Boyarin puts it, in affirming and elaborating on an argument made by Lieu so that it pertains to Jewish, as well as Christian, martyrs, "It is this moment that most completely serves to enable the martyrology to serve the production of group identity

and self-definition. . . . The confession, 'I am a Christian,' binds the martyr with all Christians everywhere, and so also the confession 'Hear O Israel, the Lord, our God, the Lord is One,' binds the martyr with all Jews everywhere and always" (*Dying for God*, 109). Cf. Lieu, *Image and Reality*, 82–83.

If we imagine these martyrdom narratives constructed in some sort of conversation, and through experimentation leading to the production of two distinct social groups, a fascinating web of connections may be traced: The dying martyr who cries for vengeance in 2 and 4 Maccabees is replaced in the rabbinic tradition of the mother and her seven sons with the affirmation that "the Name is One" (*Lam. Rab.* 1.16; *b. Git.* 57b). Acts, a document with a date and provenance near to 4 Maccabees knows the tradition of the dying martyr's cry for vengeance and substitutes, "Lord, do not hold this sin against them," a speech act that eventually gives way to the *Christianos sum*, as the producer of Christian group identity.

3. Brigitte Kahl's recent reading of Acts is noteworthy in that she both acknowledges the text's embrace of imperial discourse, while also proposing a deeply sympathetic reading of its author's situation. Noting the constraints imposed on an early Christian author who wishes to tell the story of Jesus and Paul, she observes, "[t]his story after 70 was an impossible story to tell. Yet Luke managed to tell it 'securely.' One could view Acts as a voice training, a speech exercise for a narrative whose words had been cut off by the irresistible power of Roman swords. In this regard Luke's writing is an act of resistant survival in circumstances that rendered any explicit resistance suicidal" (Kahl, "Acts of the Apostles," 149).

4. *Marcion: The Gospel of the Alien God*, 134. I follow the translation of Steely and Bierma, with slight revision.

5. Harnack's motives are complex. Heikki Räisänen, arguing that this famous thesis of Harnack's has been widely misunderstood, notes that Harnack himself wished primarily for a "critical sifting" of the contents of the Old Testament, so that its warlike God might not be used to justify present-day violence. He notes further that Harnack is on record decrying anti-Semitism in prewar Germany. See Heikki Räisänen, "Marcion and the Origins of Christian Anti-Judaism: A Reappraisal," *Tenemos* 33 (1997): 121–35, esp. 130–31. Cf. also Henning Graf Reventlow, "The Role of the Old Testament in the German Liberal Protestant Theology of the Nineteenth Century," in *Biblical Studies and the Shifting of Paradigms, 1850–1914* (ed. Henning Graf Reventlow and William Farmer; JSOTSup 192; Sheffield: Sheffield Academic Press), 132–48.

6. For critique of the influence of Girard in New Testament scholarship, see John G. Gager, "Violent Acts and Violent Language in the Apostle Paul" in *Violence in the New Testament* (ed. Shelly Matthews and E. Leigh Gibson; London: T&T Clark, 2005), 13–21. On Drewermann, see Erwin Dirscherl, "Marcions später Triumph? Bemerkungen zum Verhältnis von Dogmatik und Tiefenpsychologie," in *Gottes Offenbarung in der Welt* (ed. Friedhelm Krüger; Gütersloh: Gütersloher Verlagshaus, 1998), 246–59.

7. Slavoj Žižek, *The Sublime Object of Ideology* (London: Verso, 1988), 49.

8. See the discussion of the arguments of J. Massyngbaerde Ford and Brittany Wilson, in chap. 1, pp. 52–53.

9. Eric Osborn, *Tertullian: First Theologian of the West* (Cambridge: Cambridge University Press, 1997).

10. Ibid., 109.

11. Ibid., 248.

12. Ibid., 102. Cf. also p. 247, n. 4: "Here Tertullian remains a Christian more of the Old Testament than of the New."

13. Ibid., 246, n. 1, emphasis added.

14. Note in particular his insistence that God's goodness is primary, his justice secondary in *Marc.* 2.11.2: [with reference to fall of Genesis 2–3] "Thus the goodness of God came first, as his nature is: his sternness came afterwards, as there was reason for it. The former was ingenerate, was God's own, was freely exercised: the latter was accidental, adapted to need, an expedient (Evans) [*Ita prior bonitas dei secundum naturam, severitas posterior secundum causam. Illa ingenita, haec accidens; illa propria, haec accommodate; illa edita, haec adhibita*]."

15. The importance for Tertullian of demonstrating specifically the violence of Marcion's *Gospel* is indicated by the length of book 4, the book devoted to his version of the Gospel of Luke. Books 1 and 2, setting out Tertullian's arguments against Marcion's God on the basis of rational theological principles, contain 29 chapters each. Book 3, the proof of Christ from Old Testament prophecies, contains 24 chapters. Book 5, devoted to Marcion's "Apostle," a version of a Pauline Letter collection, is a mere 21 chapters in length. By contrast, book 4 is 43 chapters long, twice as long as the book devoted to the Pauline Letters and sizably larger than any other book of the Treatise or, for that matter, any other book in T's corpus.

16. *Marc.* 4.43.9: *Misereor tui, Marcion, frustra laborasti. Christus enim Iesus in evangelio tuo meus est.*

Bibliography

Ahn, Yong-Sung. *The Reign of God and Rome in Luke's Passion Narrative: An East Asian Global Perspective.* Biblical Interpretation Series 80. Leiden: Brill, 2006.

Aland, Barbara. "Marcion/Marcioniten." *Theologische Realenzyklopädie* 22 (1992): 89–101.

Aland, Kurt. *Synopsis Quattuor Evangeliorum.* 15th ed. Stuttgart: Deutsche Bibelgesellschaft, 1996.

Alexander, Loveday. *Acts in Its Ancient Literary Context.* Library of New Testament Studies 298. New York: T&T Clark, 2006.

———. *The Preface to Luke's Gospel: Literary Convention and Social Context in Luke 1.1–4 and Acts 1.1.* Society for New Testament Studies Monograph Series 78. Cambridge: Cambridge University Press, 1993.

Allison, Dale. *The Intertextual Jesus: Scriptures in Q.* Harrisburg, Pa.: Trinity, 2000.

Balch, David. "ΜΕΤΑΒΟΛΗ ΠΟΛΙΤΕΙΩΝ—Jesus as Founder of the Church in Luke-Acts: Form and Function." Pages 139–88 in *Contextualizing Acts: Lukan Narrative and Greco-Roman Discourse.* Edited by Todd Penner and Caroline Vander Stichele. Society of Biblical Literature Symposium Series 20. Atlanta: Society of Biblical Literature, 2003.

———. "Response to Daryl Schmidt: Luke-Acts Is Catechesis for Christians, Not Kerygma to Jews." Pages 97–110 in *Anti-Judaism and the Gospels.* Edited by William R. Farmer. Harrisburg, Pa.: Trinity, 1999.

Banks, J. S. "Professor Deissmann on Jesus at Prayer." *Expository Times* 11 (1899/1900): 270–73.

Barclay, John. "The Empire Writes Back: Josephan Rhetoric in Flavian Rome." Pages 315–32 in *Flavius Josephus and Flavian Rome.* Edited by

Jonathan Edmondson, Steve Mason, and J. B. Rives. Oxford: Oxford University Press, 2005.

Barrett, C. K. "The First New Testament?" *Novum Testamentum* 38 (1996): 94–104.

Barthes, Roland. *The Rustle of Language*. New York: Hill & Wang, 1986.

Barton, John. "Marcion Revisited." Pages 341–54 in *The Canon Debate*. Edited by Lee Martin McDonald and James A. Sanders. Peabody, Mass.: Hendrickson, 2002.

Bauckham, Richard. "For What Offence Was James Put to Death?" Pages 199–232 in *James the Just and Christian Origins*. Edited by B. Chilton and C. A. Evans. Novum Testamentum Supplements 98. Leiden: Brill, 1999.

———. "James and the Jerusalem Community." Pages 55–95 in *Jewish Believers in Jesus: The Early Centuries*. Edited by Oskar Skarsaune and Reidar Hvalvik. Peabody, Mass.: Hendrickson, 2007.

———. *Jude and the Relatives of Jesus in the Early Church*. London: T&T Clark, 2004.

Bauer, Walter. "Das Gebot der Feindesliebe und die alten Christen." *Zeitshcrift für Theologie und Kirche* 27 (1917): 37–54. Repr. pages 243–44 in *Aufsätze und Kleine Schriften*. Edited by Georg Strecker. Tübingen: Mohr, 1967.

———. *Orthodoxy and Heresy in Earliest Christianity*. Edited by Robert A. Kraft and Gerhard Krodel. Translated by a team from the Philadelphia Seminar on Christian Origins. Philadelphia: Fortress 1971.

Baur, F. C. *Paul, the Apostle of Jesus Christ, His Life and Works, His Epistles and Teachings: A Contribution to a Critical History of Primitive Christianity*. Translated by A. P. Menzies (vol. 1) and A. Menzies (vol. 2). 2 vols. London: Williams & Norgate, 1873–75.

Beavis, Mary Ann. "Christian Origins, Egalitarianism and Utopia." *Journal of Feminist Studies in Religion* 23 (2007): 27–49.

Beck, Brian E. "'Imitatio Christi' and the Lucan Passion Narrative." Pages 28–47 in *Suffering and Martyrdom in the New Testament*. Edited by William Horbury and Brian McNeil. Cambridge: Cambridge University Press, 1981.

Berkowitz, Beth. *Execution and Invention: Death Penalty Discourse in Early Rabbinic and Christian Cultures*. New York: Oxford University Press, 2006.

Betz, Hans Dieter. *The Sermon on the Mount: A Commentary on the Sermon on the Mount Including the Sermon on the Plain (Matthew 5:3–7:27 and Luke 6:20–49)*. Edited by Adela Yarbro Collins. Hermeneia. Minneapolis: Fortress, 1995.

Beyschlag, Karlmann. "Das Jakobusmartyrium und seine Verwandten in der frühchristlichen Literatur." *Zeitschrift für die neutestamentliche Wissenschaft und die Kunde der älteren Kirche* 56 (1965): 149–78.

———. "Zur Geschichte der Bergpredigt in der Alten Kirche." *Zeitschrift für Theologie und Kirche* 74 (1977): 291–322.

Bhabha, Homi. *The Location of Culture*. London: Routledge, 1994.

Blank, Sheldon H. "The Death of Zechariah in Rabbinic Literature." *Hebrew Union College Annual* 13 (1938): 327–46.

Blum, Matthais. "*. . . denn sie wissen nicht, was sie tun.*" *Zur Rezeption der Fürbitte Jesu am Kreuz (Lk 23,34a) in der antiken jüdisch-christlichen Kontroverse*. Neutestamentliche Abhandlungen. Second Series 46. Münster: Aschendorff, 2001.

Bormann, Lukas. "Die Verrechtlichung der früheste Christlichen Überlieferung im Lukanischen Schrifttum." Pages 283–311 in *Religious Propaganda and Missionary Competition in the New Testament World: Essays in Honoring Dieter Georgi.* Edited by Lukas Bormann, Kelly Del Tredici, and Angela Standhartinger. Leiden: Brill, 1994.

Bovon, François. "The Dossier on Stephen, the First Martyr." *Harvard Theological Review* 96 (2003): 279–315.

———. "Israel, the Church and the Gentiles in the Twofold Work of Luke." Pages 81–95 in *New Testament Traditions and Apocryphal Narratives.* Edited by François Bovon. Allison Park, Pa.: Pickwick, 1995.

———. "La figure de Moïse dans l'oeuvre de Luc." Pages 47–65 in *La Figure de Moïse: écriture et relectures.* Edited by Robert Martin-Achard et al. Geneva: Labor et Fides, 1978.

———. "Studies in Luke-Acts: Retrospect and Prospect." *Harvard Theological Review* 85 (1992): 175–96.

Bowersock, G. W. *Martyrdom and Rome.* Cambridge: Cambridge University Press, 1995.

Boyarin, Daniel. *Borderlines: The Partition of Judaeo-Christianity.* Divinations: Rereading Late Ancient Religion. Philadelphia: University of Pennsylvania Press, 2004.

———. *Dying for God: Martyrdom and the Making of Christianity and Judaism.* Figurae. Stanford: Stanford University Press, 1999.

Brawley, Robert. "Ethical Borderlines between Rejection and Hope: Interpreting the Jews in Luke-Acts." *Currents in Theology and Mission* 27 (2000): 414–23.

———. "The God of Promises and the Jews in Luke-Acts." Pages 279–96 in *Literary Studies in Luke-Acts: Essays in Honor of Joseph B. Tyson.* Edited by Richard. P. Thompson and Thomas E. Phillips. Macon, Ga.: Mercer University Press, 1998.

———. *Luke-Acts and the Jews: Conflict, Apology, and Conciliation.* Society of Biblical Literature Monograph Series 33. Atlanta: Scholars Press, 1987.

Brehm, Alan. "The Meaning of Ἑλληνιστής in Acts in Light of a Diachronic Analysis of ἑλληνίζειν." Pages 180–99 in *Discourse Analysis and Other Topics in Biblical Greek.* Edited by Stanley E. Porter and D. A. Carson. Journal for the Study of the New Testament: Supplement Series 113. Sheffield: Sheffield Academic Press, 1995.

Brent, Allen. *The Imperial Cult and the Development of Church Order: Concepts and Images of Authority in Paganism and Early Christianity before the Age of Cyprian.* Supplements to Vigilae Christianae 45. Leiden: Brill 1999.

Brown, Raymond. *The Birth of the Messiah.* Garden City, N.Y.: Doubleday, 1977.

Bruce, F. F. *Commentary on the Book of Acts.* Grand Rapids: Eerdmans, 1956.

Buell, Denise K. *Why This New Race: Ethnic Reasoning in Early Christianity.* New York: Columbia University Press, 2005.

Bultmann, Rudolf. "The Significance of the Historical Jesus for the Theology of Paul." Pages 220–46 in *Faith and Understanding.* 2 vols. Translated by Louise Pettibone Smith. New York: Harper & Row, 1969.

Burnett, Fred. "historiography." Pages 106–12 in *Handbook of Postmodern Biblical Interpretation.* Edited by A. K. M. Adam. St. Louis, Mo.: Chalice, 2000.

Burrus, Virginia. "The Gospel of Luke and the Acts of the Apostles." Pages 133–55 in *A Postcolonial Commentary on the New Testament Writings*. Edited by Fernando Segovia and R. S. Sugirtharahah. The Bible and Postcolonialism 13. London: T&T Clark, 2007.

Butler, Judith. *Excitable Speech: A Politics of the Performative*. London: Routledge, 1997.

Byron, Gay L. *Symbolic Blackness and Ethnic Difference in Early Christian Literature*. London: Routledge, 2002.

Campenhausen, Hans von. *The Formation of the Christian Bible*. Translated by J. A. Baker. Philadelphia: Fortress, 1972.

Cancik, Hubert. "The History of Culture, Religion and Institutions in Ancient Historiography: Philological Observations Concerning Luke's History." *Journal of Biblical Literature* 116 (1997): 673–95.

Carras, G. P. "A Pentateuchal Echo in Jesus' Prayer on the Cross: Intertextuality between Numbers 15,22–31 and Luke 23,34a." Pages 605–16 in *The Scriptures in the Gospels*. Edited by C. M. Tuckett. Bibliotheca ephemeridum theologicarum lovaniensium 131. Leuven: Leuven University Press, 1997.

Cassidy, Richard J. *Jesus, Politics and Society: A Study of Luke's Gospel*. Maryknoll, N.Y.: Orbis, 1978.

———. *Society and Politics in the Acts of the Apostles*. Maryknoll, N.Y.: Orbis, 1987.

Cassidy, Richard J. and Philip Scharper, eds. *Political Issues in Luke-Acts*. Maryknoll, N.Y.: Orbis, 1983.

Castelli, Elizabeth. *Martyrdom and Memory: Early Christian Culture Making*. Gender, Theory and Religion. New York: Columbia University Press, 2004.

Castelli, Elizabeth and Hal Taussig. "Drawing Large and Startling Figures: Reimagining Christian Origins by Painting Like Picasso." Pages 3–20 in *Reimagining Christian Origins: A Colloquium Honoring Burton L. Mack*. Edited by Elisabeth A. Castelli and Hal Taussig. Valley Forge, Penn.: Trinity, 1996.

Certeau, Michel de. *The Writing of History*. Translated by Tom Conley. New York: Columbia University Press, 1988.

Chrysostom, John. *Homilies on the Acts of the Apostles*. In vol. 11 of *The Nicene and Post-Nicene Fathers*. Series 1. Edited by Philip Schaff. 1886–1889. 14 vols. Repr., Peabody, Mass.: Hendrickson, 1994.

Clark, Elizabeth A. *History, Theory, Text: Historians and the Linguistic Turn*. Cambridge: Harvard University Press, 2004.

Conzelmann, Hans. *The Acts of the Apostles*. Hermeneia. Translated by James Limburg, A. Thomas Kraabel, and Donald H. Juel. Edited by Eldon Jay Epp. Philadelphia: Fortress, 1987.

———. *Theology of St. Luke*. Translated by Geoffrey Buswell. New York: Harper & Row, 1961. Originally published as *Die Mitte der Zeit. Studien zur Theologie des Lukas*. Beiträge zur historischen Theologie 17; Tübingen: Mohr, 1953.

Cooper, Kate. *The Virgin and the Bride: Idealized Womanhood in Late Antiquity*. Cambridge: Harvard University Press, 1996.

Crossan, John Dominic. *The Historical Jesus: The Life of a Mediterranean Jewish Peasant*. San Francisco: HarperSanFrancisco, 1991.

Cullman, Oscar, ed. and trans. "The Protevangelium of James." Pages 421–39 in *Gospels and Related Writings*. Rev. ed. Vol. 1 of *New Testament Apocrypha*. Edited by Wilhelm Schneemelcher and R. McL. Wilson. Louisville, Ky.: Westminster John Knox, 1991.

Cyprian. *On Patience*. In vol. 5 of the *Ante-Nicene Fathers*. *Hippolytus, Cyprian, Caius, Novatian, Appendix*. Translated by Ernest Wallis. Edited by Alexander Roberts and James Donaldson. 1885–1887. 10 vols. Repr. Grand Rapids: Eerdmans, 1985.

D'Angelo, Mary Rose. "The ANHP Question in Luke-Acts: Imperial Masculinity and the Deployment of Women in the Early Second Century." Pages 44–69 in *A Feminist Companion to Luke*. Edited by Amy-Jill Levine. Feminist Companion to the New Testament and Early Christian Writings 3. Sheffield: Sheffield Academic Press, 2002.

———. "Women in Luke-Acts: A Redactional View." *Journal of Biblical Literature* 109 (1990): 441–61.

Dassmann, Ernst. *Sündenvergebung durch Taufe, Busse und Martyrerfürbitte in den Zeugnissen frühchristlicher Frömmigkeit und Kunst*. Münsterische Beiträge zur Theologie 36. Münster: Aschendorff, 1973.

Datema, Cornelis. *Asterius of Amasea. Homilies I–XIV: Text, Introduction and Notes*. Leiden: Brill, 1970.

Daube, David. "'For They Know Not What They Do': Luke 23,24." *Studia Patristica* 4, no. 2 (1961): 58–70.

Dehandschutter, Boudewijn. "Asterius of Amasea." Pages 162–93 in *"Let Us Die That We May Live": Greek Homilies on Christian Martyrs from Asia Minor, Palestine and Syria c. AD 350–AD 450*. Edited by Johan Leemans, Wendy Mayer, Pauline Allen, and Boudewijn Dehandschutter. London: Routledge, 2003.

Delobel, Joël. "Luke 23:34a: A Perpetual Text-Critical Crux?" Pages 25–36 in *Sayings of Jesus: Canonical and Non-Canonical: Essays in Honour of Tjitze Baarda*. Edited by William L. Petersen, Johan S. Vos, and Henk J. De Jonge. Novum Testamentum Supplements 89. Leiden: Brill, 1997.

Dialog des Admantius. Edited by W. H. van de sande Bakhuyzen. Leipzig: Hinrichs, 1901.

Dibelius, Martin. *James: A Commentary on the Epistle of James*. Revised by Heinrich Greeven. Hermeneia. Philadelphia: Fortress, 1976.

———. *Studies in the Acts of the Apostles*. London: SCM, 1956.

Didascalia apostolorum. Translated and edited by Alistair Stewart-Sykes. Turnhout: Brepols, 2008.

Dillon, Sheila. "Women on the Columns of Trajan and Marcus Aurelius and the Visual Language of Roman Victory." Pages 244–71 in *Representations of War in Ancient Rome*. Edited by Sheila Dillon and Katherine E. Welch. Cambridge: Cambridge University Press, 2006.

Dirscherl, Erwin. "Marcions später Triumph? Bemerkungen zum Verhältnis von Dogmatik und Tiefenpsychologie." Pages 246–59 in *Gottes Offenbarung in der Welt*. Edited by Friedhelm Krüger. Gütersloh: Gütersloher Verlagshaus, 1998.

Dowling, Melissa. *Clemency and Cruelty in the Roman World*. Ann Arbor: University of Michigan Press, 2006.

Dube, Musa. *Postcolonial Feminist Interpretation of the Bible*. St. Louis, Mo.: Chalice, 2000.

Dunn, James D. G. *The Parting of the Ways: Between Christianity and Judaism and Their Significance for the Character of Christianity*. London: SCM, 1991.

Ehrman, Bart. *The Orthodox Corruption of Scripture: The Effect of Early Christological Controversies on the Text of the New Testament*. New York: Oxford University Press, 1996.

———. "The Text of the Gospels at the End of the Second Century." Pages 95–122 in *Codex Bezae: Studies from the Lunel Colloquium June 1994*. Edited by D. C. Parker and C.-B. Amphoux. New Testament Tools and Studies 22. Leiden: Brill, 1996.

Eliav, Yaron Z. "The Tomb of James, Brother of Jesus, as *Locus Memoriae*." *Harvard Theological Review* 97 (2004): 33–59.

Epp, Eldon Jay. "The 'Ignorance Motif' in Acts and Anti-Judaic Tendencies in Codex Bezae." *Harvard Theological Review* 55 (1962): 51–62.

Esler, Philip. *Community and Gospel in Luke-Acts: The Social and Political Motivations of Lucan Theology*. Society for New Testament Studies Monograph Series 57. Cambridge: Cambridge University Press, 1987.

Eusebius. *Ecclesiastical History*. Translated by Kirsopp Lake. 2 vols. Loeb Classical Library. Cambridge: Harvard University Press, 1980.

Evans, C. A. "Faith and Polemic: The New Testament and First-Century Judaism." Pages 1–17 in *Anti-Semitism and Early Christianity: Issues of Polemic and Faith*. Edited by Craig Evans and Donald Hagner. Minneapolis: Fortress, 1993.

———. "Is Luke's View of the Jewish Rejection of Jesus Anti-Semitic?" Pages 29–56 in *Reimaging the Death of the Lukan Jesus*. Edited by D. D. Sylva. Frankfurt am Main: Hain, 1990.

Fitzmyer, Joseph. *Gospel According to Luke (I–IX)*. Anchor Bible. Garden City, N.Y.: Doubleday, 1979.

Flusser, David. "'Sie wissen nicht, was sie tun': Geshichte eines Herrnwortes." Pages 393–410 in *Kontinuität und Einheit*. Edited by Paul-Gerhard Müller and Werner Stenger. Freiburg: Herder, 1981.

Ford, J. Massyngbaerde. *My Enemy Is My Guest: Jesus and Violence in Luke*. Maryknoll, N.Y.: Orbis, 1984.

Frend, W. H. C. *Martyrdom and Persecution in the Early Church: A Study of a Conflict from the Maccabees to Donatus*. New York: New York University Press, 1967.

Gager, John G. *The Origins of Anti-Semitism: Attitudes toward Judaism in Pagan and Christian Antiquity*. New York: Oxford University Press, 1983.

———. "Violent Acts and Violent Language in the Apostle Paul." Pages 13–21 in *Violence in the New Testament*. Edited by Shelly Matthews and E. Leigh Gibson. London: T&T Clark, 2005.

Gasque, W. *A History of the Criticism of the Acts of the Apostles*. Beiträge zur Geschichte der biblischen Exegese 17. Tübingen: Mohr, 1975.

Gaston, Lloyd. *No Stone on Another: Studies in the Significance of the Fall of Jerusalem in the Synoptic Gospels*. Studien zum Neuen Testament 23. Leiden: Brill, 1970.

George, Augustin. "Israël dans l'œuvre de Luc." *Revue biblique* 75 (1968): 481–525.

Gibson, E. Leigh. "Jewish Antagonism or Christian Polemic: The Case of the *Martyr-dom of Pionius.*" *Journal of Early Christian Studies* 9 (2001): 339–58.

Gilbert, Gary. "The List of Nations in Acts 2: Roman Propaganda and the Lukan Response." *Journal of Biblical Literature* 121 (2002): 497–529.

———. "Roman Propaganda and Christian Identity in the Worldview of Luke-Acts." Pages 233–56 in *Contextualizing Acts: Lukan Narrative and Greco-Roman Discourse.* Edited by Todd Penner and Caroline Vander Stichele. Society of Biblical Literature Symposium Series 20. Atlanta: Society of Biblical Literature, 2003.

Glancy, Jennifer. *Slavery in Early Christianity.* New York: Oxford University Press, 2002.

Gnilka, Joachim. *Die Verstockung Israels: Isaias 6,9–10 in der Theologie der Synoptiker.* Munich: Kösel, 1961.

Goodspeed, Edgar. *The Formation of the New Testament.* Chicago: University of Chicago Press, 1926.

Gregory, Andrew. *The Reception of Luke and Acts in the Period before Irenaeus: Looking for Luke in the Second Century.* Tübingen: Mohr, 2003.

Green, Joel. *The Gospel of Luke.* New International Commentary on the New Testament. Grand Rapids: Eerdmans, 1997.

Haacker, Klaus. "Die Stellung des Stephanus in der Geschichte des Urchristentums." *ANRW* 26.2:1515–53. Part 2, *Principat*, 26.2. Edited by H. Temporini and W. Hasse. New York: de Gruyter, 1995.

Haenchen, Ernst. *The Acts of the Apostles.* Translated by Bernard Noble and Gerald Shinn, with the translation revised and brought up to date by R. McL. Wilson. Philadelphia: Westminster, 1971.

———. "Judentum und Christentum in der Apostelgeschichte." *Zeitschrift für die neutestamentliche Wissenschaft und die Kunde der älteren Kirche* 54 (1963): 155–89.

Haines-Eitzen, Kim. *Guardians of Letters: Literacy, Power, and the Transmitters of Early Christian Literature.* New York: Oxford University Press, 2000.

Harnack, Adolf von. *The Acts of the Apostles.* Crown Theological Library. New Testament Series 3. Translated by J. R. Wilkinson. New York: Putnam, 1909.

———. *Marcion: Das Evangelium vom Fremden Gott.* Leipzig: Hinrichs, 1924. Repr., Darmstadt: Wissenschaftliche Buchgesellschaft, 1985.

———. *Marcion: The Gospel of the Alien God.* Translated by John E. Steely and Lyle D. Bierma. Durham, N.C.: Labyrinth, 1990.

———. *The Mission and Expansion of Christianity in the First Three Centuries.* Translated by James Moffatt. 1908. Repr., New York: Harper & Row, 1961.

Harootunian, Harry. *History's Disquiet: Modernity, Cultural Practice, and the Question of Everyday Life.* New York: Columbia University Press, 2000.

Hayes, Richard B. *Echoes of Scripture in the Letters of Paul.* New Haven, Conn.: Yale University Press, 1989.

Hemer, Colin J. *The Book of Acts in the Setting of Hellenistic History.* Winona Lake, Ind.: Eisenbrauns, 1990.

Henten, Jan Willem van. "Jewish and Christian Martyrs." Pages 163–81 in *Holy Persons in Judaism and Christianity.* Edited by Marcel Poorthuis and Joshua Schwartz. Leiden: Brill, 2004.

———. *The Maccabean Martyrs as Saviours of the Jewish People: A Study of 2 and 4 Maccabees*. Journal for the Study of the Pseudepigrapha: Supplement Series 57. Leiden: Brill, 1997.

———. "Zum Einfluss jüdischer Martyrien auf die Literatur des frühen Christentums, II. Die Apostolischen Väter," *ANRW* 27.1:700–23. Part 2, *Principat*, 27.1. Edited by H. Temporini and W. Haase. New York: de Gruyter, 1992.

Heschel, Susannah. *The Aryan Jesus: Christian Theologians and the Bible in Nazi Germany*. Princeton: Princeton University Press, 2008.

———."From Jesus to Shylock: Christian Supersessionism and 'The Merchant of Venice.'" *Harvard Theological Review* 99 (2006): 407–31.

———. "Theology as a Vision for Colonialism: From Supersessionism to Dejudaiza-tion in German Protestantism." Pages 148–64 in *Germany's Colonial Pasts: An Anthology in Memory of Susanne Zantop*. Edited by Marcia Klotz, Lora Wildenthal, and Eric Ames. Lincoln: University of Nebraska Press, 2005.

Heusler, Erika. *Kapitalprozesse im lukanischen Doppelwerk: Die Verfahren gegen Jesus und Paulus in exegetischer und rechtshistorischer Analyse*. Neutestamentliche Abhandlun-gen. Second Series 38. Münster: Aschendorff, 2000.

Hill, Craig C. *Hellenists and Hebrews: Reappraising Division within the Earliest Church*. Minneapolis: Fortress, 1992.

Hippolytus. *Expository Treatise against the Jews*. In vol. 5 of the *Ante-Nicene Fathers. Hippolytus, Cyprian, Caius, Novatian, Appendix*. Edited by Alexander Roberts and James Donaldson. 1885–1887. 10 vols. Repr. Grand Rapids: Eerdmans, 1985.

Hoffmann, P. "Jesus versus Menschensohn: Mt 10,32f und die synoptische Menschen-sohnüberlieferung." Pages 165–202 in *Salz der Erde, Licht der Welt: exegetische Studien zum Matthäusevangelium*. Edited by L. Oberlinner and P. Fiedler. Stut-tgart: Verlag katholisches Bibelwerk, 1991.

Holmås, Geir Otto. "'My House Shall Be a House of Prayer,' Regarding the Temple as a Place of Prayer in Acts within the Context of Luke's Apologetical Objective." *Journal for the Study of the New Testament* 27 (2005): 393–416.

Horn, Fredrich W. "Die Haltung des Lukas zum Römischen Staat im Evangelium und in der Apostelgeschichte." Pages 203–24 in *The Unity of Luke-Acts*. Edited by J. Verheyden. Bibliotheca ephemeridum theologicarum lovaniensium 142. Leuven: Leuven University Press, 1999.

Horsley, Richard A. *The Liberation of Christmas: The Infancy Narratives in Social Context*. New York: Crossroad, 1989.

———. "'Like One of the Prophets of Old:' Two Types of Popular Prophets at the Time of Jesus." *Catholic Biblical Quarterly* 47 (1985): 435–63.

Hubbard, Moyer V. "Urban Uprisings in the Roman World: The Social Setting of the Mobbing of Sosthenes." *New Testament Studies* 51 (2005): 416–28.

Irenaeus. *Against All Heresies*. In vol. 1 of the *Ante-Nicene Fathers. The Apostolic Fathers, Justin Martyr, Irenaeus*. Edited by Alexander Roberts and James Donaldson. 1885. Repr. Grand Rapids: Eerdmans, 1985.

Jenkins, Keith. *On "What Is History?": From Carr to Elton to Rorty and White*. London: Routledge, 1995.

Jervell, Jacob. *Die Apostelgeschichte*. Kritisch-exegetischer Kommentar über das Neue Testament 3. Göttingen: Vandenhoeck & Ruprecht, 1998.

———. *Luke and the People of God: A New Look at Luke-Acts*. Minneapolis: Augsburg, 1972.

———. *The Unknown Paul: Essays in Luke-Acts and Early Christian History*. Minneapolis, Augsburg, 1984.

Johnson, Luke Timothy. *The Acts of the Apostles*. Sacra Pagina 5. Collegeville, Minn.: Liturgical Press, 1992.

Johnson-DeBaufre, Melanie. "The Blood Required of This Generation: Interpreting Communal Blame in a Colonial Context." Pages 22–34 in *Violence in the New Testament*. Edited by E. Leigh Gibson and Shelly Matthews. New York: T&T Clark, 2005.

———. *Jesus among Her Children: Q, Eschatology and the Construction of Christian Origins*. Harvard Theological Studies 55. Cambridge: Harvard University Press, 2005.

Jones, F. Stanley. "An Ancient Jewish Christian Rejoinder to Luke's Acts of the Apostles: Pseudo-Clementine *Recognitions* 1.27–71." *Semeia* 80 (1997): 223–245.

———. *An Ancient Jewish Christian Source on the History of Christianity: Pseudo-Clementine Recognitions 1.27–71*. Society of Biblical Literature Texts and Translations 37. Christian Apocrypha Series 2. Atlanta: Scholars Press, 1995.

———. "Hegesippus as a Source for the History of Jewish Christianity." Pages 201–12 in *Le judéo-christianisme dans tous ses états: Actes du collogque de Jérusalem 6–10 Juillet 1998*. Edited by Simon C. Mimouni and F. Stanley Jones. Paris: Cerf, 2001.

———. "The Martyrdom of James in Hegesippus, Clement of Alexandria, and Christian Apocrypha, Including nag Hammadi: A Study of the Textual Relations." Pages 322–35 in *SBL Seminar Papers, 1990*. Society of Biblical Literature Seminar Papers 29. Atlanta: Scholars Press, 1990.

Josephus. *Jewish Antiquities Book 20*. Translated by L. H. Feldman. Loeb Classical Library. Cambridge: Harvard University Press, 1965. Repr. 1985.

Justin Martyr. *Dialogue with Trypho*. Translated by Thomas B. Falls. Revised and with a New Introduction by Thomas P. Halton. Edited by Michael Slusser. Washington, D.C.: Catholic University Press, 2003.

———. *Dialogus cum Tryphone*. Edited by Miroslav Marcovich. Patristische Texte und Studien 47. Berlin: de Gruyter, 1997.

Kahl, Brigitte. "Acts of the Apostles: Pro(to)-Imperial Script and Hidden Transcript." Pages 137–56 in *In the Shadow of Empire: Reclaiming the Bible as a History of Faithful Resistance*. Edited by Richard Horsley. Louisville, Ky.: Westminster John Knox, 2008.

Kellermann, Ulrich. "Das Danielbuch und die Märtyrertheologie der Auferstehung." Pages 51–75 in *Die Entstehung der jüdischen Martyrologie*. Edited by J. W. van Henten. Studia post-biblica 38. Leiden: Brill, 1989.

Kelley, Nicole. *Knowledge and Religious Authority in the Pseudo-Clementines: Situating the Recognitions in Fourth Century Syria*. Wissenschaftliche Untersuchungen zum Neuen Testament. Second Series 213. Tübingen: Mohr, 2006.

Kelley, Shawn. *Racializing Jesus: Race, Ideology and the Formation of Modern Biblical Scholarship*. Biblical Limits. London: Routledge, 2002.

Kilgallen, J. J. "The Function of Stephen's Speech (Acts, 2–53)." *Biblica* 70 (1989): 177–81.

Kimelman, Reuven. "*Birkat Ha-Minim* and the Lack of Evidence for an Anti-Christian Jewish Prayer in Late Antiquity." Pages 2.226–44, 2.391–403 in *Jewish and Christian Self-definition*. Edited by E. P. Sanders. 2 vols. Philadelphia: Fortress, 1981.

King, Karen. *What Is Gnosticism?* Cambridge: Harvard University Press, 2003.

Klassen, William. *Love of Enemies: The Way to Peace*. Overtures to Biblical Theology 15. Philadelphia: Fortress, 1984.

Kloppenborg, John S. "The Death of Jesus in Luke." *Toronto Journal of Theology* 8 (1992): 121–33.

Knox, John. *Marcion and the New Testament: An Essay in the Early History of the Canon*. Chicago: University of Chicago Press, 1942.

Koester, Helmut. *Synoptische Überlieferung bei den apostolischen Vätern*. Berlin: Akademie, 1957.

Lake, Kirsopp and Henry Cadbury. *English Translation and Commentary*. Vol. 4 of *The Beginnings of Christianity Part I: The Acts of the Apostles*. Edited by F. J. Foakes Jackson and Kirsopp Lake. 5 vols. 1920–1933. Repr., Grand Rapids: Baker, 1979.

Lapide, P. E. "Die Bergpredigt—Theorie und Praxis." *Zeitschrift für evangelische Ethik* 17 (1973): 369–72.

Larsson, Edvin. "Temple-Criticism and the Jewish Heritage: Some Reflections on Acts 6–7." *NTS* 39 (1993): 379–95.

Le Boulluec, Alain. *La notion d'hérésie dans la littérature qrecque IIᵉ-IIIᵉsiècles*. 2 vols. Paris: Études Augustiniennes, 1985.

Lefkowitz, M. R. *The Lives of the Greek Poets*. London: Duckworth, 1981.

Levine, Amy-Jill. "Anti-Judaism and the Gospel of Matthew." Pages 9–36 in *Anti-Judaism and the Gospels*. Edited by William R. Farmer. Harrisburg, Pa.: Trinity, 1999.

Licht, J. "Taxo, Or the Apocalyptic Doctrine of Vengeance." *Journal of Jewish Studies* 12 (1961): 95–103.

Lieu, Judith. "Accusations of Jewish Persecution in Early Christian Sources, with Particular Reference to Justin Martyr and the *Martyrdom of Polycarp*." Pages 279–95 in *Tolerance and Intolerance in Early Judaism and Christianity*. Edited by Graham N. Stanton and Guy G. Stroumsa. Cambridge: Cambridge University Press, 1998.

———. *Image and Reality: The Jews in the World of the Christians in the Second Century*. Edinburgh: T&T Clark, 1996.

———. *Neither Jew Nor Greek?: Constructing Early Christianity*. London: T&T Clark, 2002.

Liew, Tat-siong Benny. "Acts." Pages 420–23 in *Global Bible Commentary*. Edited by Daniel Patte et al. Nashville: Abingdon, 2004.

Lightfoot, J. B. "St. Paul and the Three." Pages 291–374 of the author's *Saint Paul's Epistle to the Galatians*. 7th ed. London: MacMillan, 1881. Originally published in 1865 in *Dissertations on the Apostolic Age*.

Lohfink, Gerhard. *Die Sammlung Israels: Eine Untersuchung zur lukanischen Ekklesiologie*. Munich: Kösel, 1975.

Löhr, Winrich. "Did Marcion Distinguish between a Just God and a Good God?" Pages 131–46 in *Marcion und seine kirchengeschictliche Wirkung: Vorträge der Internationalen Fachkonferenz zu Marcion, gehalten vom 15–18. August 2001 in Mainz*. Edited by Gerhard May and Katharina Greschat; Texte und Untersuchungen zur Geschichte der altchristlichen Literatur 150. Berlin: de Gruyter, 2002.

Loisy, Alfred. *Les Actes des apôtres*. Paris: E. Nourry, 1920.

Lüdemann, Gerd. *Early Christianity according to the Traditions in Acts: A Commentary*. Translated by John Bowden. Minneapolis: Fortress, 1989.

———. *Opposition to Paul in Jewish Christianity*. Translated by M. Eugene Boring. Minneapolis: Fortress, 1989.

Luz, Ulrich. *Das Evangelium nach Matthäus*. Evangelisch-katholischer Kommentar zum Neuen Testament 1. 3 vols. Neukirchen-Vluyn: Neukirchener Verlag, 1997.

———. *Matthew 1–7: A Commentary*. Vol. 1 of *Matthew, A Commentary*. Translated by James E. Crouch. Edited by Helmut Koester. Hermeneia. Minneapolis: Fortress, 2007.

MacDonald, Dennis R. "Apocryphal and Canonical Narratives about Paul." Pages 55–70 in *Paul and the Legacies of Paul*. Edited by William S. Babcock. Dallas: Southern Methodist University Press, 1990.

Mack, Burton. "A Jewish Jesus School in Jerusalem?" Pages 253–62 in *Redescribing Christian Origins*. Edited by Ron Cameron and Merrill P. Miller. Symposium 28. Atlanta: Society of Biblical Literature, 2004.

Maddox, Robert. *The Purpose of Luke-Acts*. Studies in the New Testament World. Edinburgh: T & T Clark, 1982.

Marcus, Joel. "Crucifixion as Parodic Exaltation," *Journal of Biblical Literature* 125 (2006): 73–87.

———. "The Old Testament and the Death of Jesus: The Role of Scripture in the Gospel Passion Narratives." Pages 205–33 in *The Death of Jesus in Early Christianity*. Edited by John T. Carroll and Joel B. Green. Peabody, Mass.: Hendrickson, 1995.

Marguerat, Daniel. *The First Christian Historian: Writing the 'Acts of the Apostles'*. Society for New Testament Studies Monograph Series 121. Cambridge: Cambridge University Press, 2002.

Martin, Dale. *Sex and the Single Savior: Gender and Sexuality in Biblical Interpretation*. Louisville, Ky.: Westminster John Knox, 2006.

Martyn, Louis. *History and Theology in the Fourth Gospel*. 2d ed. Nashville: Abingdon, 1979.

Mason, Steve. *Josephus and the New Testament*. Peabody, Mass.: Hendrickson, 1992.

Massey, Doreen. *World City*. Malden, Mass.: Polity, 2007.

Mathys, Hans-Peter. *Liebe deinen Nächsten wie dich selbst. Untersuchungen zum alttestamentlichen Gebot der Nächstenliebe (Lev 19.18)*. Orbis biblicus et orientalis 71. Göttingen: Vandenhoeck & Ruprecht, 1986.

Matthews, Shelly. "Ethical Issues in Reconstructing Intrareligious Violence in Antiquity: The Gospel of Matthew as a Test Case." Pages 334–50 in *Walk in the Ways of*

Wisdom: Essays in Honor of Elisabeth Schüssler Fiorenza. Edited by Shelly Matthews, Cynthia Kittredge, and Melanie Johnson-DeBaufre. Harrisburg, Pa.: Trinity, 2003.

———. *First Converts: Rich Pagan Women and the Rhetoric of Mission in Early Judaism and Christianity.* Contraversions. Stanford: Stanford University Press, 2001.

———. "The Need for the Stoning of Stephen." Pages 124–39 of *Violence in the New Testament.* Edited by Shelly Matthews and E. Leigh Gibson. London: T&T Clark, 2005.

May, Gerhard and Katharina Greschat, eds. *Marcion und seine kirchengeschichtliche Wirkung: Vorträge der Internationalen Fachkonferenz zu Marcion.* Berlin: de Gruyter, 2002.

McLaren, James. "Ananus, James, and Earliest Christianity: Josephus' Account of the Death of James." *Journal of Theological Studies* 52 (2001): 1–25.

———. "Constructing Judaean History in the Diaspora: Josephus's Accounts of Judas." Pages 90–108 in *Negotiating Diaspora.* Edited by John Barclay. London: T&T Clark, 2004.

———. "Josephus on Titus: The Vanquished Writing about the Victor." Pages 279–96 in *Josephus and Jewish History in Flavian Rome and Beyond.* Edited by Joseph Sievers and Gaia Lembi. Supplements to the Journal for the Study of Judaism in the Persian, Hellenistic, and Roman Periods 104. Leiden: Brill, 2005.

Meeks, Wayne A. and Robert L. Wilken. *Jews and Christians in Antioch in the First Four Centuries of the Common Era.* Society of Biblical Literature Sources for Biblical Study 13. Missoula, Mont.: Scholars Press, 1978.

Meier, J. P. "Jesus in Josephus: A Modest Proposal." *Catholic Biblical Quarterly* 52 (1990): 76–103.

Metzger, Bruce. *A Textual Commentary on the Greek New Testament.* Stuttgart: Biblia-Druck GmbH, 1975.

Miller, Merrill P. "Antioch, Paul and Jerusalem: Diaspora Myths of Origins in the Homeland." Pages 177–235 in *Redescribing Christian Origins.* Edited by Ron Cameron and Merrill P. Miller. Symposium 28. Atlanta: Society of Biblical Literature, 2004.

Moessner, David. "'The Christ Must Suffer': New Light on the Jesus—Peter, Stephen, Paul Parallels in Luke-Acts." *Novum Testamentum* 28 (1986): 220–56.

———. "'Completed End[s]ings' of Historiographical Narrative: Diodorus Siculus and the End[ing] of Acts." Pages 193–221 in *Apostelgeschichte und die hellenistische Geschichtsschreibung: Festschrift für Eckhard Plümacher zu seinem 65. Geburtstag.* Edited by Ciliers Breytenbach and Jens Schröter. Arbeiten zur Geschichte des antiken Judentums und des Urchristentums 57. Leiden: Brill, 2004.

———. "The 'Script' of the Scriptures in Acts: Suffering as God's 'Plan' (Βουλή) for the World for the 'Release of Sins.'" Pages 218–50 in *History, Literature, and Society in the Book of Acts.* Edited by Ben Witherington. Cambridge: Cambridge University Press, 1996.

Moffitt, David M. "Righteous Bloodshed, Matthew's Passion Narrative, and the Temple's Destruction: Lamentations as a Matthean Intertext." *Journal of Biblical Literature* 125 (2006): 299–320.

Mommsen, Theodor. *Römisches strafrecht.* Leipzig: Duncker & Humblot, 1899.

Moore, Stephen D. and Janice C. Anderson. "Taking It Like a Man: Masculinity in 4 Maccabees." *Journal of Biblical Literature* 117 (1998): 249–73.

Moore, Stephen D. and Fernando F. Segovia, eds. *Postcolonial Biblical Criticism: Interdisciplinary Intersections.* London: T&T Clark, 2005.

Mount, Christopher. *Pauline Christianity: Luke-Acts and the Legacy of Paul.* Novum Testamentum Supplements 104. Leiden: Brill, 2002.

Müller, Mogens. "The Reception of the Old Testament in Matthew and Luke-Acts: From Interpretation to Proof from Scripture." *Novum Testamentum* 43 (2001): 315–30.

Nasrallah, Laura. "The Acts of the Apostles, Greek Cities, and Hadrian's Panhellenion." *Journal of Biblical Literature* 27 (2008): 533–66.

———. *Christian Responses to Roman Art and Architecture: The Second-Century Church amid the Spaces of Empire.* New York: Cambridge University Press, 2010.

Neusner, Jacob. *What Is Midrash?* Philadelphia: Fortress, 1987.

Novum Testamentum Graece. Nestle-Aland. 27th ed. Stuttgart: Deutsche Bibelgesellschaft, 1993.

O'Neill, J. C. *The Theology of Acts in Its Historical Setting.* 2d ed. London: SPCK, 1970.

Osborn, Eric. *Tertullian: First Theologian of the West.* Cambridge: Cambridge University Press, 1997.

Painter, John. *Just James: The Brother of Jesus in History and Tradition.* Columbia: University of South Carolina Press, 1997. Repr., Minneapolis: Fortress, 1999.

Parsons, Mikeal and Richard Pervo. *Rethinking the Unity of Luke and Acts.* Minneapolis: Fortress, 1993.

Pelikan, Jaroslav. *Acts.* Brazos Theological Commentary on the Bible. Grand Rapids: Brazos, 2005.

Penner, Todd. "Civilizing Discourse: Acts, Declamation, and the Rhetoric of the Polis." Pages 65–104 in *Contextualizing Acts: Lukan Narrative and Greco-Roman Discourse.* Edited by Todd Penner and Caroline Vander Stichele. Society of Biblical Literature Symposium Series 20. Atlanta: Scholars Press, 2003.

———. *In Praise of Christian Origins: Stephen and the Hellenists in Lukan Apologetic Historiography.* New York: T&T Clark, 2004.

Perkins, Judith. "The Rhetoric of the Maternal Body in the *Passion of Perpetua.*" Pages 313–32 in *Mapping Gender in Ancient Religious Discourses.* Edited by Todd Penner and Caroline Vander Stichele. Leiden: Brill, 2007.

———. *The Suffering Self: Pain and Narrative Representation in the Early Christian Era.* London: Routledge, 1995.

Pervo, Richard. *Acts.* Hermeneia. Edited by Harold W. Attridge. Minneapolis: Fortress, 2009.

———. "'Antioch, Farewell! For Wisdom Sees. . .': Traces of a Source Describing the Early Gentile Mission in Acts 1–15." Paper read at the fall meeting of the Westar Institute. Sonoma, Calif., 2006.

———. *Dating Acts: Between the Evangelists and the Apologists.* Santa Rosa, Calif.: Polebridge, 2006.

———. "A Hard Act to Follow: The Acts of Paul and the Canonical Acts." *Journal of Higher Criticism* 2, no. 2 (1995): 3–32.

———. *Profit with Delight: The Literary Genre of the Acts of the Apostles.* Philadelphia: Fortress, 1987.

———. Review of Joseph B. Tyson, *Marcion and Luke-Acts: A Defining Struggle. Journal of Religion* 87 (2007): 435–36.

Petzer, Jacobus H. "Anti-Judaism and the Textual Problem of Luke 23:34." *Filología Neotestamentaria* 5 (1992): 199–204.

Piper, John. *'Love Your Enemies': Jesus' Love Command in the Synoptic Gospels and in the Early Christian Paraenesis.* Society for New Testament Studies Monograph Series 38. Cambridge: Cambridge University Press, 1979.

Plett, Heinrich. "Intertextualities." Pages 3–29 in *Intertexuality.* Edited by Heinrich Plett. Research in Text Theory 15. Berlin: de Gruyter, 1991.

Polycarp. *To the Philippians.* In *The Apostolic Fathers.* Edited and Translated by Bart D. Ehrman. 2 vols. Loeb Classical Library. Cambridge: Harvard University Press, 2003.

Pratscher, Wilhelm. *Der Herrenbruder Jakobus und die Jakobustradition.* Forschungen zur Religion und Literatur des Alten und Neuen Testaments 139. Göttingen: Vandenhoeck & Ruprecht, 1987.

Räisänen, Heikki. "The 'Hellenists': A Bridge between Jesus and Paul?" Pages 149–202 in *Jesus, Paul and Torah: Collected Essays.* Journal for the Study of the New Testament: Supplement Series 43. Sheffield: Sheffield Academic Press, 1992.

———. "Marcion." Pages 100–24 in *A Companion to Second-Century Christian 'Heretics'.* Edited by Antti Marjanen and Petri Loumanen. Leiden: Brill, 2008.

———. "Marcion and the Origins of Christian Anti-Judaism: A Reappraisal." *Tenemos* 33 (1997): 121–35.

Rajak, Tessa. "Friends, Romans, Subjects: Agrippa II's Speech in Josephus's *Jewish War.*" Pages 122–34 in *Images of Empire.* Edited by Loveday Alexander. Journal for the Study of the Old Testament: Supplement Series 122. Sheffield: Sheffield University Press, 1991.

Reed, Annette Yoshiko. "'Jewish Christianity' after the 'Parting of the Ways': Approaches to Historiography and Self-definition in the Pseudo-Clementines." Pages 189–231 in *The Ways That Never Parted.* Edited by Adam H. Becker and Annette Yoshiko Reed. Texte und Studien zum antiken Judentum 95. Tübingen: Mohr, 2003.

Rehm, Bernard, ed. *Die Pseudoklementinen II: Rekognitionen in Rufins Übersetzung.* Edited by Georg Strecker. 2d ed., rev. Die griechischen christlichen Schriftsteller der ersten Jahrhunderte 51. Berlin: Akademie, 1994.

Reicke, B. "Judaeo-Christianity and the Jewish Establishment, A.D. 33–66." Pages 145–52 in *Jesus and the Politics of His Day.* Edited by Ernst Bammel and C. F. D. Moule. Cambridge: Cambridge University Press, 1984.

Reid, Barbara. "The Power of the Widows and How to Suppress It (Acts 6.1–7)." Pages 71–88 in *A Feminist Companion to the Acts of the Apostles.* Edited by Amy-Jill Levine. Feminist Companion to the New Testament and Early Christian Writings 9. London: T&T Clark, 2004.

Reimer, Ivoni Richter. *Women in the Acts of the Apostles: A Feminist Liberation Perspective.* Minneapolis: Fortress, 1995.

Reinhartz, Adele. "Love, Hate, and Violence in the Gospel of John." Pages 109–23 in *Violence in the New Testament.* Edited by E. Leigh Gibson and Shelly Matthews. New York: T&T Clark, 2005.

———. "The New Testament and Anti-Judaism: A Literary Critical Approach." *Journal of Ecumenical Studies* 25 (1988): 524–37.

Reiser, Marius. "Love of Enemies in the Context of Antiquity." *New Testament Studies* 47 (2001): 411–27.

Reventlow, Henning Graf. "The Role of the Old Testament in the German Liberal Protestant Theology of the Nineteenth Century." Pages 132–48 in *Biblical Studies and the Shifting of Paradigms, 1850–1914.* Edited by Henning Graf Reventlow and William Farmer. Journal for the Study of the Old Testament: Supplement Series 192. Sheffield: Sheffield Academic Press.

Richard, Earl. *Acts 6:1–8:4: The Author's Method of Composition.* Society of Biblical Literature Dissertation Series 41. Missoula, Mont.: Scholars Press, 1978.

Roloff, J. "Die Paulus-Darstellung des Lukas. Ihre geschichtlichen Vorausetzungen und ihr theologisches Ziel." *Evangelische Theologie* 39 (1979): 510–31.

Rossi, Andreola. "The Tears of Marcellus: History of a Literary Motif in Livy." *Greece and Rome* 47 (2000): 56–66.

Rothschild, Clare K. *Luke-Acts and the Rhetoric of History: An Investigation of Early Christian Historiography.* Wissenschaftliche Untersuchungen zum Neuen Testament. Second Series 175. Tübingen: Mohr, 2004.

Rowe, C. Kavin. "Luke-Acts and the Imperial Cult: A Way Through the Conundrum?" *Journal for the Study of the New Testament* 27 (2005): 279–300.

Salmon, Marilyn. "Insider or Outsider? Luke's Relationship with Judaism." Pages 76–82 in *Luke-Acts and the Jewish People: Eight Critical Perspectives.* Edited by Joseph B. Tyson. Minneapolis: Augsburg, 1988.

Sanders, Jack T. *The Jews in Luke-Acts.* Philadelphia: Fortress, 1987.

———. "The Parable of the Pounds and Lucan Anti-Semitism." *Theological Studies* 42 (1981): 667.

Schaberg, Jane. *The Resurrection of Mary Magdalene: Legends, Apocrypha, and the Christian Testament.* New York: Continuum, 2004.

Schmid, Ulrich. *Marcion und sein Apostlos: Rekonstruction und historische Einordnung der marcionitischen Paulusbriefausgabe.* Arbeiten zur neutestamentlichen Textforschung 25. Berlin: de Gruyter, 1995.

Schmidt, Daryl. "Anti-Judaism and the Gospel of Luke." Pages 63–96 in *Anti-Judaism and the Gospels.* Edited by William R. Farmer. Harrisburg, Pa.: Trinity, 1999.

Schneemelcher, Wilhelm, ed. and trans. "The Acts of Peter." Pages 259–322 in *Writings Related to the Apostles: Apocalypses and Related Subjects.* Vol. 2 of *New Testament Apocrypha.* Edited by Edgar Hennecke, Wilhelm Schneemlecher, and R. McL. Wilson. Philadelphia: Westminster, 1965.

Schoeps, Hans Joachim. *Theologie und Geschichte des Judenchristentums.* Tübingen: Mohr, 1949.

Schreckenberg, Heinz. "Flavius Josephus und die Lukanischen Schriften." Pages 179–209 in *Wort in der Zeit: Neutestamentliche Studien. Festgabe für Karl Heinrich Rengstorf zum 75. Geburtstag.* Edited by Wilfrid Haubeck and Michael Bachmann. Leiden: Brill, 1980.

Schüssler Fiorenza, Elisabeth. "A Feminist Critical Interpretation for Liberation: Martha and Mary: Luke 10:38–42." *Religion and Intellectual Life* 3, no. 2 (1986): 21–36.

———. *Jesus and the Politics of Interpretation.* New York: Continuum, 2000.

———. "Revisioning Christian Origins: *In Memory of Her* Revisited." Pages 225–50 in *Christian Beginnings: Worship, Belief and Society.* Edited by Kieran O'Mahoney. London: Continuum, 2003.

———. *Rhetoric and Ethic: The Politics of Biblical Studies.* Minneapolis: Fortress, 1999.

Schwartz, Regina. *The Curse of Cain: The Violent Legacy of Monotheism.* Chicago: University of Chicago Press, 1997.

Schwartz, Seth. *Imperialism and Jewish Society 200 B.C.E. to 600 C.E.* Princeton: Princeton University Press, 2001.

Scott, James C. *Domination and the Arts of Resistance: Hidden Transcripts.* New Haven, Conn: Yale University Press, 1990.

Seim, Turid Karlsen. *The Double Message: Patterns of Gender in Luke-Acts.* Studies of the New Testament and Its World. Edinburgh: T&T Clark, 1994.

Seneca. *On Mercy.* In *Moral Essays.* Translated by John W. Basore. 3 vols. Loeb Classical Library. New York: Putnam, 1928.

Skarsaune, Oskar. *The Proof from Prophecy: A Study in Justin Martyr's Proof-Text Tradition: Text-Type, Provenance, Theological Profile.* Novum Testamentum Supplements 56. Leiden: Brill, 1987.

Slingerland, Dixon. "'The Jews' in the Pauline Portion of Acts." *Journal of the American Academy of Religion* 54 (1986): 305–21.

———. "The Composition of Acts: Some Redaction-Critical Observations." *Journal of the American Academy of Religion* 56 (1988): 99–113.

Squires, John T. *The Plan of God in Luke-Acts.* Society for New Testament Studies Monograph Series 76. Cambridge: Cambridge University Press, 1993.

Stanton, Graham. "Jewish Christian Elements in the Pseudo-Clementine Writings." Pages 305–24 in *Jewish Believers in Jesus: The Early Centuries.* Edited by Oskar Skarsaune and Reidar Hvalvik. Peabody, Mass.: Hendrickson, 2007.

Steck, Odil Hannes. *Israel und das gewaltsame Geschick der Propheten: Untersuchungen zur Überlieferung des deuteronomistischen Geschichtsbildes im Alten Testament, Spätjudentum und Urchristentum.* Wissenschaftliche Monographien zum Alten und Neuen Testament 23. Neukirchen-Vluyn: Neukirchener Verlag, 1967.

Stendahl, Krister. "Hate, Non-retaliation, and Love: 1QS x,17–20 and Rom. 12:19–21." *Harvard Theological Review* 55 (1962): 337–55.

Sterling, Gregory E. *Historiography and Self-definition: Josephus, Luke-Acts and Apologetic Historiography.* New Testament Studies 64. Leiden: Brill, 1992.

———. "'Opening the Scriptures': The Legitimation of the Jewish Diaspora and the Early Christian Mission." Pages 199–217 in *Jesus and the Heritage of Israel: Luke's*

Narrative Claim upon Israel's Legacy. Edited by David P. Moessner. Harrisburg, Pa.: Trinity, 1999.

Stewart, Zeph. "Greek Crowns and Christian Martyrs." Pages 119–23 in *Mémorial André-Jean Festugière; Antiquité Païenne et Chrétienne*. Edited by E. Lucchesi and H. D. Saffrey. Geneva: P. Cramer, 1984.

Stoler, Ann Laura. "Racial Histories and Their Regimes of Truth." *Political Power and Social Theory* 11 (1997): 183–206.

Stoops, Robert. "Riot and Assembly: The Social Context of Acts 19:23–41." *Journal of Biblical Literature* 108 (1989): 73–91.

Stowers, Stan. "Comment: What Does *Unpauline* Mean?" Pages 70–77 in *Paul and the Legacies of Paul*. Edited by William S. Babcock. Dallas: Southern Methodist University Press, 1990.

Swartley, Willard M. "War and Peace in the New Testament." *ANRW* 26.3:2298–408. Part 2, *Principat*, 26.3. Edited by H. Temporini and W. Haase. New York: de Gruyter, 1996.

Sylva, Dennis D. "The Meaning and Function of Acts 7.46–50." *Journal of Biblical Literature* 106 (1987): 261–75.

Tajra, H. W. *The Martyrdom of St. Paul: Historical and Judicial Context, Traditions, and Legends*. Wissenschaftliche Untersuchungen zum Alten und Neuen Testament. Second Series 67. Tübingen: Mohr, 1994.

Talbert, Charles. *Literary Patterns, Theological Themes and the Genre of Luke-Acts*. Missoula, Mont.: SBL & Scholar's Pres, 1974.

———. "Martyrdom in Luke-Acts and the Lukan Social Ethic." Pages 99–110 in *Political Issues in Luke-Acts*. Edited by Richard J. Cassidy and P. J. Scharper. Maryknoll, N.Y.: Orbis, 1983.

Tannehill, Robert C. "Israel in Luke-Acts: A Tragic Story." *Journal of Biblical Literature* 104 (1985): 69–85.

———. *The Narrative Unity of Luke-Acts: A Literary Interpretation*. 2 vols. Philadelphia: Fortress, 1986–90.

Taylor, N. H. "Stephen, the Temple, and Early Christian Eschatology." *Revue biblique* 110 (2003): 62–85.

Tertullian. *Adversus Marcionem*. Books 1–5. 2 vols. Edited and translated by Ernest Evans. Oxford Early Christian Texts. Oxford: Clarendon, 1972.

Thompson, John B. *Ideology and Modern Culture: Critical Social Theory in the Era of Mass Communication*. Stanford: Stanford University Press, 1990.

Tiede, David. "'Fighting Against God': Luke's Interpretation of Jewish Rejection of the Messiah Jesus." Pages 102–12 in *Anti-Semitism and Early Christianity: Issues of Polemic and Faith*. Edited by Craig Evans and Donald Hagner. Minneapolis: Fortress, 1993.

———. *Prophecy and History in Luke-Acts*. Philadelphia: Fortress, 1980.

Tomson, Peter J. "Gamaliel's Counsel and the Apologetic Strategy of Luke-Acts." Pages 585–604 in *The Unity of Luke-Acts*. Edited by J. Verheyden. Bibliotheca ephemeridum theologicarum lovaniensium 142. Leuven: Leuven University Press 1999).

Tyson, Joseph B. *Luke, Judaism, and the Scholars: Critical Approaches to Luke-Acts.* Columbia: University of South Carolina Press, 1999.

———. *Marcion and Luke-Acts: A Defining Struggle.* Columbia: University of South Carolina Press, 2006.

Unnik, W. C. van. "Die Motivierung der Feindesliebe in Lukas 6:32–35." *Novum Testamentum* 8 (1966): 284–300.

Vielhauer, Philipp and Georg Strecker, eds. and trans. "Jewish-Christian Gospels." Pages 134–78 in *Gospels and Related Writings.* Rev. ed. Vol. 1 of *New Testament Apocrypha.* Edited by Wilhelm Schneemelcher and R. McL. Wilson. Louisville, Ky.: Westminster John Knox, 1991.

Virgil. *The Aeneid.* Translated by Robert Fitzgerald. New York: Random House, 1983.

Visotzky, Burton L. *Fathers of the World: Essays in Rabbinic and Patristic Literatures.* Tübingen: Mohr, 1995.

Walaskay, Paul W. *'And So We Came to Rome': The Political Perspective of St. Luke.* Cambridge: Cambridge University Press, 1987.

Walker, William O. "The Portrayal of Aquila and Priscilla in Acts: The Question of Sources." *New Testament Studies* 54 (2008): 479–95.

Walter, Nikolaos. "Proselyt aus Antiochen, und die Nikolaiten in Ephesos und Pergamon: Ein Beitrag auch zum Thema: Paulus und Ephesos." *Zeitschrift für die neutestamentliche Wissenschaft und die Kunde der älteren Kirche* 93 (2002): 200–206.

Walton, Steve. *Leadership and Lifestyle: The Portrait of Paul in the Miletus Speech and I Thessalonians.* Society for New Testament Studies Monograph Series 108. Cambridge: Cambridge University Press, 2000.

———. "The State They Were In: Luke's View of the Roman Empire." Pages 1–41 in *Rome and the Bible in the Early Church.* Edited by Peter Oakes. Grand Rapids: Baker, 2002.

Wasserberg, Günter. *Aus Israels Mitte—Heil für die Welt: Eine narrativ-exegetische Studie zur Theologie des Lukas.* Beihefte zur Zeitschrift für die neutestamentliche Wissenschaft 92. Berlin: de Gruyter, 1998.

Weatherly, Jon A. *Jewish Responsibility for the Death of Jesus in Luke-Acts.* Journal for the Study of the New Testament: Supplement Series 106. Sheffield: Sheffield Academic Press, 1994.

Wengst, Klaus. *Pax Romana and the Peace of Jesus Christ.* Translated by John Bowden. Philadelphia: Fortress, 1987.

White, Hayden. *The Content of the Form: Narrative Discourse and Historical Representation.* Baltimore: John Hopkins University Press, 1987.

White, L. Michael. "The Pentecost Event: Lukan Redaction and Themes in Acts 2." *Forum* 3 (2000): 75–103.

Whitlark, Jason A. and Mikeal C. Parsons. "The 'Seven' Last Words: A Numerical Motivation for the Insertion of Luke 23.34a." *New Testament Studies* 52 (2006): 188–204.

Whittaker, John. "Christianity and Morality in the Roman Empire." *Vigiliae christianae* 33 (1979): 209–25.

Williams, Demetrius K. "*The Acts of the Apostles.*" Pages 213–48 in *True to Our Native Land: An African American New Testament Commentary.* Edited by Brian K. Blount et al. Minneapolis: Fortress, 2007.

Wills, Lawrence. "The Depiction of the Jews in Acts." *Journal of Biblical Literature* 110 (1991): 631–54.

———. *Not God's People: Insiders and Outsiders in the Biblical World.* Lanham, Md.: Rowman & Littlefield: 2008.

Wilson, Brittany E. "Pugnacious Precursors and the Bearer of Peace: Jael, Judith, and Mary in Luke 1:42." *Catholic Biblical Quarterly* 68 (2006): 436–56.

Wilson, Stephen G. "The Jews and the Death of Jesus in Acts." Pages 155–64 in *Paul and the Gospels.* Vol. 1 of *Anti-Judaism in Early Christianity.* Edited by Peter Richardson with David Granskou. Studies in Christianity and Judaism 2. Waterloo, Ontario: Wilfrid Laurier University Press, 1986.

———. "Marcion and the Jews." Pages 45–58 in *Separation and Polemic.* Vol. 2 of *Anti-Judaism in Early Christianity.* Edited by Stephen G. Wilson. Studies in Christianity and Judaism 2. Waterloo, Ontario: Wilfrid Laurier University Press, 1986.

Wimbush, Vincent L. "Reading Texts as Reading Ourselves: A Chapter in the History of African-American Biblical Interpretation." Pages 95–108 in *Social Location and Biblical Interpretation in the United States.* Vol. 1 of *Reading From This Place.* Edited by Fernando F. Segovia and Mary Ann Tolbert. Minneapolis: Fortress, 1995.

Winter, Paul. "Magnificat and Benedictus—Maccabean Psalms?" *Bulletin of the John Rylands University Library of Manchester* 37 (1954–55): 328–47.

Wiseman, T. P. "Lying Historians: Seven Types of Mendacity." Pages 122–46 in *Lies and Fiction in the Ancient World.* Edited by C. Gill and T. P. Wiseman. Austin: University of Texas Press, 1993.

Woodman, A. J. "From Hannibal to Hitler, the Literature of War." *University of Leeds Review* 26 (1983): 107–24.

———. *Rhetoric in Classical Historiography: Four Studies.* London: Croon Helm, 1988.

Wordleman, Amy. "Cultural Divides and Dual Realities: A Greco-Roman Context for Acts 14." Pages 205–32 in *Contextualizing Acts: Lukan Narrative and Greco-Roman Discourse.* Edited by Todd Penner and Caroline Vander Stichele. Society of Biblical Literature Symposium Series 20. Atlanta: Society of Biblical Literature, 2003.

Wrege, H.-T. "Zur Rolle des Geisteswortes in frühchristlichen Traditionen (LC 12,10 parr.)." Pages 373–77 in *Logia: les paroles de Jésus.* Edited by J. Coppens, J. Delobel, and T. Baarda. Louvain: Peeters, 1982.

Zeller, Eduard. *The Contents and Origin of the Acts of the Apostles Critically Investigated.* 2 vols. Translated by Joseph Dare. Edinburgh: Williams & Norgate, 1875–1976. Translation of *Die Apostelgeschichte nach ihrem Inhalt und Ursprung kritisch Untersucht.* Stuttgart: Carl Mäcken, 1854.

Zerbe, Gordon M. *Non-retaliation in Early Jewish and New Testament Texts: Ethical Themes in Social Contexts.* Journal for the Study of the Pseudepigrapha: Supplement Series 13. Sheffield: Sheffield Academic Press, 1993.

Zizek, Slavoj. *The Sublime Object of Ideology.* London: Verso, 1988.

Index of Scripture Citations

Index of Ancient Sources

General Index